Accentuating Veneer Countervailed Prodigiosity

Talh M.

AF720567

Accentuating Veneer Countervailed Prodigiosity

First Edition November 2025

Written by Talh M.

Table of Contents

TOPIC/CHAPTER NAME	PAGE NO.
Chapter 1- Introduction	1
1.1 History of Printing	2
1.2 Invention of Paper	3
1.2.1 What is Paper Used For?	5
1.3 Lithography	6
1.3.1 Basic Principles of Lithography	7
1.4 Lithographic-Offset Printing	7
1.4.1 Functioning of Sheet-Fed Offset Printing Press	8
1.4.2 Advantages and Disadvantages of Offset Printing	9
1.4.3 Offset Printing Remains the Dominant Technology on the Market	9
1.4.4 New Generation Offset Machines	10
1.5 Offset Printing Press Operations	11
1.6 Sheet Fed Offset Press Design	11
1.7 Scenario of Indian Printing Industry	12
1.8 Scenario of Global Printing Industry	12
1.9 Productivity	13
1.9.1 Meaning of Production and Productivity	14
1.9.2 Productivity Growth is not Production Growth	15
1.9.3 Concept of Productivity	16
1.9.4 Measurement of Productivity	17
1.9.5 Factors Affecting Productivity	18
1.9.6 Ways to Improve Productivity	19
1.10 Concept of Productivity in Printing Industry	20

1.11 Productivity Enhancement	22
1.12 Productivity Enhancement in Printing Industry	24
1.13 Present Scenario of Productivity in Printing Industry	25
1.14 Components of Print Productivity	27
1.14.1 Printing Machine Efficiency	27
1.14.2 Human Performance	28
1.14.3 Machine Availability	29
1.14.4 Production Breakdown	30
1.14.5 Maintenance of Equipment	31
1.14.6 Press Automation	33
1.14.7 Training	34
1.15 Internal Situation of Print Production	35
1.15.1 Printing Machine Speed	35
1.15.2 Make-ready	35
1.15.2.1 Make the Make-ready more Efficient	36
1.15.2.2 Taking Control of Waste inside the Pressroom	37
1.15.2.3 Faster Offset Press Make-ready	37
1.15.3 Equipment Performance/ Utilization	38
1.16 Print Productivity direct in relation with Waste in all Forms	38
1.17 Potential of Printing Sector and Enhancement of Print Productivity	39
Chapter 2- Review of Literature	41
Chapter 3- Research Problem	57
Chapter 4- Research Objectives	58
Chapter 5- Research Methodology	59
Chapter 6- Data Collection and Analysis	69
Chapter 7- Result and Discussion	148
Chapter 8- Conclusion and Future Scope	162
References	165

This is the first chapter of the thesis and it represents the introductory part of the research work. Sheet fed offset printing is one of the major forms of printing techniques and is basically preferred for producing high quality printing output with cost efficiencies. This chapter indicates the necessary background and context for the particular piece of research. It outlines the existing state of knowledge in the field of offset printing technology, starting from the historical background to the principles of operation and the various points relating to the press productivity. This chapter justifies the topic and context of the research work in the areas of sheet fed offset printing technology.

Knowledge of environment and more specifically gradual accumulation of essential knowledge of the nature earth is considered to be the growth and progress of our historical, social and cultural change. Environment generally fulfils our needs and requirements and hence the human society thereof keeps moving to live a better life in a very systematic, efficient and effective manner. In order to live a healthy and social life, we the humans need to communicate, and after writing, printing certainly made it possible to communicate in a highly effective manner. Printing is one of the strongest medium of mass communication and the role and importance of printing in modern society cannot be overlooked. Invention of printing is considered to be one of the highly important inventions to the whole mankind in order to dissemination of knowledge and information to the people at large thereby reducing the possible geographical barriers among the nations (Forrester, 2020).

Printing in a very simplest term can be defined as one of the effective forms of presentation for the human communications. It is the presentation of one's ideas, thoughts, knowledge, and expression to the people at large or mass people. It is the art, science and technology of reproducing "n" number of copies identical to the original. The number of reproductions can vary from as low as one (with the digital printing technology printing of single copy is very much possible) to any quantity. Maybe it is the first of such kind in the whole spectrum of manufacturing industry, where all the three forms; art, science, and technology co-exist side by side to compliment and enrich the whole printing production process (Baral, 2010).

Without creativity and artistic approach, print output may not be able to produce the print with the unique art touch. Without the science (physics, chemistry, environment, ecology, principles) printing may not have progressed to the present form. Technology is certainly playing a bigger role in the recent years to standardize the whole print production process. It is the right blend of art, science, and technology which makes printing vibrant, unique and effective appealing to the all groups of society (Baral, 2010). Printing is continued to grow to cater the various needs and requirements of the society in many forms and a modern society cannot think of its very existence without the use and applications of printing. Over the years, technological advancements in this field continues to dominate the various press functions.

1.1 History of Printing

Printing has a very unique, rich and long history and all the milestones on its journey have helped printing to evolve and grow with time (Prepressure, 2012). Printing is not a new concept, for thousands of years it has existed in various forms like; signet rings, seals by royal family and various designed punches being used by the goldsmiths and silversmiths. It has evolved with time and it came out each time with added features and facilities to cater a wide array of needs and requirements of the print end-users (Forrester, 2020).

Movable type is considered as one of the greatest milestones in the history of printing and it has certainly made the invention of printing machines to took place in the subsequent period of time, to speed up the printing techniques. As per the historical records, Bi Sheng of Chine, around 1040 AD, created movable types with ceramic materials and in the subsequent years around 1434 AD, Johannes Gutenberg of Germany invented metal movable types to further accelerate the printing. Success of printing as an industry is credited to Gutenberg for his historic metallic movable types (Wikipedia, 2022).

Fig. 1.1: Johannes Gutenberg (Wikipedia, 2022)

Movable types gave birth to the Letterpress process of printing and for the next 350 years it was the only dominant forms of printing for taking care of various printing products. Around 1796 AD, Lithographic process of printing was invented by Alois Senefelder, with a motive for printing theatrical works, in low cost. Unlike the letterpress printing technique, where the printing and non-printing areas are separated physically, lithography is a chemical printing process in which both the areas lie on the same plane or surface (Sciencephotolibrary, 2023).

Fig. 1.2: Alois Senefelder (Science photolibrary), 2023)

Over the years, with refinement and fine tuning, still lithographic process is a major and dominant form of printing all over the globe. Invention of lithography has changed the face of the printing industry and is considered as the turning point in the history of printing (Science photolibrary, 2023).

Fig. 1.3: Heidelberg Tiegel (Daydaynews, 2020)

1.2 Invention of Paper

Printing has been playing a major role towards developing the human civilization in the form of favourite and effective form of mass communication and disseminating knowledge and information (Deshpande, 2011). Paper is highly important when it comes to printing and it is basically a network of plant fibres which are being laid down in the form of flat sheets. Paper is generally prepared from pulp and the potential source for pulp preparation for paper manufacturing is wood; which hence makes paper to be recycled and environmentally friendly. Hemp, cotton, esparto grass, sugar cane bagasse and bamboo are some of the plant-based sources for the pulp for paper manufacturing applications (Kew, 2018).

From 3100 BC onwards, long before the invention of paper, writing was first developed on the river plains of Mesopotamia. As clay was available abundantly in these areas, hence it was also used as the writing materials of the temple scribes. With the help of hard materials, the clay tablets were given the particular character shapes which when dried the particular characters were resulted. This style of writing was known as Cuneiform. Under the sunlight, these clay tablets were stored and exposed for dry and hard tablet formation. But it was not convenient and so easy to convey messages in this method (Woods, 2015).

Around the 3000 BC, in Egypt, a portable writing substance was invented for easy writing and giving a momentum in this area. Near the popular Nile River, an aquatic plant, popularly known as Cyperus papyrus, was identified for making a very smooth and flexible surface for writing purpose. One of the most characteristics of this plant is that, the surface accepts and retains ink without smudging and blurring, which is certainly an important point for the writing to take place (Oxford Dictionaries, 2023).

In the later days, paper was invented and the word "Paper" is accordingly derived from the Latin world "Papyrus". In the subsequent years, paper and particularly manufacturing process started identifying various sources, both natural and manmade, for preparation of pulp for the paper production. Paper is basically hygroscopic nature due the essential properties and characteristics of the fibres sourced from the plant bodies, which suits to the basic requirements of most of the printing techniques (Oxford Dictionaries, 2023).

Around 1500 BC, Bamboo books were very famous, in which thin strips of bamboo were used to write in a single column or two lines of threads which were linked to each other for the longer size documents; as it was as convenient as writing on the Papyrus. It was a very popular forms of writing in China during the "Shang Dynasty", and for almost next one thousand years it was used in China (Boltz, 2017).

History also indicates that, using mulberry and other bast fibers with old rags, hemp waste and fishnets, sheets of papers were prepared in China during the Han Dynasty (202 BC-AD 220), which were traced from some of the court documents during the above period of time. This gives us a general view and idea regarding the papermaking in the ancient times and how writing evolved with evolution of papermaking from various sources by different people and different geographical locations (Britannica, 2007).

Last four decades have witnessed the ever-increasing worldwide consumption of paper, and research data indicates it has risen by 400 percent, which is certainly an important point to note. Around 35 percent of the harvested trees, is used by the paper industry for manufacturing of paper. For taking care of the sustainability related issues of paper industry, these companies are also planting new trees for re-growing of the forests (Martin, 2004). Although, invention of paper was centred around giving a momentum to writing and reading, but in the recent years packaging accounts for more than 41 percent applications of all global paper use. Packaging is one of the fastest growing fields in the recent times, and from the sustainability front, it is the need of the hour to shift towards paper-based packaging applications (Beckline et al., 2016).

Research indicates that, around 400 million tons of paper and paperboards are being produced globally on annual basis and Asia is considered as the fastest growing market in this sector (FAO, 2014). Per capita average consumption of paper and paperboard in global scenario is 57 kg and in India it is little over 13 kg. At the same time, in 2021, global consumption of paper and paperboard was at 408 million tons and is projected to reach 476 million tons by 2032. This show in coming years, there will be high consumption of paper and paperboard products, as in most of the nations have putting restrictions on use of plastics and its by-products for various environmental reasons (Giampiero, 2010 & Forestindustries, 2013).

1.2.1 What is Paper Used For?

When it comes to the printing substrates, paper is ranked one, as because of potential benefits it offers in comparison to other similar substrates. It is available in a wide variety of sizes, colours, thicknesses, basis weights, and surface and strength properties, to take care of the operational and process requirements of different printing processes. Due to the above characteristics, paper and paper-based substrates are highly suitable for printing of a wide range of printing products. Ranging from books, journals, magazines, security printing, packaging printing, posters, commercial printing to special application printing are printed very effectively with the use of paper as the printing substrates (Kew, 2018).

Based on the applications paper can be grouped into four categories; papers for various printing applications, writing papers for various stationery requirements, wrapping papers for the physical protection of goods and merchandise, and speciality papers (toilet tissue, cigarette paper and other specific industrial applications). All these papers are being manufactured with the particular end-user needs and requirements in mind. The paper which is meant for printing, the surface and strength properties needs to be controlled critically as per the basic principles of the particular printing technique (Graphic Arts Collection, 2016).

1.3 Lithography

In 1798, Alois Senefelder invented one of the very important inventions in the history of printing, "Lithography". Although in the beginning it was not so popular, but as the time progressed, it became one of the most significant printing process and printing industry segment, also. In the present times, lithography-offset printing is a widely used printing technique for printing of a wide array of printing works (University of Houston, 2019). During the early days of the invention, limestone was used as the printing plate and accordingly the applications were confined to flat and porous surfaces only.

Lithography is derived its name from two words, "Litho" and "Graph", which means printing from a stone surface. Even though, invention of lithographic printing was accidental, Senefelder devoted his major part of his life for the refinement of this particular printing technique. Around 1817, he was able to designed a lithographic press featuring dampening and inking of the stone surface with a suitable means. For his outstanding contributions in this field, he was honoured with many prizes and recognitions from various prestigious quarters.

Fig. 1.4: Litho-stone (Graphic Arts Collection, 2016)

In the gradual years, lithographic printing technique got transformed into offset printing process and the original process which is a direct process of printing also shifted to indirect process of printing (offset printing process). Around 1904 to 1905, Ira Ruble discovered the offset printing press for printing of paper with the use of a flatbed litho stone machine. He was very successful in designing the impression cylinder with a rubber covering for transfer of image from the stone surface to paper. This indirect approach of printing, from the plate surface to blanket and then from blanket to paper, was considered as the turning point in the areas of printing technology (University of Houston, 2019).

Fig. 1.5: Lithographic offset press, Rubel (Smithsonian, 2016)

1.3.1 Basic Principles of Lithography

Lithography printing is basically a chemical printing technique, where both the image and non-image areas lie on the same surface or plane. Unlike the other printing processes, where printing and non-printing areas are separated physically, in lithography, both the areas are on the same plane and they are separated chemically. The basic principle states that, grease and water repel to each other, whether they are in contact on the same surface. The image areas on the litho-stone are made to attract greasy type of ink and the non-image like-wise is treated to accept water; even though both the areas are on the same plane but essentially, they do not get mixed with each other.

More specifically, lithographic printing process works on the basic principles of mutual repulsion of ink and water. The image areas accepts and transfers oil-based inks and the non-image areas accordingly accepts and transfers water from the stone surface to printing paper, to effect printing cycle. The inks for lithography printing applications are a greasy type of ink and high viscosity, for effective printing and keeping water from the image areas.

1.4 Lithographic-Offset Printing

In offset printing, the inked image is first transferred from the plate surface onto the rubber blanket surface and finally onto the substrate for effecting printing cycle. Offset essentially indicates, the image from the plate surface is first "off" onto the rubber blanket and from the blanket the transferred image is set onto the printing substrate along with the impression surface. Offset printing is the refined version of the lithographic printing technique and the basic working principles of both the system are same; mutual repulsion of oil and water. (Wikipedia, 2020).

Suitable arrangements are made to apply a thin and even layer of ink and water onto the plate surface and both the inked image and water layer from the non-image areas get transferred onto the blanket surface during the printing cycle. Development of offset printing process have taken place in two phases; printing on tin sheets by this printing process by Robert Barclay of England in 1875 and printing on paper by Ira Washington Rubel in 1904. The real momentum to offset printing was occurred with effective printing on paper and the subsequent developments in this area helped to formulate various grades of paper for different printing applications.

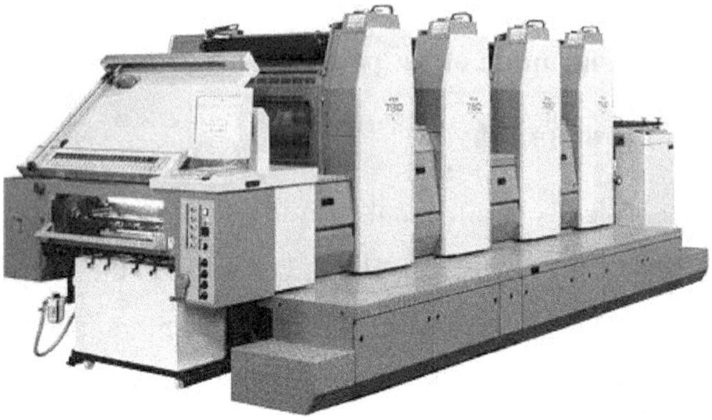

Fig. 1.6: Sheet Fed Offset Press (Prepressure, 2012)

Offset printing technique is further classified into two categories; sheet fed offset and web fed offset presses. In sheet fed offset presses, individual sheets are fed into press for printing and web fed offset presses are designed to print web of paper. In general, sheet fed offset presses are designed for high quality printing output and web fed is meant for high-speed print operations (Wikipedia, 2020). Sheet fed offset presses are quite popular in the printing industry and in the recent years, number of innovative technologies are added into the press configuration for making the press high speed, reliable and printing of high-quality printing.

1.4.1 Functioning of Sheet-Fed Offset Printing Press

Sheet fed offset printing is one of the mostly used forms of printing and it equally true in India and worldwide printing market scenario. Offset is known for high quality printing along with advanced technology for press functions and compatible with printing of wide range of printing jobs. The market share of offset printing is roughly around 40-45 percent market share of all printing markets. After the World War-II, the market share of offset printing was around 50 percent, but gradually the market share is being replaced by other printing techniques like; gravure, flexography, screen and different digital printing techniques (Offset printing technology, 2019).

In the recent years, digital printing techniques are slowly penetrating into the offset printing market as because of short run jobs and low job changeover related market trends. In order to take care of possible challenges posed by the digital printing, the new generation offset presses are equipped with advanced level technology and moreover, these machines are capable of handling the above challenges very effectively (Offset printing technology, 2019).

1.4.2 Advantages and Disadvantages of Offset Printing

Offset printing process being one of the dominant forms of printing has number of merits and limitations also. As it is a matured printing technique, over the years it has successfully absorbed and introduced number of technological advancements into the press configuration and process aspects for making the press, simple and easy to operate, maintain and calibrate for higher press productivity and enhanced print quality. Some of the potential advantages of offset printing can be summarized as; high-end printing quality, simpler and fast method of preparation of offset plates with low/minimum use of processing chemicals, unit cost of printing is low especially in long run print jobs, longer plate life and high level of press productivity (Wikipedia, 2022).

There are some limitations of these presses also; specialized press operators are required to operate, handle and maintain the press, higher fixed cost of operation in comparison to other printing process presses, more time for the press set-up especially while comparing with modern digital printing presses, press operation is not suitable for small run printing jobs and the modern automatic offset presses are of higher cost. This is one of the limiting factors for the small sized printers for not opting the multi-colour sheet fed offset presses, especially the high-end presses for installing into their workplace.

1.4.3 Offset Printing Remains the Dominant Technology on the Market

Offset printing technology is one of the major printing industries and moreover it is a mature form of printing, catering a wide range of printing requirements. But in the recent years, there is a stiff competition in the printing industry for the survival and growth of sheet fed offset printing segment. Job order quantity is shrinking day by day, commercial printing applications are also decreasing and there is a continuous pressure to absorb the pressure given by the digital printing segment. But there is a lot of scope for improving for the sheet fed offset printing industry in order to survive and grow in the marketplace. In spite of all the above points, sheet fed offset printing is still going strong and it roughly comprises half of the world's consumption of printed applications (Statista, 2023).

In terms of the growth of the digital printing presses, even though the percentage growth is convincing, but when it comes to volume of printing, offset printing is much ahead than the digital printing. Technological advancements in this segment are quite high and will continue to influence the market considerably in the coming years also. Altogether, sheet fed offset has a brighter future and will continue to serve the printing market in an innovative and effective manner, in the years to come.

1.4.4 New Generation Offset Machines

Being a matured industry, offset presses have evolved over the period of time and continues to adopt new and innovative technologies for serving the printing industry in a more meaningful and productive manner. Starting from the invention of lithography to offset to sheet fed offset and web fed offset presses, it has travelled a long distance. The time line of lithography-offset printing indicates the entire relevant and important milestone during the long journey.

Each step has contributed its own bit and the present generation offset presses are nowhere behind the advanced manufacturing equipment and devices. Credit goes to the machine and equipment manufacturers in this segment for their continued research and development activities for producing next generation offset presses with innovative added features to support process optimization and enhancing the level of print quality with low cost of print production and lowest press setup time.

According to a research publication by Smithers (The Future of Digital versus Offset Printing to 2024), until 2024, digital printing segment in terms of printing volume, is going to be limited to 10 percent whereas offset printing to dominate with more than two-thirds of all global print volume. With all the positive points; short run jobs, shorter press set-up time and lowest wastage level of digital presses, offset printing process is still going strong and will continue to grow in the coming years also (Smithers, 2023). In the recent times, technological advances in the offset press technology have certainly made to manufacture presses with easier operational features coupled with significant reduction in press set-up time. Press make-ready/set-up time is one of the major concerns for the offset press for optimization of press productivity, reduction of raw materials and completing higher number of jobs in shorter period of time.

Prices of offset plates tend to be reducing to accommodate short-run jobs with the digital printing systems with cost justification. It is not only the next generation offset presses with shorter make-ready time and speed of operation, but also it is the generation of possible waste during the print production cycle; it is rightly mentioned that these presses are designed to result into as low as six times less waste reduction, leading to generating high proportion of profitability of the entire print production process. These machines are being manufactured with intelligent software for controlling the entire production systems and also can be operated and monitored remotely, thereby able to monitor all the activities with ease and reducing machine downtime caused by possible failure of the press.

1.5 Offset Printing Press Operations

Various press operations are performed on the offset printing press to print a job. It includes feeding the press sheet where the paper sheet are accurately fed into the feeder of the press, registering the press sheet where the paper sheet are registered accurately on registration board with the help of various control devices, delivering the press sheet where the printed sheets are delivered on the delivery board with the help of various control devices, preparing the printing unit where inking and dampening systems are adjusted to control ink and water balance and others, attaching the printing plates where the printing plates are mounted around the plate cylinders and starting up and proofing where make-ready sheets are printed to get Ok paper sheet. (Adams & Dolin, 2002).

1.6 Sheet Fed Offset Press Design

Almost all sheet fed offset press have common five main units; feeding unit, registration unit, inking & dampening unit, printing unit, and delivery unit. A single-colour sheet fed offset press has only one printing unit that can print one color at a time. Multi-color sheet fed offset presses are designed with two or more printing units. One of the primary advantages of a multi-colour press is to print more than one color on a substrate at a time. A Multi-colour printing press consumes less operation time and reduces registration problem as compared to a single-color sheet fed offset press used for multi-color jobs. Now a day, almost all fully automated or semi-automated multi-color presses are being monitored by the use of computers (Adams & Dolin, 2002).

Automated presses are attached various automated features such as plate changing, registration, colour control, ink delivery & distribution, feeder setting, and ink delivery and distribution. In single colour sheet fed offset printing press various operations of feeding, registration, ink and water balance and delivery can be controlled easily but in case of multi-colour offset printing press registration becomes a big issue and it is solved by new generation printing presses. Therefore, the computer-controlled presses reduce make-ready time and wastages. In fully automated printing presses, details of job in digital form to be printed is sent to the press from the press console and setting and adjustments from in-feed unit to delivery unit are done automatically resulting into the reduction of make-ready time or set-up time and wastages on the press (Adams & Dolin, 2002).

1.7 Scenario of Indian Printing Industry

Indian printing is very active and vibrant industry and is the nation with highest number of printers in the worldwide scenario. Roughly more than 2,50,000 printers are being operated across the nation and most of them are either small or medium in nature. Interestingly, a larger portion of all the printing houses is of family-owned business units. This industry has undergone a major transformation in the last three decades, especially after 1990, in which India initiated the process of reforms. The aim behind privatization is to open-up the market for integrating with the world economy. This step has certainly made the Indian printing industry to modernize their printing establishments in the way of investing in the latest and advanced printing equipment and devices. As per the research date, Indian printing industry has registered around 12 percent compounded annual growth over the last two decades.

India is considered as one of the major printing production and manufacturing of printed paper catering to the world market. It is not only the print volume, moreover the quality standards of printing output have improved dramatically over the last few years and now it is nowhere below than the international printing standards. As per the statistical data, annual turnover of all the components engaged in all printing related activities in the Indian printing industry are estimated more than 50,000 crores Indian rupees (Wikipedia, 2022).

1.8 Scenario of Global Printing Industry

There is an ever-changing scenario of global printing markets, especially in the last few years; electronic versions are taking the place of print volumes. Circulation of newspaper is shrinking day by day, so is the case of journals, magazines, catalogues, brochures, posters and folders; all of their electronic versions in the marketplace. Currency, once used to be frequent in physical mode, is now gradually getting transformed into electronic transaction mode; advertising expenditure once one of the major uses of printing applications is now moving into new areas including on-line. Continued growth of different social networking platforms resulting into declining of print products volumes, but the other side of the story indicates that there is a continuous growth of packaging and labels applications in the recent years (Smithers, 2023).

Digital printing is continued to grow as because of; customization, mass versioning, economic cost of production especially in small print run jobs, print-on-demand and more prominently it is much closer to the print end-users. Research data indicates that, during 2017, market share of digital printing was at 15.7 percent and it has gone to 19. 3 percent in 2022, of the whole print market segment. This is possible mainly due to the next generation digital presses are power-packed with bundles of facilities to boost the press productivity along with the high print quality level (Smithers, 2023).

In 2019, the value of global commercial printing market was valued at USD 400.46 billion and is projected to touch USD 460.28 billion by 2025, with a compounded annual growth rate of 2.24 percent during the 2020-2025 assessment period. There will be remarkable growth of commercial printing sector in the coming years, because of technological advancements and adoption process into the press environment is getting increased over the period of time. This will help to accelerate the demand of sheet fed offset presses with high level of press automation in coming years. As the customer demand is shifting towards short run commercially printed jibs; such as books, magazines, journals, brochures, catalogues, etc., it is certainly going to help the commercial printing sector to prosper in coming times, which is a very good sign altogether (Research and Markets, 2020).

1.9 Productivity

Modern business is all about effective management of unpredictable set of varying factors, that affects the business set-up either directly or indirectly. Economy is in continuous state of change and struggling to balance the national scenario with the international/global prospective. It is the critical analysis of the individual circumstances and the nature of particular business in question, for its survival, growth and development. To take care of such situation, productivity comes into picture. As a general rule, the higher the productivity, the higher the effective utilization of various resources during the production cycle. Higher productivity level eventually leads to higher national economy. In the recent years, higher importance is given to the various productivity optimization process for keeping the national economy progressing (Salman et al., 2008).

In order to be in the race and competitive in the marketplace, it is demanded to opt for the sustainable development on the socio-economic front. Over the years, a wide range of productivity enhancing tools, methods, processes, techniques and practices have been developed and adopted by numerous organizations all over the globe covering the manufacturing and service industries for accelerating the growth and development of their business entities (Antonio, 2015).

Especially in manufacturing industry, productivity and production are two most commonly used terms, because these two terms are highly relevant towards effective utilization of resources in the various conversion processes. In industrial engineering, the term productivity is most commonly used and it is a measure how the available resources are utilized for the production of output (Antonio, 2015).

1.9.1 Meaning of Production and Productivity

Production and productivity even-though looks similar on the surface, but they carry different meaning and hence are different from each other. Production is related to process of converting input into finished products for the customers and consumers. Input may be the different raw materials, machine & equipment, tolls, man power, tools, money, energy, etc., and products as the output that carries a certain value for the benefit of prospective consumers. There are basically a series of steps and most prominently each step adds value to the inputs and helps the material to reach to the desired state of product (Tangen, 2002).

On the other hand, productivity is concerned with the relationship between output and input. Input is the quantity or number of resources being used for the process of production and output is the quantity being produced, thereof. In the very basic sense, productivity is associated with the ratio between the output of the particular goods or services being produced and the input of different resources got consumed during the conversion process (Misterek et al., 1992).

It can also be expressed as the ratio between an output value and an input value which are essentially used for the production of output. Utmost care and attention are being given by each business set-up for enhancing the productivity for their growth and development, which in-turn adds value to the national economy (Misterek et al., 1992).

While analysing productivity, it is clearly shown that, it has a direct relationship with the effective identification and utilization of various resources that are required for the production process. Accordingly, the productivity of a printing press is reduced if the resources required for printing are not used properly. It can be concluded that, productivity is linked with the creation of value. High productivity essentially helps to add added value to the produced products (Tangen, 2002). In most of the time, for the measuring of production, productivity concept is used and followed, this leads to a general perception of increased production means increased productivity, which is not true. Unless and until a comparison is made, one cannot conclude that the productivity is increased or decreased (Tangen, 2002).

Productivity and more specifically improvement of productivity is of greater importance for any business set-up, in terms of sustainability and growth. There are five different aspects by which the productivity of any organization can be affected; both the input and output increases, input remains the same but the output increases, input reduced with increase in output, input decreases while the output remains the same, and output decreases while the input decreases even more (Misterek et al., 1992). These five stages need to be studied thoroughly so that the particular condition can be identified for enhancing the productivity. The underlying point is to address the particular situation where with low level of resource utilization the output needs to be maximized (Misterek et al., 1992).

1.9.2 Productivity Growth is not Production Growth

There should be a clear-cut distinction between the two words; production and productivity, so that they can be applied to the appropriate situations to address the particular problem in hand. Productivity is a relative concept whereas production is considered as absolute. Productivity is best explained when the various inputs in the production process and utilized optimally so as to achieve higher levels of output. For working with longer labour hours does not guarantee high productivity, rather it will result in a measure of greater inputs for every output, in which the basic aim and purpose of productivity is lost. Production growth relates to an increase in output of goods and services over a span of time period. It is taken as a measure of improvements in quality or quantity of production in a particular sector (Aph, 2009).

There are number of factors that relates to the production growth; technological progress and advancements, nature and characteristics of capital goods, infrastructure, skilled labour force, and efficient production processes. As a general rule, higher growth rate of production indicates a healthy economic condition of the state and it leads to increased employment, higher income of the people residing in the nation, and higher standard of living. Productivity growth is the increase in output per unit of input, over a particular span of time. It is in relation with how effectively all the resources are in use for the production of goods and services. Better organizational management practices always lead to higher productivity and it is true equally to printing industry, also. This helps to generating higher amount of output with the same or fewer inputs.

1.9.3 Concept of Productivity

The concept of productivity is aimed at measuring the efficiency and effectiveness of utilization of various resources for achieving the desired results or outcomes. This is considered to be one of the very important and crucial factors for calculating and thereby achieving the economic growth of any business entity. At its core, it is relating to maximizing output with minimized output. The central aim lies on utilization of all the resources in best possible manner and it is equally applicable to all the business activities covering manufacturing and service sectors (Singh et al., 2000).

Productivity can be applied to any business establishments irrespective of, small, medium or large business houses. With the adoption of suitable productivity measures, it is highly possible to deliver the product or service at the lowest possible cost (Shital, 2018). Survival of fittest, is still holds the same meaning and weightage as it was, before many years. In order to be competitive in the marketplace, productivity should be taken into consideration at the individual as well as industries level. Higher productivity or enhanced productivity certainly leads to higher cost savings, high quality products with competitive pricing factors.

This certainly led to capturing larger market shares and thereby maintains a competitive advantage over the other players in the particular industry segment. With higher productivity, the living standards of individuals and the particular society can also be enlarged into the next level. Accordingly, with the improved productivity, the higher profits being generated can be utilized among the workers in the form of higher wage packages, which will certainly boost the morale of the employee for further improvement of quality and productivity.

Innovation and technological advancements always go along with productivity growth. In order to opt for higher productivity, it is advised to invest in new and advanced technologies, research and development activities, improving and optimizing production processes. To strengthen and fostering technological advancements & progress and innovations, the organization should invest in acquisition of skilled professional manpower to execute the various concepts of productivity. The perfect combination of press with high level of automation and the highly skilled manpower to handle these machines will certainly help to produce high quality printing with greater efficiency and thereby justifying the unit cost of print output.

1.9.4 Measurement of Productivity

Measurement of productivity is a challenging task and it can be only measured indirectly; first calculating other variables and then by using these variables, productivity can be calculated. The root cause of difficulty in measuring the productivity is in not only defining the various inputs and outputs, but at the same time it is very difficult to quantifying them. It essentially involves in quantifying the relationship among the inputs and outputs being involved in the particular production system. Depending upon the inputs and outputs and the context of business, the specific methods of productivity measure can also vary considerably (Yadav and Marwa, 2015).

In particular, when there are multiple inputs and outputs are involved or considering the qualitative aspects of productivity measures, measuring the resultant productivity can be complex. Productivity measurement should be ideally consistent over the period of time, so that meaningful comparison can be made. In the very simplest form, productivity can be expressed as the ratio of output to the resources being used for producing the output. Mathematically it can be shown as;

$$\text{Productivity} = \frac{\text{Quality of Goods and Services Produced}}{\text{Amount of Resource Used}}$$

Mathematically, $\mathrm{P} = \frac{\mathrm{O}}{\mathrm{I}}$, where "P" denotes productivity, "O" denotes output, and "I" denotes input (Shital, 2018).

Measurement of productivity is aimed at quantification way of evaluating the effectiveness of utilization of various resources, identification of areas of improvement, and finally setting targets for improved productivity. Progress of any organization is linked with measuring and quantifications of productivity, to assess their progress and future planning to enhance performance, for successive growth and development. It also guides to effective allocations of resources for its optimal utilization for improving the press productivity.

Measurement of productivity allows for benchmarking, so that proper comparison can be made against the top performers. This certainly helps to learn from others and adopting best practices, in order to set and achieve higher level of productivity. Regular measurement of productivity helps to monitor performance over period of time, which may help towards tracking trends, progress and assess the various factors that affect productivity. In general, productivity measurement can be linked with; effective resource allocation, performance evaluation, effective planning & decision making, and finally fostering efficiency and competitiveness.

1.9.5 Factors Affecting Productivity

There are number of factors that affects and influence productivity and some of the factors are; technology and technological advancements always play a major role in enhancing the productivity. Identification, selection and proper applications of suitable technology will certainly help to enhance production efficiency, reduction of various associated costs, streamlining the processes with new and improved products and services. Workforce always plays an important and crucial role towards attending enhanced productivity. Skill, expertise and knowledge base of the workforce are the essential factors for productivity. Besides to these points, other factors like; experience, training, education and motivation plays an important role that affects productivity level.

Capital infrastructures in the form of machinery, equipment, tools and infrastructure are also highly factors affecting productivity. Care must be observed to maintain all the physical capital assets for their easy availability and reliability. Production efficiency, minimization of machine down time and effective utilization of various resources are the results of well-maintained capital assets. Identification and availability of raw materials, land and energy sources are some of the points to be taken into account for improving productivity. Effective management of all resources is the first step towards waste minimization and lowering the possible environmental burden.

Besides the above-mentioned factors, effective organizational structures coupled with best management practices can have significant impact on print productivity. Local government rules, regulations and policies can influence the output of the printing press, also. Adequate infrastructure like; communication systems, power supply, transportation networks, and logistic support are vital for achieving press efficiencies. Natural factors including; geographical locations, climatic conditions, physical infrastructure plays an important role on the functioning of the printing units. The nature of the industry should also be taken into account while considering the industrial productivity (Kalpana, 2019). The very existence of any printing press is highly dependent upon the identification of the above mentioned factors which directly contributes to the press functioning and subsequently analysing them in detail and finally devising suitable action plan to overcome the possible deficiencies will result into enhanced printing press production cycle.

1.9.6 Ways to Improve Productivity

All the business houses irrespective of manufacturing or service sector, needs to take care of their productivity in order to stay competitive and grow and develop in their areas of operation. In today's cut throat competition market scenario, one has to identify and work on innovative methods which will result into higher productivity (Shabat, 2019). There are some points which needs to be taken into account for improving productivity; proper identification and selection of equipment and machines, continuous training of the workforce, review of workflow on a continuous basis, adoption of latest technology, optimization of the shop floor, introduction of smart work culture, disposal of old and unused machineries, productive inventory management and effective communication within the organization and to the outer world (Shabat, 2019).

The secrets to great manufacturing are to focus and doing simple things exceptionally well, which leads to great results in the form of mastering on the simple techniques and more prominently applying these techniques consistently all the time for achieving the best possible results. Higher the productivity within shorter span of time, more money can be generated and this is the bottom line of all the business units. Small changes being adopted and implemented in various areas will certainly lead to big and productive improvements and the visible changes in overall productivity (Michael, 2020).

Some of the possible ways by which productivity can be improved could be; adoption of suitable management practice towards elimination of waste, shifting focus on different value-added activities, possible reduction of inventory & inventory carrying costs, optimization of production flow systems and continuous involvement of employees in the activities relating to process streamlining. Introduction of automated and advanced technologies towards increasing process efficiency and possible reduction of manual labour are some of the points needs to be taken care for increasing industrial productivity.

Investing in modular and comprehensive training programs for enhancing the skill and knowledge base of the workforce will lead to improving the efficiency of the people to perform and handle various tasks and activities in a productive manner. The employees must be encouraged to identify various areas to be taken into account for improvement and to provide useful suggestions in this context. The communication channel needs to be enhanced and encouraged within the various working groups, among the groups for improving coordination and sharing of knowledge and information.

At a regular interval of time all the machines and equipment need to be calibrated and maintained for achieving highest level of device performance towards achieving high productivity. Care must be given to upgrade the machines and equipment whenever necessary for reaping the benefits of new and advanced technologies towards enhanced productivity. Strict quality control measures must be followed and adopted for ensuring high level of product or service, for higher acceptance and creation of brand value in the marketplace.

It is much better to implement effective quality management systems, conducting inspections at every possible point, and thereby establishing checkpoints throughout the entire production process, so that it will be easy to inspect, measure, convey and control various quality parameters. In the recent years, energy efficient advanced technologies and practices are being used to reduce possible burden on energy consumption and lowering the final cost of production or service. All the above points need to be analysed and accordingly implemented for moving in the direction of improving productivity.

1.10 Concept of Productivity in Printing Industry

Printing industry is a progressive and growing industry and is also capital-intensive industry for taking care of hybrid forms of print production, distribution, and other related ancillary services. In the recent years, digital penetration is putting hard time for the traditional printing systems to survive and grow in the print marketplace (Michael, 2020). Digital printing possibly puts pressure in the forms of shorter press set-up time, low level of wastage, lower print order quantity, print on demand, customization and on the top, environmental friendliness. In order to take care of the array of benefits offered by the digital printing, offset printing industry is taking all possible measures to enhance productivity thereby proving low-cost print solutions to the prospective end-users (Michael, 2020).

Printing industry is intended to function with many complex and interconnected systems to generate the final print products. Customers need and requirements are changing with time and the printing companies are expected to fulfil their expectations without compromising on quality, pricing and delivery time front. It is not fulfilling the very expectations of the print buyers/end-users, but at the same time, competing successfully the modern modes of communications, also.

Printing companies which are very successful in the marketplace have evolved beyond producing the print output to complete solution providers, thereby educating and guiding the prospective print buyers with the options and facilities that can be effectively incorporated into the print for making the output unique and effective while performing its intended use (Tomljanovic, 2015). With the deep penetration of digital media and platforms, the print customers are expecting instant information from the printers on the print products and present generation printers are successfully doing these activities in an effective manner (Tomljanovic, 2015).

In the recent times, all the major printing industries are under the pressure of producing print outputs faster, cheaper in cost, and with better print quality. Globalization has certainly lessened the physical distance and the geographical distance is not at all a constraint for the printing company to operate on any part of the world. In order to stay competitive, all the printing companies need to focus on high productivity. To be a market leader, a printing establishment is expected to produce printing with low cost and still maintain the desired levels of quality standards (Uribe, 2008).

But as most of the printing companies are either small or medium in nature, due to capital and resource constraints, it is not possible them to install modern automatic machines and equipment along with standardized work culture. For them to be in the marketplace means a lot and they should fine tune their work environment with focus on small changes in the work-culture to be productive (Uribe, 2008). Printing industry is essentially highly different than the other industry; as because it is diverse, complex and dynamic in nature. Unlike the other manufacturing industries, printing industry caters to a wide array of print products, and this is the very reason of existence of small print shops in every part and corners.

This is not true in the case of other traditional industries, where small firms generally do not exist. One can easily list down a complete range of printing products, which are essentially differ from each other in terms of appearance, functions, end-use, etc. In other traditional industries, the market is generally ruled by the market leaders and small units are of no importance. At the same time, printing industry also falls under mass production industry for producing voluminous print outputs. The first complexity is related to the print product diversity coupled with mass/volume of production. In most of the cases, this particular blend does not exist at all.

In printing essentially caters to make-to-order production system mostly with customized print products. Due to the above factor, it is difficult to implement productivity improvement programs in the printing industry. As per the general rule, manufacturing industries are classified under either capital intensive or labour-intensive industries. But printing industry generally accommodates the above two things; labour and capital-intensive industries into their establishment successfully. Printing industries essentially employs high-cost machines and equipment for print production activities and at the same time in binding & finishing sections employs lot of manpower to perform various value-added post-press operations (Uribe, 2008).

The third complexity of printing press is related to workflows and business models. There are numerous workflow models and business models designed for different printing units to perform various print related operations to suit to the particular establishment. It is practically impossible to find a single business model to be used as solution which is to be useful and effective for the whole printing industry. Rather, it is the different combination of resources and equipment specific to the printing house for carrying out their press operations. Product specialization, labour cost, technological level, target print market and scale of operation are some of the potential factors which decide the particular business model to be designed and formulated for use.

All the three factors essentially indicate and explain the complexity and diverse nature of printing industry. Other side of the coin tells the abundance of opportunities that are available for improvement towards better decision-making process in the printing industry. It is the particular printing establishment to analyse and explore the various possibilities and to select the particular business model for achieving higher productivity. At the same time, low productivity of printing industry is caused mainly by the complex nature of the business. In the recent years, the technological advancements in the press configuration are certainly boosting the press productivity by undercutting the manual nature of press operations.

1.11 Productivity Enhancement

Printing industry is undergoing through structural changes and higher importance is given to improve print productivity by the top management, also. As printing is evolving, it is expected that the printing industry will certainly adopt innovative approaches to serve its potential print buyers/end-users in a better and effective manner while not compromising the level of print quality. Cut throat competition makes the situation more complex and the printing industry should take necessary measures to overcome such difficulties and transforming them into opportunities (Gornam,2019).

In order to survive and prosper in the marketplace, print establishment continually push their workforce to work for longer working hours, work harder, to increase the final productivity. In reality it may be helpful to some extent, but in long run it leads to risk of employee burnout. Off late, it is underlined that higher productivity is not about working harder, rather it is all for adoption of smart work culture (Gornam,2019).

Productivity enhancement is one of the basic requirements for printing industry in order to grow and stay competitive in the print marketplace. It is basic need of the hour to increase output while reducing the possible utilization of various resources. Resources are limited and one has to find various means to conserve these resources while increasing the output. Printing business is very different than the other industries and it needs special care and attention for operational functioning (Sarokin, 2020).

Printing market is highly price sensitive and accordingly the individual printing establishment should identify the various means and ways to reduce the print manufacturing cost, so that the need for expensive overtime can be brought down. This is one of the major issues being faced by most of the printing units all over the globe. These possible cost savings coupled with higher productivity are some of the points which will certainly help printing companies to stay competitive in the market (Sarokin, 2020).

Waste is a major concern especially for the printing industry and moreover it applies equally to the printing presses operating various parts of the globe. In the printing company, waste refers to any kind of materials or resources that are essentially discarded or not being utilized effectively during the printing cycle. Even though one cannot make the wastage to zero percent, but ways and means must be identified to bringing down the wastage percentage to minimum level. For any printing company, profitability is linked with the waste being generated during the printing cycle. Waste is not restricted to only material, rather it is an umbrella term covering, time, labour and the various resources that are required for carrying out printing operations in typical printing organizations.

Improper planning, bad inventory management, poor layout of the shop floor and the warehouse are some of the points which needs utmost care and attention for possible reduction of waste in a printing press. In a simpler term, waste is associated with the effort or expenses that do not help to transform the raw materials into the output or the intended finished product. By optimizing the printing process operations and eliminating the waste, in each phase, value addition can be carried out in phase of operations (Sarokin, 2020).

Reducing waste in a printing industry is not associated with cost-cutting and cost effectiveness rather it extends to crucial environmental sustainability aspects also. For successful implementation and adoption of waste minimization programs, printing companies are expected to adopt innovative practices and approaches like; investment in energy-efficient equipment, recycling of paper and chemicals, optimizing the process, process standardization programs, efficient and effective inventory management programs, use of eco-friendly chemicals, inks and printing substrates, etc. (Sarokin, 2020).

1.12 Productivity Enhancement in Printing Industry

To continue printing business, it is expected that the printing press should operate at higher press productivity by effective utilization of available and existing resources without increasing the final sale price of the print products. Print product pricing is a major issue and in order to acquire the particular job, in most of the time, printer try to quote low price and this situation is highly noticed all over the globe, as because of low level of business ethics in this sector (Andrade, 2012). But one has to be very much in the marketplace with minimizing the print manufacturing cost by essentially reducing the various manufacturing losses and finding key areas which can be taken into account for improvement towards reducing the waste and maximizing net profit for the particular printing press (Andrade, 2012).

In this digital age, value addition to the print output is one of the potential solutions for enlarging the base and maximizing profit with innovative printing solutions. In the last twenty years, traditional printing is being continuously challenged by the various digital media and the paper printing segment needs to adjust its business model in order to stay and progress in the print market (Varma and Lal, 2019).

Besides these possible challenges by the digital printing segment, environmental concern also pushing hard to the printing industry to readjust themselves. Different regulatory bodies are being engaged to take care of the sustainability related issues specific to the printing industry, to produce green, eco-friendly and sustainable printing solutions. Care must be taken so that the raw material that are required for the printing operations are not hazardous to the environment, rather it should complement the environment for a sustainable earth to live (Varma and Lal, 2019).

Regular printing inks, plate processing chemicals, paper and substrate coatings, and other consumables which are the basic requirements for any printing industry to operate are being compelled to use green and eco-friendly substitutes for printing operations. Present generation printing machines are manufactured with an eye to reduce carbon foot print and they are mainly operating on energy-efficient mode. Atomization has certainly made it possible to undercut or minimize the manual work or more specifically reducing human contact/touch with the machine, thereby reducing possible errors considerably.

Once the doing of errors are minimized, then the machine is able to produce the desired print output with less wastage. Less wastage leads to produce print output with lower cost of production and less environmental burden while continuing the print production activities. During the printing operation, various scraps that are being generated needs to be handled and recycled, so as to minimize the resource wastage, leading to enhance the overall press productivity and final profit margin (Varma and Lal, 2019). By adoption of these changes, it is very much possible to overcome the pricing challenges and taking care of the environment in an effective manner. Various standards are being developed at the national and international levels to standardize the workflow and enhancing printing quality and the productivity of the particular printing process and printing environment (Varma and Lal, 2019).

1.13 Present Scenario of Productivity in Printing Industry

As the competition within the printing industry is growing day-by-day, it is highly demanded to increase the core competency and capability of the print organization, so that they can sustain in the marketplace. Competitive capability of any printing establishment can be attained through improving productive performance by adopting innovative methods and organizational practices. After thorough research in this area, it is found that enhancing printing press productivity is the only solution for the continuous growth and development of the particular business set-up. This will lead to; enhanced print quality, potential cost savings, better service, reduction of lead time and innovative print out-put (Sneed and Verhoef, 2001).

It is underlined that, in the very first step, the production workflow of the printing industry needs to be studied and analysed thoroughly for determining the changes that are required for improvements towards increasing press productivity. In a printing unit, a workflow indicates the sequence of steps or activities that are required to be followed to produce a complete or final printed product (Bellander, 1997). It essentially outlines the movement of essential materials, resources and information through various stages of the printing press. The task starts with receiving the print job order, critical analysis of the print job, job planning, pre-press, press, post-press, quality control & assurance, logistics and executing the whole plan to deliver the final print output. Workflow management of a printing press needs to be given higher importance for improving press productivity (Bellander, 1997).

In the recent times, sophisticated print production systems and with the introduction of highly skilled manpower into press organization have certainly demanding to manage and monitor the entire printing production process in a very scientific manner. To grow in the print marketplace, all the essential resources (equipment, machines, materials, workforce and core competencies) need to be analysed and managed effectively for sustainable growth in this area. But, in most of the printing establishments still focus on acquiring and installing very high-cost printing machines and equipment, instead of focusing on the complete printing production workflow. The aim of systematic and scientific workflow should focus on; optimization of process efficiency, possible reduction of all kinds of waste, ensuring high level of print quality, fulfilling the requirements & expectations of the print buyers/customers, for streamlining the print process, sustainable growth and development of the printing organization.

In the present era of digital communication, it is expected to fulfil two basic points; on-time delivery and flexible approach to respond the needs & requirements of the print customers. Job order quantities are shrinking day-by-day, and the varieties/number of print jobs are increasing and at the same time the delivery period of the print jobs is getting reduced. Print consumers are expecting the delivery period of the printed products should be as low as possible. Just-in-time delivery approach is penetrating into the printing industry, and digital print engines are very successful in this regard (Hwei, 2014).

Concepts like, print-on-demand (pod), are very popular in the printing industry, and digital printing presses are very much into it. For the traditional forms of printing presses, they need to think out-of-the-box, for fulfilling the on-demand delivery of various print products. This can be effectively addressed by implementing scientific workflow systems into traditional printing shops. By proper identification, selection and implementation of right workflow system, will certainly help to enhance the press productivity and minimizing delivery period. It is not only following a better workflow system, rather efficiency of the particular workflow system is very important to optimize the production cycle time.

There are basically three sections for any printing establishment; pre-press, press and post-press activities. All these three departments need to work with greater co-ordination and cohesive manner for effecting improved press productivity with low level of wastage and lower processing waiting time. Workflow management for all the three sections needs to be formulated and managed effectively, so that minimum waiting period should be observed during the production cycle (Hwei, 2014).

There are number of sub-steps or activities needs to be performed in pre-press, press and post-press departments and they are highly dependent on each other. Effective workflow will certainly take care of these activities to be executed without much delay or waiting. Proper planning coupled with tracking of the activities will help to reducing repetition of information, possible generation of errors, unwanted waiting time and integration of activities for the fulfilment of the final print jobs.

1.14 Components of Print Productivity

Print productivity is a hot topic of discussion in the printing industry and hence it needs utmost care and attention, for its survival and growth in the print marketplace. Printing industry is highly unique in many respects, and the level of press automation is quite high in the recent times for taking care of process efficiency and press productivity related issues. While discussing and analysing the printing press productivity following components are required to be taken into account.

1.14.1 Printing Machine Efficiency

Press efficiency is not taken into consideration by most of the printing press management and it is basically overlooked in press environment. Even though the offset presses are manufactured with various levels of technological advancements, but they are generally less productive as because of proper care and attention is not given to this equipment in terms of timely care and maintenance are not followed strictly. Rather than following and adopting pro-active machine maintenance policies in most of the cases, breakdown maintenance policies are generally adopted. In long run, this approach does not yield the intended equipment productivity (Konopka and Trybula,1996).

Multi-colour sheet fed offset presses are very costly and speed of operation is also high in comparison with other printing process presses. These presses are manufactured to handle complexed nature printing jobs with greater efficiency and with high speed of press operation. Such machines need effective workflow management systems, proper sequencing of jobs, regular maintenance and check-up and proper setting and handling for giving the desired level of print output with higher press productivity. Present generation offset machines are nowhere behind the other similar manufacturing machines being used by other progressive industry.

There are certain ways and means by which the efficiency of offset presses can be improved. One of the ways could be the impact of technology and automation on the press. By incorporating advanced technologies and automation to the presses like; automated colour management systems, computerized settings and controls in various sections of the press, automatic plate loading systems, and increased press speed, etc. the efficiency of the press can be increased considerably. Timely servicing, maintenance scheduling at a regular interval of time, and in-time press calibration are some of the best practices to be followed strictly for achieving higher press efficiency. These points not only help to increase the press efficiency, but also directly contribute to extending the life span of the machine.

1.14.2 Human Performance

It is related to the overall effectiveness and capabilities of individuals engaged in a printing press for performing specific activities in print-production. It is all about an individual person's ability to perform certain tasks efficiently and finally contributing to the productivity and quality of the printing products. Human performance essentially varies from person to persons and time to time, depending upon the duration of work and their individual capabilities. There is a one-to-one relationship between the human performance and the production output. When the performance of workers increases, so is the increase in press production output and vice-versa (Subramaniam et al., 2007).

Continuous monitoring of the performance of the workers results into better standards of production out-put. As a general rule, most of the workers tend to perform in an average manner which leads to low press productivity, generation of high wastage of the valuable production time. By optimizing human performance in printing industries, printing companies can certainly able to achieve higher press productivity, better printing quality, reducing possible wastages, enhanced safety, and moreover the increased level of employee satisfactions. By providing appropriate training and opportunities to sharpen their understanding, knowledge and skills relating to various aspects of printing, employees will certainly get a chance to upgrade their knowledge base and stay updated with latest information of printing industry practice.

Effective communication and collaboration among the various levels of people (workers, supervisors, middle and top-level management), with clear-cut instructions, feedback systems, open culture to facilitate problem-solving and timely decision making are some of the points which needs to be taken into consideration for enhancing human performance in a printing establishment. Worker's motivation is one of the areas which directly affect the human performance in the workplace. This can be effectively achieved by various recognition programs, incentive systems, career advancement path and opportunities, and creating a positive organizational culture (Subramaniam et al., 2007).

Workers should feel safe about their career with the organization and the growth of the printing company should reflect with the growth of the individual being employed in it. Job satisfaction is very important when discussing on human performance, a satisfied and happy mind will certainly contribute effectively to the performance of the press organization. A happy mind is a productive mind and the print shop should identify all the factors which have a direct relationship with the well-being of the workforce employed in it for higher press productivity. By optimizing the human performance in printing industry, printing presses can certainly achieve higher press productivity, improved print quality, reduction of wastages, enhanced safety of the workplace, and increased employee satisfaction.

1.14.3 Machine Availability

Machine availability/equipment availability/uptime is indicated as the percentage of time that a particular machine/equipment is available for utilization or production purpose. It is basically used in the printing industry for assessing the reliability and performance of the particular machine/equipment used in the shop floor (Ziemerink & Bodenstein,1998). High machine availability makes sure that the particular machine/equipment is consistent in operational and ready for use; thereby maximizing the production capacity of the machine and minimizing possible production disruptions. In the same manner, low machine/equipment availability indicates frequent machine breakdown, maintenance related issues, and factors limiting the production capability of the particular machine/equipment (Ziemerink & Bodenstein,1998).

Monitoring, analysis and improving the availability of the machine should be taken into account for productivity optimization, reduction of possible delays, and meeting customers' needs and requirements effectively and timely. This essentially helps to identify the possible bottlenecks, planning for effective & timely maintenance schedule, and implementation of various measures to enhance the reliability and uptime of the particular machine/equipment installed in the print shop floor. It essentially takes into account the possible losses due to downtime and drawing the possible causes of such unwanted machine downtime, so that appropriate measures can be taken to improve the availability of the machine/equipment.

There are certain activities which are basically time consuming and with higher machine availability percentage such activities can be addressed effectively towards reducing the time. Make-ready or press set-up is one of such activities in a multi-colour sheet fed offset press, which generally consumes more time to execute. With high level of press availability coupled with greater degree of press automation, it is certainly possible to perform this activity in a shorter period of time (Ziemerink & Bodenstein,1998).

Most of the sheet fed offset press manufacturers are working hard to manufacture such presses with high level of machine availability. This will certainly make the machine reliable and reducing the machine down time considerably, so that the press operator has the liberty to run the press at a higher speed with less job changeover time towards achieving high press productivity (Ziemerink & Bodenstein,1998).

1.14.4 Production Breakdown

Planned shift length in printing industry can vary from eight hour to twelve hours depending upon several factors; local labor regulations, company policy, nature of printing work. However, the common shift length in manufacturing industry is typically eight hours, with scheduled breaks and a lunch break during their shift. It has to be noted that, the shift lengths can vary considerably between different printing companies and geographical locations (Tom, 2006). There are some printing presses may operate on multiple shifts for carrying out production around the clock, other may restrict to standard daytime shift. The planned shift length can be divided into two parts for effective operation of the press; planned downtime and planned operational time (Tom, 2006).

Planned down time is related to scheduled periods in which production activities are halted/paused intentionally. This is required for; maintenance of machine/equipment, job changeover/set-up, cleaning, employee break time, and inventory management purposes. It essentially helps the print companies to make it sure that, machines/equipment are function effectively, reduction of risk of possible accidents/breakdowns, and maintaining a safer and efficient working environment. On the other hand, planned operational time relates to scheduled periods during which print production activities are carried out. It is the time in which, labor, equipment, and machinery are engaged in the manufacturing of print products.

Right balance between the planned operational time and planned downtime is highly crucial for the printing companies in order to optimize press productivity, so as the meet production target within particular time and minimum utilization of various resources. By proper planning, downtime can be minimized with minimizing disruptions to the production activities. Unplanned downtime like; failure of equipment, unforeseen disruptions, power outages can certainly occur in the printing industry. These situations may lead to delays and disruptions in production schedules. Both these factors; actual operational time and unplanned downtime are major concern for the printing press management, when discussing on press and manpower utilization (Tom, 2006).

Production breakdown which is also known as equipment failure or production failure relates to a situation in the printing industries where the particular equipment or machine does not function effectively or results into significant disruption that leads to preventing it from performing its intended functions. As a result, the production process is halted or interrupted resulting into temporary stoppage of printing operations. Production breakdown in a printing press may come into picture due to the following reasons; electrical faults, mechanical failures, material shortage, human error, unforeseen circumstances, and software glitches.

1.14.5 Maintenance of Equipment

Maintenance of equipment is very crucial and especially machines and equipment used in the printing presses are of high cost and needs special care and attention. Timely maintenance of these high-cost machines and equipment will certainly help to discard any major problems. Moreover, regular maintenance certainly helps to ensure that the printing machines are in optimal working condition and hence availability of the press is high. It also leads into unexpected failures/breakdowns, which leads into improved reliability. On the other hand, unplanned machine downtime can be very costly; which results into loss of production, missing the delivery deadlines, and customer dissatisfaction. Well maintained printing machines and equipment results into efficient operation, reducing operational cost, and consumes less energy.

Regular and proper maintenance essentially helps to extend the life span of the machine, so that cost of the machine is distributed for a longer period of time. Regular cleaning, servicing, and calibration results into preventing possible wear and tear, deterioration of components, and corrosion. This will certainly undercut the problem of replacement of expensive parts and thereby saves money. In nutshell, maintenance of printing machines and equipment is highly essential for reducing the machine downtime, maximizing operational efficiency, minimizing production cost, maintain the longevity of equipment, and ensuring overall safety (Kulshrestha and Pant, 2014).

By doing regular maintenance of machines, printing press can certainly optimize their press operations, enhance overall equipment reliability and performance, and improving the bottom-line of press organizations. Printing industries that regularly carryout maintenance with good follow-up always attracts the print customers by the way of full utilization of their machines and equipment as well as good housekeeping safety (Kulshrestha and Pant, 2014).

With regular maintenance of printing machines and equipment, performance aspects of business like; profitability and productivity of the press can be increased considerably. Unplanned stoppage of machine is a big concern of worry for most of the printing presses and it results into going for overtime and hence adds additional cost to the business, which is very difficult to recover (Al-Najjar, 1998).

Opportunity lost is a not good the health of the printing press and the customer accordingly get shifted to some other press for getting the job done, and in most of the cases the customer never returns back, also. In the recent times, the role and importance of maintenance function in a typical printing press has increased considerably, due to its contributions towards in keeping and improving the availability, high print quality products, performance efficiency of the equipment, on-time delivery of the printed products, fulfilling the safety & environmental requirements, and cost effectiveness of the complete printing press at high levels (Al-Najjar, 1998).

In the olden days, maintenance was considered as a necessary evil, but in the recent years with the introduction of high cost and high-end automatic press machines and equipment this perception is changing, rather than just unavoidable and unpredicted expenses, it is considered as a profit centre. By the use of regular, pro-active and effective maintenance policies and programs, it is very much possible to reduce the failure of the press equipment considerably, which will enhance the availability and reliability level of the machines towards higher press productivity (Al-Najjar, 2002).

All these will lead to greater savings and higher profit margin for the printing press. In order to attain the long-term goal of registering higher profit, it is expected that the printing presses should adopt scientific methods for maintaining the various machines and equipment being installed for carrying out the print production activities. Maintenance has a direct impact on the cost, quality, capacity utilization, safety and environmental aspects of printing business (Al-Najjar, 2002).

1.14.6 Press Automation

Press automation is related to the integration of technologies and automated systems in the operation of a printing press. It is essentially aimed at streamlining and optimizing the printing process, reducing possible human contacts/intervention and finally increasing the efficiency of the printing press. There are basically three stages being followed in a typical printing establishment; pre-press, press and post-press along with planning and co-ordination functions. Automation is equally applicable to all the areas of press sections, for setting up printing press activities quickly and efficiently for executing different printing jobs.

Press set-up time or make-ready is a very time-consuming press activity and press automation certainly helps to reduce this time, so that the saved time can be utilized for the other productive activities. In totality, printing press automations results into; higher press productivity, reduced manpower cost, improved printing quality coupled with consistency, faster press set-up time, and overall enhanced press productivity (Subramaniam et al., 2014). Press automation has certainly encouraged and helped the printing presses to handle and execute a wide variety of printing jobs, reacting and responding to the changing demands and requirements of the prospective consumers and moreover staying very much competitive in the printing market place (Subramaniam et al., 2014).

In order to take care of short run jobs, high print quality, shorter delivery time, and cost-effective printing output, modern offset printing presses are highly equipped with automatic systems, which has certainly improved press performance, reducing the wastage level, reducing possible use of power consumption to run the machine, and increasing the speed of press operations. While discussing about the conventional printing press, all the five units; in-feed, inking, dampening, printing and deliver units were adjusted and controlled manually by the press operator. But the present generation presses perform most of the activities with greater degree of press automation (Kipphan, 2001).

The use of automated press equipment certainly helps to achieve press productivity along with reduced material wastage level and much cost savings. Level of automation can be essentially divided into two heads; semi-automatic and fully automatic press operations (Groover, 2008). In the next generation high-tech sheet fed offset presses, removing and fixing the printing plates in the different printing stations are carried out automatically without much human interference. Moreover, simultaneous plate loading options are also available to save the precious press time. Efforts are made to bring down the make-ready time as low as possible, so that press productivity can be enhanced with less material wastage and higher cost savings (Dejidas and Destree, 2005). In the recent years, in order to compete with other available printing technologies in the marketplace, there is a greater pressure on the sheet fed offset printing machine to prepare machine with greater degree of automation.

Automated sheet fed offset presses have certainly numerous potential advantages over the conventional/traditional presses; high quality print products, higher colour and ink consistency, higher productivity, reduced machine downtime, lesser production time to executing printing jobs, and finally saving the operational costs (Waller, 1999). While ordering a multi-colour sheet fed offset printing press, all the printing variables need to be planned and checked thoroughly with the press manufacture or equipment supplier, so that the same can be checked with the standard operating procedure, for enhancing the press set-up time. Possible reduction of the press make-ready time is very crucial and this will result into improving the final printing quality, increasing the level of customer satisfaction and moreover giving a competitive edge to the printing establishment over other printing firms (Kareem, 2015).

1.14.7 Training

It is one of the most neglected areas in any printing establishment and it is considered as non-productive activity and it has very low level of contribution towards the press productivity. Unless and until the workforce working in the press is not trained properly, it is very difficult to achieve the desired result. Training is not one time activity; rather it should be a continuous activity towards getting desired press output. Learning, unlearning and relearning process should be followed for better press productivity results (Hashmicro, 2022).

Press efficiency is resulted by the proper blend and coordination of people and processes. In order to achieve high press productivity, training component should be given topmost priority, as most of the machines are being installed with high level of automation and proper handling and functioning of these equipment demands press operator with same level of knowledge and expertise. A log book should be maintained for scheduling the training programs for all level of employees being working in the press environment (Corning Data, 2021).

The success level of any printing press is highly attributed to productivity of its employees. Employee productivity is related to the output being generated in a specific period of time. Employees should be encouraged to take active participation in various training programs being organized and conducted from time to time so that their knowledge base can be enlarged. A training calendar should be prepared for the complete year, well in advance, and a considerable time must be devoted for arranging value added training to its prospective employees. Such training programs are aimed at to enhance the productivity of the employee which in turn contributes to the press productivity (Gross, 2018).

1.15 Internal Situation of Print Production

Printing industry is highly different from other similar manufacturing industries in many respects. As mentioned earlier, complex nature of printing business demands clearcut business models specific to each individual press set-up to function and productivity related issue. A wide range of printing jobs are being handled by the individual printing presses and this makes this particular industry highly different from the other industries. As day by day, the job order quantity is decreasing and the varieties of the jobs are increasing, it is generally required to adopt innovative approaches to handle such complex situations. Some of the internal situations in a typical printing house can be identified as; speed of the printing machine, press set-up/make-ready, and utilization or performance of the press equipment.

1.15.1 Printing Machine Speed

Most of the printers generally prefer to run the press at an increasing press speed, and this may lead to some of the unforeseen problems and printing defects. The press should run at a speed at which the desired level of print quality is achieved along with productivity optimizations. The speed of the press is mainly dependent upon; the technological level of automation, age of the press, maintenance practices, reliability and availability of the press, and more. Most of the modern sheet fed offset presses are manufactured to run at 18,000 sheets per hour.

1.15.2 Make-ready

Press make-ready of set-up is related to adjusting the printing press in relation to the particular printing substrate, ink, and printing specifications prior to the actual press run. This essentially includes setting the in-feed unit as per the size, thickness, basis weight, grain direction of the substrate to be printed, setting the inking and dampening unit as per the nature of the printing job, proper ink & water balance, setting of the printing units, sequence of colours to be printed, colour registration, colour matching, setting of the delivery unit, and making it sure that the press print matches well with the proof print (Printing Tips, 2023).

It also indicates all the steps and processes to be performed to set the press to print a particular job in hand. It takes care of all the activities that the press technician should perform between accepting the printing plates for printing till the ok sheet is signed by the press supervisor (Dietz, 1942). The essential steps that are followed in a typical multi-colour sheet fed offset press during the press make-ready can be summarized as; preparation of the pile, pile board setting, feed board setting, setting the double sheet detector, setting the sheet forwarding and conveying path, setting the side lay & front lay, setting the sheet transfer systems to the printing unit, fixing the printing plates, ink sequence and setting, preparation and setting of inkers & dampers, registration of colours, colour matching, printing unit setting, delivery board preparation, dryer setting, and matching the printed sheet with the standards or proof sheets for starting the actual printing cycle (Dietz, 1942).

1.15.2.1 Make the Make-ready more Efficient

A good make-ready is all about systematic and effective coordination all the activities that are needed to press set-up, and moreover it comes with experience and time. Most of the modern high speed and automatic multi-colour sheet fed offset presses are equipped with latest technology to take care of make-ready procedure and time, effectively. In recent time, simultaneous plate loading, automatic colour management and control, automatic plate, blanket and impression cylinder wash-up, and automatic in-feed unit setting are some of the facilities being incorporated into the machine configuration to shorten the make-ready time considerably.

A well performed press make-ready not only saves precious machine time, but also helps to reduce material wastes and saves money during the whole process. Efficient make-ready is given utmost importance in the recent times, as because the job run quantity is getting reduced and the consumers are demanding faster delivery time without compromising the final printing quality. In order to stay alive in the competitive print marketplace, the cost of the print production also needs to be brought down. With proper and systematic make-ready, one can certainly save precious machine time and other resources, which will result into higher press output with much cost savings (Offset Pressman, 2011).

1.15.2.2 Taking Control of Waste inside the Pressroom

Most of the present generation sheet fed offset presses are focussing on controlling waste time and resources for their survival and growth in the printing marketplace. Typical analysis of a printing job essentially indicates that, labor cost ten percent, material cost is seventy percent, and fixed cost is twenty percent. Identification of source of generation of waste and effective management of these wastes will certainly help to reduce the waste in a typical sheet fed offset press. Make-ready process is one of the major contributors of waste in a multi-colour sheet fed offset press. The length of make-ready time has a direct impact on the amount of waste to be generated in the particular press (Offset Pressman, 2012). Waste in nay form is not at all desirable in any press set-up, they need to be reduced to the lowest possible limit, for effective functioning of the press organization and generating more profit.

The skill of the press operator plays an important role in performing the press make-ready and thereby controlling the amount of waste to be resulted in make-ready. One of the recent surveys indicates that a typical multi-colour sheet fed offset press is not running for 40 percent of time; breaking down into 23 percent on make-ready and 17 percent on delays. This indicates the importance of a properly planned and executed make-ready operation in a typical sheet fed offset press, towards minimizing wastes and making the print output cost effective (Offset Pressman, 2012).

1.15.2.3 Faster Offset Press Make-ready

As per the general observation, if the multi-colour sheet fed offset press is not running (i.e., idle), then it not generating any revenue. This statement certainly indicates the role and importance of press make-ready operation and moreover the whole activity faster and more efficient in terms of saving the precious press time and raw materials. By preparing a proper and workable checklist, be ready for the next job in terms of printing plates, ink, substrates, etc., use of manpower wisely, setting the press set-up standards, and motivation of the press crew are some of the important points to be taken into account for a faster press make-ready (Offset Pressman, 2014).

Critical analysis of the job before loading the plates, setting the various units of the press, sequence of printing colours, colour management, etc., is very important. As the length of the print run is getting reduced day by day coupled with increasing in the number of jobs, it is expected that, the make-ready should be faster, so that a greater number of printing jobs can be accommodated within particular span of time without compromising the print quality and cost factors.

1.15.3 Equipment Performance/Utilization

Equipment performance/utilization essentially refers to how efficiently and effectively the sheet fed offset press is being used in the print production process along with its degree of performance to the intended press functions and contribution to the overall press productivity. Multi-colour sheet fed offset presses are very costly, and the high cost of the equipment is justified if and only if, it is able to delivering the desired print output. There are number of factors which indicate equipment performance; print throughputs, speed of the press, accuracy, availability, reliability, and the final produced printing quality. higher values of offset press performance indicates that the particular machine is operating optimally and with desired results efficiency (Heidelberg, 2016).

There are many factors to be taken into account for achieving higher equipment performance rate. Training of the press operator, well managed workflow system, total productive maintenance systems, and proper job planning along with automated multi-colour sheet fed offset presses are some of the factors which needs utmost care and attention for the higher utilization of presses. Proper printing job scheduling and planning also helps to enhance the equipment performance. As a general rule, sequencing of the similar nature of jobs, generally compliments not to change the ink colour sequence of the various units of the press. This helps to save precious press time and hence higher rate of equipment utilization (Offset Pressman, 2014).

1.16 Print Productivity direct in relation with Waste in all Forms

Printing press is credited with generating more wastes than many other manufacturing industries. The list could be; waste printing substrates, ink, fountain solution, plate cleaners, blanket wash, packaging from the incoming supplies, adhesives, binding & finishing wastes, pre-press materials and chemicals, and printing plates, etc. It is rightly calculated that; the true cost of the waste can be as much as twenty-five times the cost of disposal of the same. Proper planning should be outlined for the reducing the printing press waste as low as possible; so that profit can be maximized and protecting the environment. As a general rule, anything that leaves the printing press the print buyer pays for it is print output and anything that leaves the press and the printing press pays is a waste (Alberta, 1995).

An ideal waste management practice is to have plan for preventing waste generation from its source. Waste prevention should be the utmost priority for any printing press. High-tech modern multi-colour sheet fed offset presses are manufactured with an eye to reduce the waste at its source point during the whole print production cycle. Waste reduction also addresses the environmental related issues effectively. The last option should be sending the waste to the landfill. Prior to this, all other options should be taken into consideration; reduce, reuse, recycle, and recover. Poor printing, poor press make-ready, operator error, changing requirements of the customers, over production, and mismatch between the paper required and printed are some of the possible factors which contributes to the substrate waste in a typical sheet fed offset press organization.

As substrate constitutes a major portion of the final cost of the print production, care must be observed to minimize possible wastage of printing substrate. Rising cost of raw materials always puts pressure on the printing industry to increase the efficiency of the press to justify the final cost of print production. Reduction of substrate waste is one of the better options to save resources and taking care of the environment as per the government regulations (Lundberg & Wallin, 2016). In printing industry, there is a continuous pressure from the local government to adopt sustainable practices, so that possible negative impact on the nature earth can be lessened. Besides this, the printer's worldwide in the recent times are facing sharp increase in raw material cost. In order to continue printing business, print house should focus on minimizing material waste (Thompson, 2014).

Printing industry in the recent years are under government scanner in terms of production of green and environment printing solutions with low level of carbon footprint and sustainability related issues (Thornhill, 2014). By successful utilization of the various resources required for the print production systems, printing industry can certainly address various issues relating to cost reduction, productivity enhancement, and print sustainability effectively (Envirowise, 2004).

1.17 Potential of Printing Sector and Enhancement of Print Productivity

Indian printing and paper industry is showing a positive growth trend in the recent years and it is also projected to have a better future also. As the demand for packaged products is increasing day by day, so is the demand of package printing and paper production. By 2025, paper consumption is going to increase by approximately 50 percent. The same is true for the printing industry also, as the demand for high quality printing products are increasing day by day, in India (Maiervidorno, 2023).

With the fast increasing of digitalization in India, there is common perception among the Indian people is that, physical printing especially books, magazines, newspapers, etc. are going to be declined considerably. But the adoption of high-tech automatic machines and equipment in the press organization, it is very much possible to produce eco-friendly, low-cost printing products to take care of the Indian consumers. It is very much sure that, Indian printing industry will be in the good shape and size in coming years also (Maiervidorno, 2022). The printing industry in India is growing at an annual growth rate of 12 percent per annum and essentially generates an annual turnover of over $11 billion. With rapid modernization and urbanisation, it is highly possible to achieve higher growth rate, in coming years (Maiervidorno, 2020).

This chapter has successfully covered the theoretical aspects relating to the topic of the research work. It outlined the historical background of the printing, lithographic printing technique, basic principles of offset printing, invention of paper, importance of paper for the printing process, applications of offset printing in the printing marketplace, design of sheet-fed offset printing press, Indian and global scenario of sheet fed offset printing. This chapter also covers the meaning and concepts of productivity, production vs productivity, measurement of productivity, possible factors that affects productivity, concept of productivity in printing industry, enhancing productivity, components of offset press productivity, press efficiency and the factors affecting offset press productivity, press automation and the impact of automation on the productivity of the sheet fed offset presses. This chapter has certainly formed the basic understanding of the theoretical aspects of the topic of the research work.

CHAPTER-2 REVIEW OF LITERATURE

This chapter is about the literature review part relating to the research work. The purpose of literature review is to show the subject-matter competence, highlight gaps and research requirements, and place the study within a larger academic framework for moving further to carry out the research work systematically. It also serves to inform the research design. It summarizes and synthesizes the body of information that already exists on the research topic and thereby giving the research the essential context. It is aimed to understand the key concepts, points of contention, and historical development of the area of the chosen topic of the research. The chapter highlights relevant theories and conceptual frameworks that inform the research study's approach.

Author (Forrester, 2020), explained that, from the invention of movable type by Gutenberg to laser printing and digital printing, printing is serving the whole world as a mass media for communication. Much before the invention of printing, written word was the only method being widely used for the preparation of books, which was a very time-consuming process and months together was required for preparing a single book. If some errors are occurred, then the whole process was repeated from the beginning. Historical record indicates that before printing was invented, the European libraries would often contain less than five hundred books. Invention of printing has certainly given a momentum in the direction of mass production of books with less time and making knowledge and information to the mass people, cutting down the geographical barriers.

Author (Baral, 2010), explained that, invention of paper is one of the strongest milestones in the history of mankind which in the later stage made printing to grow and progress. Initially, paper was made out from papyrus, which grows in Africa, way back in 2600 BC, and the real invention of paper made from the plant fibers such as; cambric grass or bamboo fibers dates back to 105 AD. Printing substrate is very important for effecting printing operation. Due to the structural and surface characteristics of paper, it provides a better option for printing applications. As the main ingredient for papermaking is fiber and it is essentially sources from plant bodies, it is natural, bio-degradable, recyclable and easy to carry and use. This makes paper as one of the most suitable printing substrates for various printing applications.

Author (Kew, 2018), pointed out that, in the recent times, packaging industry is largely dependent upon the paper as one of the major base materials for various packaging printing and converting processes. In order to provide multi functions it is combined with metallic foils, plastic films, wood, boards, which is popularly known as laminations. Sometimes the paper surface can be made glazed, waxed, water-proofed, embossed, coloured, coated, and printed for taking care of the packaging consumers.

Author (Kew, 2018), further mentioned that, in the recent times, packaging industry is registering higher growth percentage in comparison to printing industry, and packaging printing is one of the areas which are very important in the present context. Paper manufacturers are highly engaged in preparing very high-quality paper for taking care of a wide range of requirements of printing as well as packaging industry. Paper manufacturing process is also adopting innovative practices for manufacturing papers which are cost effective, eco-friendly and with highest level of surface and strength properties.

As per (University of Houston, 2019) critically pointed that, there are four stages contributing to the history and growth of lithographic printing process; the very invention of lithographic process of printing and its early use, subsequent introduction of photographic principles to the printing process, successful addition of offset press into the printing system, and development of metallic offset printing plates. Alois Senefelder, inventor of Lithographic printing process was highly involved for the subsequent refinement of this printing technique and his contributions to this work is highly remarkable. In the later stage, the printing process was noticed by the printing industry as one of the most widely acceptable form of printing.

As per (Offset printing technology, 2019), pointed out that, the basic construction or configuration of a typical sheet fed offset consist of one printing station, for printing one colour at a time. The number of printing stations can be increased to eight to ten, depending upon the nature of work to be printed in that particular machine. Each printing station essentially contain; one inking unit, one dampening unit, and three cylinders for effecting printing.

Offset printing technology, 2019, further mentioned that, most of the large sized printing establishments generally install multi-colour sheet fed offset presses for printing complex nature jobs with high speed of operation. Further, offset printing presses are grouped under two subheadings; sheet fed offset press and web fed offset press. Sheet fed offset presses are generally used for commercial and packaging printing applications, whereas web fed offset presses are used for publication, label printing, etc.

According to (Wikipedia, 2022), explained that, India is a vast country and its population is its strength. Growing literacy rate coupled with growing economy always demands for higher volume of books, journals, newspapers, packaging and other printed products. Indian economy in the recent years is showing positive growth and the purchasing power of the common man is also increasing. For education one need physical books and hence the growth of printing industry is accelerated. This is the case of other printed products consumption also, in terms of its growth. In India, there are numerous regional languages besides English and Hindi, so the demand of educational related printed materials is also equally high to meet the demands of the particular geographical region.

Author (Salman et al., 2008), very rightly pointed that, a number of techniques and methodologies are in the marketplace to improve the operational efficiency of any manufacturing and service industries. As printing is highly unique in many respects than the other manufacturing industries, it is highly important to select the most appropriate method and process for enhancing the press productivity and efficiency. Care must be given to analyse the internal environment of the particular printing establishment and according identify the particular model to suit to the requirement of the press for improving the process efficiency. In the recent times, higher importance is given for attaining high productivity with the available resources and that too with minimum utilization of various resources so as to generate high proportion of profit.

Author (Womack and Jones, 1998), explained that, Lean thinking is highly beneficial to printing industry for promoting and achieving continuous improvements in methodology of doing the various activities in a typical offset press organization. Lean thinking was originated from Toyota Production System concept, which was aimed at continuous improvement philosophy of eliminating all types of waste from a system. The beauty of the Lean that it is not only restricted to manufacturing industry, rather it is well enlarged to all other aspects of any business. In printing industry, elimination of waste is a major issue, and if it taken care, no doubt the ease of doing printing business certainly can be enhanced.

Author (Nicholas, 1997), mentioned that, Lean thinking is associated with providing the customer the option of pulling the demand when it is essentially needed and the supplier with the option to supply only when it is required. This situation certainly helps both the parties; both the customer and the supplier with potential capital savings on investments in inventory and lead times. This is the basic requirements for the printing industry in the recent years for their growth and development in the print marketplace. As it is aimed at continuous improvements, so both the print consumers and press are at a better position when it comes to cost saving without compromising print quality and delivery time.

Author (Antonio, 2015), explained that, productivity concept has certainly evolved over the last few years aiming at effectiveness rather than an efficiency ratio only. Rather than restricting to only to cost and quality related issues, it has successfully expanded into other areas also; poverty alleviations, job security, job creation, conservation of essential resources, fulfilling various social responsibilities, attainment of business excellence, good governance, and environmental protection initiatives. Some of the other concepts like; knowledge productivity and social productivity are also being evolved over time to complement the business environment. Printing industry is also taking the benefits of all these productivity concepts for providing innovative printing solutions with waste reduction, value added print products which are environmentally sustainable.

Author (Tangen, 2002), explained that, the two terminologies, efficiency and effectiveness are highly crucial for the printing industry in order to stay competitive in the marketplace. However, in a very simple terms, "doing the right things" is related to effectiveness and "doing things right" describes the term efficiency. When considering the term efficiency, it is highly linked with the utilization of resources and specific to printing industry, it essentially relates to minimum resource level that is required to produce the desired output. Effectiveness is all about the minimum utilization of all the resources that are required for the typical offset press and achieving higher level of print output, i.e., enhanced press productivity. These two factors are highly interrelated and crucial to the success of the press productivity ratio.

Author (Misterek et al., 1992), pointed out that, it is highly relevant to identify the most important characteristics of productivity measures that are responsible for the change in overall press productivity. By establishing the various relationships like; decrease, increase and no change in press productivity with number of different combinations of changes in input and output levels can be worked out well in advance. The particular combination of input and output should be evaluated before adoption of the same to the press organization. Productivity enhancement should be aimed at saving of the resources and maximizing the press output with minimum use of resources, so that the effective cost of print production can be lowered down towards attaining higher profit margin.

Author (Gammarano, 2018), explained that, the economic growth and development of any nation is highly achieved through either increased level of employment of the effective work being done by the employed workforce. In nutshell, labor productivity is highly linked with the economic performance of the particular business unit and in turn it contributes to national economy. Health of the workers, the ergonomics of the work area, continuous training of the workforce, motivation and increased satisfaction level are some of the basic factors which contribute to higher labor productivity. In present time, much cost, highly automated offset presses are employed in a printing press for handling complex natured printing jobs with greater press productivity. As the cost of this equipment is very high, it is highly demanded that the press operators with high level of satisfaction can certainly lead to high press productivity.

Author (Aph, 2009), explained about the two concepts; partial productivity and overall productivity relating to the manufacturing and service industries. Partial productivity factors related to the individual factors which in turn contribute to the overall productivity of a press organization. Individual input factors like; materials, labor and overheads are easily correlated with associated cost factors and easy to calculate, measure and take necessary steps to control them. Printing uses utilizes various resources for making the final print output, and in recent times the cost of these resources is getting increased day by day.

Author (Aph, 2009), further mentioned that, effective utilization and moreover minimum uses of these resources are highly demanded for cost saving purpose. By suitable identification of various inputs to partial productivity and ranking them in terms of their value and importance, it will lead to control them in a productive manner. In turn, overall productivity can be controlled and enhanced for higher press productivity with best possible way of cost savings.

Author (Singh, 2000), explained that, in industrial engineering, productivity is defined as the produced goods to resources consumes, more specifically the relationship between the output to input in the transformation process in the manufacturing process. It is highly connected with the utilization of available resources, more specifically the effective utilization of all resources that are required for the conversion process. When the resources are properly used the productivity factor is also high and vice-versa. This clearly indicates productivity; more specifically enhanced productivity is linked to creation of value to the organization. By adding value to the printed output, certainly high press productivity can be achieved. Utmost care must be observed to devise innovative methods to reduce the utilization of various resources for the production of print output.

Author (Shital, 2018), mentioned that, possible wastage of time and resources is the result of lower press productivity. It should be noted that, vital resources like; time and capital are very important, and hence should be used wisely for achieving higher press output. In order to give a long-term growth and momentum to the particular firm, a high level of productivity should be maintained years after years. When the resources are utilized wisely and effectively with minimum wastage level, then certainly the firm attain high press productivity. This essentially results into possible reduction of production cost and providing high quality printed products to the consumers at a lower price, creating a wining-wining situation to both to the firm and the consumer. More profits means that more earnings to the firm, which can be passed to the various stakeholders for wealth creation.

Author (Aph, 2009), mentioned that, in any business, in order to compete with other competitors within the particular segment and also to maintain international level competitiveness, productivity growth should be utmost importance. At the firm level, it helps to offer a better salary package and incentives to its employees and stakeholders and keep the funds reserved for possible investment in capital goods and equipment. Through productivity growth, the printing press is able to generate extra amount of profit and accommodate a greater number of printing jobs without compromising desired quality level and delivery time. With the transition to a more open economy, the government all over the globe are shifting their focus on higher productivity level, so that the national economy can be boosted. Printing industry is under scanner for fulfilling the above factor with sustainability aspects.

Author (Yadav and Marwa, 2015), explained that, productivity is not a subjective concept, rather it is an objective concept. Being the objective in nature, it can be measured against either national or international standard. As it is measurable, the same data can be used for monitoring purpose such as; planning at the organizational level, organizational improvement, and comparison to the competitors in the particular industry segment. Productivity is basically a scientific concept, and hence needs to be defined logically and followed with utmost care in order to get high benefits from it. Being measured in quantitative terms, it is essentially qualifying as a variable, and can be defined and measured in relative or absolute terms. Printing industry certainly is utilizing these concepts for achieving higher productivity.

Author (Kalpana, 2019), pointed out that, the local government always play an important role for framing various industrial policies for providing momentum to the industrial productivity of the particular industry segment. It is the sole responsibility of the government to formulate such policies which will create favourable condition for investment, flow of capital, savings and conversion of national resources. In certain industrial sectors, incentive schemes may be encouraged for the growth and development of the particular industry segment, in keeping view of the national interest. One of the incentive schemes could be taxation policy which essentially encourages further expansion of the particular business segment.

Author (Shabat, 2019), explained that, it is not always possible to replace the machines and equipment with new ones, because it can be very expensive, particularly most of the press equipment are very costly. This problem can be effectively addressed with implementing a suitable and effective maintenance program in the press environment. Along with productive maintenance programs, the competency of the press crew is very important in order to achieve higher press productivity.

Author (Shabat, 2019), further explained that most of the printing machines and equipment are high-tech machines with high level of press automation to perform complex natured printing work with high degree of press efficiency. Such machines and equipment essentially demand for press crew with advanced knowledge and expertise to handle and operate with utmost care and attention for achieving optimum press productivity. If they are not motivated and trained properly, then it will be very difficult to attain the desired press output.

Author (Michael, 2020), explained the role and importance of scheduling of regular maintenance programs for enhancing the reliability and availability of the particular equipment or machine. Regular maintenance is highly important for the optimal functioning and performance of a piece of equipment. It is expected that all the equipment and machines installed in the press room should be checked regularly to take care of any unwanted or sudden breakdown, which will affect heavily to the print production systems. Scheduled maintenance will certainly take care of such unwanted situations and thereby less downtime and leading more machine times for production related activities. Regular maintenance should be planned and scheduled in such a manner so that it will have least impact on the production activities.

Author (Tomljanovic, 2015), explained that, printing industry is in constant transforming mode to take care the present need and requirements of the print consumers. Modern modes of communication are changing at a greater pace, so printing industry need to change and adjust accordingly in order to stay competitive in the communication platforms. Traditional printing is all about much of human touch, but with the penetration of internet, the dynamics of printing business is changing constantly, in particular the job ordering process and technique.

Author (Tomljanovic, 2015), further mentioned that, it should not be considered as a burden or hurdle to carrying out business, rather it should be considered as compliment to perform the print production with ease and effective manner with generating high profit margin. Suitable arrangements need to be made to accept job orders through online mode and executing them with the traditional method with greater degree of accuracy and sticking to the delivery time lone for on-time delivery of the print products.

Author (Uribe, 2008), explained that, printing press environment is highly complex, as the type and nature of each job is quite different from one another, and moreover the job order quantities are also highly segregated ranging from few numbers to few millions also. Due to high complexity of the system, decision of running the business also rests on the decisions of the shop floor managers. Almost all the decisions are based on mental models rather than data-based models. When evaluated, most of the decisions are not usually optimal, but with trial-and-error basis over a period of time, it is being used for carrying out various operational activities.

Author (Uribe, 2008), stated that in recent times, introduction of high-tech machines and equipment's in the print shop floor is changing the old methods of decision-making and making the process more systematic and productive. This essentially helps to reduce possible errors that may happen during the print production process and making the decision-making process more systematic and effective. Sheet fed offset printing industry is adopting these automatic and technologically advanced machines and equipment to perform printing production work in more scientific manner.

Author (Gornam, 2019), mentioned that, training is one of the important factors which contributes to enhancing the press productivity. Most of the multi-colour sheet fed offset presses are equipped with greater level of automation and high speed. These high-tech offset presses are manufactured to perform most of the setting and press functions automatically without much human contacts. To maintain and operate these machines the press crew needs to be trained and retrained at a regular interval of time, so that much delay these machines can be operated to its rated efficiencies. In these presses, retention of employees is also very important, with regular up gradation of employee skill and expertise, this can be certainly improved and hence the press productivity is enhanced.

Author (Sarokin, 2020), explained that, technology is one of the important fundamental factors to be taken into account when discussing the press productivity. It is well established that, with proper selection of technology, press productivity can be enhanced. Before investment in advanced technology and high-cost machines, the overall productivity level should be taken into account. Sometimes, the high cost is justified with the productivity that can be achieved from the particular equipment. Money invested must be recovered with the output, as per the particular press set-up. All the pros and cons must be evaluated and analysed properly before selecting, installing and putting the particular machine into the printing shop floor.

Author (Varma and Lal, 2019), explained that, in the recent years, printing machine manufacturers are working hard to prepare multi-colour sheet fed offset presses equipped with advanced technology to take care of complex nature printing jobs, with cost and resource savings. During the press make-ready operation/ job changeover process, it is generally expected that resource waste cannot be avoided. But these machines are equipped with facilities where minimum human interference is observed and most of the press setting and adjustments are automatic in nature, paving the path for possible reduction of materials required for press set-up. This is mainly aimed at minimizing resource waste and maximizing cost savings during the whole print production cycle.

Author (Varma and Lal, 2019), in today's competitive printing marketplace, it is the survival of fittest and innovative methods and approaches for maximizing profit margin without much disturbing the quality standard and putting unwanted burden to the environment. As the digital printing machines are highly capable of printing short run jobs, low press set-uptime, lowest level of waste generation, meeting the customer's delivery deadline effectively, the new generation offset presses are designed and manufactured to take care of such opportunities being offered by different digital printing presses, effectively. Shorter make-ready time leads to low level of wastage generation during the process and certainly helps to generate more profit and accommodating a higher number of printing jobs within a particular period of production time.

Author (Sneed and Verhoef, 2001), mentioned that, with the introduction, advancement and penetration of Internet into our daily lives, and in order to carrying out printing business in such environment, it is highly demanded to automate the business process, so that the possible challenges posed by Internet can be effectively taken care. It is the advanced technology, but the working property and reliability of technology embedded into the multi-colour sheet fed offset press, that matters the most for getting the desired result towards achieving desired print productivity. The result indicates, the present generation sheet fed offset presses are highly capable of producing the print output with greater efficiency.

Author (Bellander, 1997), explained that, the graphic arts industry is following the essential path of development what other similar manufacturing industries are following, in order to take the benefits of advanced technology in this segment. This industrialised process view of the production is certainly helping this industry to grow and prosper in terms of advanced fully automatic presses capable of operating at very high speed and attaining highest levels of print quality.

Author (Bellander, 1997) further indicated that, it will create a different situation in the marketplace, the small sized printing companies which are using the handicraft tradition may not able to absorb the shock of installation of high-speed automatic offset presses, due the cost of the equipment, leaving few big sized printers in the market. In order to survive, maintain profit and grow in the printing marketplace, the presses should invest in very high-cost sophisticated press equipment for various press operations.

Author (Hwei, 2014), mentioned that, the efficiency of the press production process and performance of the machine in terms of cycle time of production is highly crucial for producing the desired press output. The particular press business model that results into longer cycle time may be due to the fact that, the three departments; pre-press, press and post-press are separated for the job production. They are not treated as single entity due to which waiting time for transfer of raw or semi-finished materials from one department to the other finally results into delay errors, and longer production cycle time. Proper co-ordination, planning and workflow will certainly help to result into a better press productivity factor.

Author (Konopka and Trybula,1996), explained that, in sheet fed offset presses, the efficiency of the production lines is very important and crucial for achieving improved production and effective utilization of all available resources. There are two important factors which the press production line efficiency; machine efficiency and manpower utilization.

Care must be given to measure these two factors with greater accuracy. Accurate and relevant production data of the particular press should be taken into account for identification and analysis of various faults at the different production lines and to take immediate measures to rectify them, so that the overall press productivity can be increased. In most of the cases, the production data is manipulated to hide the reality, but in long term this is not good for the health of the particular printing establishment.

Author (Subramaniam et al., 2007), explained that the importance of production monitoring system of any printing press is highly crucial. A real time production monitoring system is aimed at gathering and distributing the information to each and every one employed in the print shop floor in real-time as the various events are happening. It essentially helps the particular printing press to achieve realistic production goals, at reduced machine downtime and increased press output. The aim and objectives of the real time production monitoring system should be to monitor the press system for providing the right information at right time to the concerned personal for taking appropriate actions.

Author (Subramaniam et al., 2014) mentioned that, in the manufacturing process, machines are very common for producing the output. In the recent times, in order to achieve high press productivity, machines are selected with higher level of press automation and higher speed of press functioning. Since, the investment in these machines and equipment are very high, the cost is justified if high press output is achieved within the shortest possible time period. This is not only restricted to printing industry, but extended to all other manufacturing industries for reaping the possible benefits of high-cost equipment in terms of meeting the desired targets with cost savings.

Author (Groover, 2008), explained that, press automation is related to the technology concerned with the various applications of mechanical, electrical, electronic, and computer-based systems to operate and control. It is essentially can be separated into two sub-heads; automation of the press manufacturing system and computerization of the manufacturing support system. In modern press environment, these two categories overlap to some extent. Terms like computer integrated press manufacturing is used to indicate the extensive use of computers in the print production system for achieving better workflow management and higher press productivity. By implementing these two systems, possible human contact with the press machinery gets reduced and the workflow is automated. These points certainly help to streamline the complete production cycle and the end-result is press output with greater effectiveness and optimum utilization of resources.

Author (Kareem, 2015), mentioned that, there are number of problems which may occur in a typical sheet fed offset press are due to; faulty press operation, the substrate related issues, and the operator's error during the press functions. Other possible problems may be due to; mechanical, chemical, and physical variables. Therefore, the success of the offset press operation mainly relies on the in-time identification and analysis and taking prompt decisions of these variable well in advance and taking suitable measures during the press make-ready and press operations. These pro-active measures will certainly help to reduce overtime costs, increase press efficiency, press productivity, and press productivity. Most of the problems encountered in a multi-colour sheet fed offset press originates in inking, dampening, operating conditions, and machine maintenance practices.

Author (Hashmicro, 2022), explained that, and for the long-term success of a typical sheet fed offset press is highly dependent upon the employee productivity. Most of the manufacturing industries employ lean manufacturing practices for increasing employee productivity. But in reality, this alone is not sufficient to achieve higher press productivity. It is believed that, technology plays a bigger role towards increasing press productivity. In the recent times, most of the major sheet fed offset printing machines are incorporating high level of technology into their press configuration for performing most of the press settings and adjustments automatically, thereby reducing human dependency on various press functional activities. Automatic presses combined with high employee productivity certainly helps to achieve high press productivity.

Author (Gross, 2018), mentioned that, well trained, experienced and knowledgeable workforce will contribute better towards increased press productivity. The aim and goal of any sheet fed offset press organization is to enhance the productivity in order to be competitive in the print market place. The training functions should not be confined to the shop floor only, rather it should be enlarged to all the areas or sections of the press, so that all the people employed in the particular establishment are equipped with the latest knowledge and expertise to carry out the desired role and responsibility. All the sections of a typical press establishment should work in combination, rather than competing with each other. All these factors will certainly help to increase press productivity, systematically and effectively.

Author (Groover, 2008), explained that, a fully automatic printing press is achieved when the whole machine or equipment system is a motorised integrated system, without much human attention or interference. The whole press activities and operations are monitored and controlled through the central console system. A fully automatic multi-colour sheet fed offset press, claims that; a press crew is not required to be present during the production cycle. But at the same time, it is expected that the press crew may need to attend the particular machine every tenth cycle or every hundredth cycle of print production system.

Author (Smyth, 2003), mentioned that, press make-ready is related to the processes that are essentially used to organize the multi-colour sheet fed offset press to print a particular job in hand. It covers all the activities that the press crew performs between the staring of the job till running the job for actual print production. Press make-ready is all about preparation of the offset press to be ready for printing operations. It all begins with, when the last printed job is completed and the press is set-up for the new production of the next job. These arrays of activities are highly interrelated with each other, and in modern sheet fed offset presses, suitable arrangements are provided to perform these functions automatically without less human interference. The ultimate aim lies to shorten the press make-ready time for higher press productivity.

Author (Shadiya, 2012), explained that, by utilizing different reduction techniques, waste reduction can be highly achieved in a typical sheet fed offset organization. Waste management and reduction is an important point for the success of any printing organization. Raw materials used for the print production activities are generally of high cost, and it is expected to reduce possible wastages being generated throughout the production cycle. In today's competitive print market place, cost savings is major point for reducing the cost of the production of printing output. For effective management of various resources, the key areas need to be identified which contributes towards generating possible wastage and accordingly suitable actions may be devised to reduce the same from the point of origination.

Author (Lundeberg & Wallin, 2016), explained that, there is a continuous pressure to increase the press efficiency as because the cost of essential raw materials that are required for print production activities are increasing day-by-day. Along with this, there is a continuous pressure from the government side to producing print products which are environmentally friendly and also contributes to the national productivity for giving a momentum to the national economy. In order to take care of all these factors, the press needs to adopt business practices which conserve the natural resources while reducing the final cost of print products and helping directly to the national economy to grow and prosper in long-term basis.

Author (Diana et al., 2011), mentioned that, quality system basically comprises a set of rules and norms applied within the particular print house. These norms and rules are formulated to take care of aimed quality demands and thereby achieving printing business excellence. Modern business environment essentially demands for considering quality system as an important part of organizational culture. As each printing establishment is quite different from the others, they can develop its own quality system for adoption towards achieving higher press productivity.

Author (Poksinska, 2010), explained the role and importance of involvement of people for achieving higher press productivity. The top management should always be committed towards demonstrating the importance of quality printing jobs to the people working in the press organization. With the support and coordination from the top management, a conductive work-culture can be made to involve its employee for producing high quality printing jobs. A quality manager may be employed to act as facilitator and drive the improvement of work culture towards maintaining and producing consistent print quality throughout the various printing jobs. Everybody should be encouraged to take active participation in problem solving activities towards achieving high print quality. This will certainly result into positive results for the effective organizational performance, thereby development of the organization and the people employed in it.

Author (Daniel, 2023), mentioned that there are essentially seven types of wastes, or processes and resources, that generally do not add value to the organization as well as for the customer. They are summarized as; excess and unnecessary inventory of raw materials, unnecessary transportation, unproductive & unnecessary movement of people within the organization, waiting time (whether it is related to people waiting or idle press equipment or machine), over production of printed products, over-processing time than the required, and underutilization of the installed machine or equipment. All these should be taken into account for the possible reduction of wastages, so that the costs associated to them can be converted into profit, thereby increasing the press productivity.

Author (Mauro, 2007), explained that, for managing and controlling printer's business, it is advised to adopt Print Management Information Systems (MIS). It is considered as the staring, central, and end point in the printing business and production workflow systems. It is a system which essentially helps the printing organizations to collect, process, store, and distribute all the information that support the decision making, planning, and control purpose within the printing establishment. It also helps to streamline various press operations, enhance the press efficiency, and improves the overall press productivity. In general, MIS in the printing establishment brings press automation, reduces the final cost of print production, and enhances the customer satisfaction level. It also helps in managing the complex workflows being involved in the printing process and thereby contributing to the success of printing business.

Author (Mauro, 2007), further explained that, printing presses are engaged in using a wide range of raw materials; paper, paperboards, ink, chemicals, plates, rollers, and other consumables. MIS essentially helps to manage the inventory levels, tracking of the stock movement from the warehouse, and optimizing procurement processes. It also makes sure that, right kind of materials is available when needed, which essentially minimizes delays and takes care of stock outs. It also helps for job scheduling, allocation of essential resources, and optimization of print production sequences to increase overall press productivity.

Author (Ryan, 2022), explained that, computer aided manufacturing is helping the new generation automatic multi-colour sheet fed offset presses towards streamlining the print production processes, which results into; reduced cost of printing production, improved job scheduling flexibility, reduced downtime, and maintain correct inventory levels of various materials. Ultimate goal of adoption of such system is to achieve maximum press efficiency along with gathering relevant, real-time data from the production shop floor and improving press productivity.

Author (Ryan, 2022), further explained that, in the recent times, integrated production facilitated multi-colour sheet fed offset presses are becoming the first choice for the presses, for achieving high level of press productivity. As the job quantities are getting smaller and the delivery time is shortening, there is a continuous pressure to integrate computer aided manufacturing practices into the various machines and equipment, so that all the above issues can be addressed properly and without affecting much to the press productivity. Automated and high-speed presses are certainly demanding offset presses to integrate into these systems for higher productivity without compromising the desired level of printing quality and final cost of production.

This chapter has essentially outlined the findings of various works that were carried out by different researchers in the fields of productivity of sheet fed offset presses, at different points of time. Productivity is an important issue while discussing the operations of multi colour sheet fed offset presses; because of high cost factor associated with the procurement of these type of printing presses. Over the years, for enhancing the productivity levels of multi colour sheet fed offset presses, number of factors are taken into consideration by the press manufacturers and incorporation of press automation is one of such area. Various researchers have pointed out different options and systems to reduce the possible press set-up time, reduction of use of resources and to improve the productivity of the multi colour sheet fed offset presses.

CHAPTER-3 RESEARCH PROBLEM

This chapter indicates the research problem which led to the selection of the particular research topic. It certainly talks about the positioning of the printing industry at the Indian as well as worldwide market scenario. It mentions about the growth aspects of Indian printing industry in the coming years. This chapter also underlines the very importance of production enhancement of the printing presses in India in the present time.

Printing industry is the fourth largest industry in India and the same is true in the worldwide market scenario also. In the coming years, there is a good scope of printing industry, particularly in India, and is also expected to grow in the same pace and even more. Most of the printing presses are either small or medium in nature in India, and mostly are of family owned business.

In the recent times, production enhancement techniques are getting wider acceptance, because the print productivity in various presses in India are in the process of increasing productivity in their respective presses. Most of the presses, till-date are being deprived from various technological adoption programs, due to low level of technical expertise and the possible cost involved in these adoption process. It is the need of the hour to identify and find out various options available in the technology front and their impact on productivity enhancement in sheet fed offset presses.

This chapter of the thesis concludes the present status of printing industry both in Indian and worldwide context. India is showing a positive trend in the fields of printing industry in the recent times with a bright future ahead. But most of the sheet fed offset presses with high capital investment are not able to justify from the press productivity front. In order to compete in the print marketplace, the multi colour sheet fed offset presses needs to incorporate innovative ideas and options so as to enhance their respective press productivity for continued growth and development. This certainly justifies the base for selecting the topic of the research work to take care of the potential problems faced by the Indian printers with multi colour sheet fed offset press installations in their presses.

CHAPTER-4 RESEARCH OBJECTIVES

Sheet fed offset printing technology is the major printing process being used extensively by most of the printing presses in India. This is because of combination of superior print quality factors and print run length; this printing system has a strong edge over the other printing systems. Even though, digital printing systems are posing a challenge to the sheet fed offset printing system, but the recent technological developments in this segment is well equipped to face these challenges effectively. Certainly, the effective adoption of these technologies will help to enhance print productivity in the sheet fed offset presses.

Objectives of this research work are:

1. To identify, study and analyze critically various print productivity related issues being used and faced in various sheet fed offset presses.
2. To identify and analyze the recent technological developments in the sheet fed offset presses and adopting them (as at point no. 1) for enhancing productivity in the sheet fed offset presses.

CHAPTER-5 RESEARCH METHODOLOGY

This chapter is the research methodology section of the research work. It is fundamentally the methodical process used to carry out studies, provide answers, or resolve issues. It acts as a guide, describing the techniques, steps, and resources that were used to gather, examine, and interpret data for carrying out the research work. The ability of research methodology to lay a strong basis for scholarly work is one of its core characteristics. Based upon the research topic, review of literature, research problem and research objectives, the detailed materials, equipment and the various phases of carrying out the whole research work is mentioned in detail in this chapter.

Research methodology relates to the process and techniques being used for the particular research work towards the scientific investigations, data collection, information analysis, result discussion and finally to the drawing of conclusion. It is basically a structured outline for the planning and execution of the research work. Printing industry is one of the major manufacturing industries and in recent times it is undergoing structural changes in terms of adoption of advanced technology to perform the various tasks more systematically with an eye to improve press productivity.

Sheet fed offset printing is one of the major forms of printing method which is being used for printing of print output with high print quality and on a wide range of printing substrates to cater an array of printing market segments. Print productivity of multi-colour sheet fed offset presses is one of the major concern and discussion in the recent times for its very survival, growth and development in the printing market place.

Single colour sheet fed offset presses are designed to print one colour, and moreover these presses are used extensively for printing black colour or one spot colour as the requirement of the particular job in hand. Most of the small and medium sized printing presses install these presses for single colour printing. On the other hand, multi-colour sheet fed offset presses are designed to print multiple colours simultaneously, at one go. Usually four or more colours (cyan, magenta, yellow and black) and special colours (spot colours) are printed effectively by multi-colour sheet fed offset presses. This clearly indicates that in single colour sheet fed offset press only one plate is used whereas in multi-colour sheet fed offset presses multiple plates are used; one for each colour relating to the printing job.

Most of the modern multi-colour sheet fed offset presses are equipped with advanced registration systems to maintain accurate and précised registration of all the print colours, thereby possible reduction of colour shifts and misalignments. Multi-colour sheet fed offset presses are designed with much higher press speed in comparison to single colour sheet fed offset presses, which results into producing more printed sheets per colour per hour.

This particular research is centred around the level of technological advancements in the areas of multi-colour sheet fed offset and their possible impact on the press productivity. Last three decades witnessed press automation from different levels and it continues to move into further advanced levels in the coming years. Sheet fed offset manufacturers are trying hard to incorporate these technical advancements for improving the press performance to compete with the possible challenges being posed by other printing techniques from time to time. In the multi-colour sheet fed offset presses, technological advancements have certainly helped to transform the industry resulting into improved press efficiency, print quality and press productivity.

Multi-colour sheet fed offset presses have certainly evolved multi-fold over the years, thereby absorbing various levels of technology for enhancing press capabilities and leading to enhanced print quality with possible reduction of paper wastage during the print production process with an eye on possible reduction of print production cost. All the different levels of technologies in multi-colour sheet fed offset presses have certainly made it possible for the industry to achieve high print quality with fine resolution, faster print production cycle, improved press efficiency, and complimenting the nature earth in terms of environmental sustainability.

During the research work, multi-colour sheet fed offset printing presses were identified and three presses with different levels of technology incorporated into them were selected accordingly for conducting the study, collection of data relating to press productivity and wastage of paper during the printing cycle. The whole research work was carried out into the following phases;

Phase I

After visiting a number of printing presses employing multi-colour sheet fed offset presses, three prominent multi-colour presses all with six colour printing stations were identified and selected for carrying out the research work. These presses are in good running condition and are installed & operated in different print organizations under standard operating environment. All these presses are able to handle a wide range and variety of printing jobs with highest level of print quality. Care was taken to select the press organization in which multi-colour sheet fed offset presses are being operated throughout the year, without much machine breakdown and job scarcity. All these selected presses are of same size and they were manufactured at different point of time with different level of press automation embedded into the machines.

Three presses are designated as, Machine one (M-I), Machine two (M-II) and Machine three (M-III). M-I is equipped with high level of press automation, M-II is equipped with medium level of press automation and M-III is equipped with low level of press automation, when they are being compared with each other. Machine one (M-I) was procured in 2016 with a price of 6 Cr INR and in 2022 the cost of the machine calculated at 3.19 Cr INR (with an annual depreciation of 10%). Machine two (M-II) was procured in 2018 with a price of 3.50 Cr INR and in 2022 the cost of machine calculated at 2.30 Cr INR (with an annual depreciation of 10%). Machine three (M-III) was procured in 2016 with a price of 2.5 Cr INR and in 2022 the cost of machine calculated at 1.34 Cr INR (at an annual depreciation of 10%).

Phase II

Print production related data for one year (twelve months) was collected from each of the above selected three multi-colour sheet-fed offset printing presses (as indicated at phase I). The collected data then was presented in day-wise and month-wise into suitable tabular forms by taking various parameters related to print productivity as; Number of make-readies, Make-ready Time, Press Speed, Press print output, Time for press production, Press Performance, Capacity and Real printing rate of production for all of the above three multi-colour sheet-fed offset printing presses in line with the objectives of the research study.

Phase III

Paper is one of the primary substrates for the printing press and the same is equally true for the sheet fed offset presses. Paper essentially provides a smooth and consistent surface which results into accurate ink transfer of ink and thereby high-quality print output. There are quite a good number of factors which decides the importance of cost percentage of paper in final print product cost; type & nature of the print job, the job order quantity, quality of the paper, condition and automation level of the offset press. As a general principle, paper contributes a sizeable portion of the total cost of the printing product. The cost of the paper varies from 30-50% or even more of the total printing production cost and it may go up especially for printing of certain jobs like; catalogues, publications and magazines.

Paper wastage for the above three multi-colour sheet fed offset presses were taken into account and correlated with the cost of the particular press to indicate and recommend which press is suitable for the particular job order quantity. 100 print jobs of varying job order quantity were identified for each press from the twelve months production data; accordingly, three tables were prepared with the job order quantity, total paper used for completing the particular job and wastage of paper for executing the same job. Jobs with the print quantity up to 5000, from 5001 to 10,000, from 10.001 to 20,000, 20,001 to 50,000 and above 50,000 were the brackets being taken into considerations for all the three presses, so as to find out the percentage of paper wastage of the three multi-colour sheet fed offset presses.

Phase IV

To analysis and compare the above-mentioned parameters related to print productivity for the above three multi-colour sheet fed offset printing presses, the print production related data is presented in suitable tables and graphs form for the data analysis purpose. Descriptive statistics tool was used or analyzing the data in more scientific way to evaluate the print productivity of above-mentioned printing presses with the impact of technologies incorporated into these machines. The percentage of paper wastage as per the particular print run quantity for all the three selected multi-colour sheet fed offset presses were analyzed in relation to the cost of the particular machine.

Sheet Fed Offset Press Specifications

Number of six-colour sheet fed offset presses were identified and finally three presses were selected with different levels of press automation for collecting the data related to print production and paper wastage during the various print jobs. All the three presses possess some common specifications and they are as follows;

Printing units

- Six Colour printing stations with high pile delivery
- Size: 28 x 40 inch (720 x 1030 mm)

Technical features

▪ Maximum paper size:	720 x 1020 mm
▪ Minimum paper size:	280 x 420 mm
▪ Thickness of printing substrate:	0.03-1.0 mm
▪ Print area size:	700 x 1020 mm
▪ Plate size:	790 x 1030 mm Thickness 0.30 mm
▪ Blanket size:	1045 x 790 mm Thickness 1.90 mm

However, all the three presses selected for the research purpose have incorporated different levels of press automation into them to offer various facilities complementing the press print productivity and paper wastage for printing a job in hand. Machine one (M-I) is selected with high automation followed by Machine two (M-II) with moderate/medium automation and the Machine three (M-III) with low level of press automation, when the above three multi-colour sheet fed offset presses are evaluated along with the automation level.

Specific features of the Machine one (M-I), with high level of press automation are as follows;

- Prinect Press Centre with 19² TFT Touch Screen
- Intellistart Job Preparation
- Press Center Instant Gate
- Press Center DryStar Advanced
- Press Center Color Assistant Pro
- Sheetfed Control System
- Alcolor with Vario Damping
- Pre-set Plus Feeder [for short make-ready times and high production speed], suction belt feeder with three sections of transport of sheets to the frontal registers, double sheet detector - pulling device, non-stop on feeder, Ultrasonic Double Sheet Detector.
- Static-Star Compact: antistatic bar on feeder, two ionizator heads on feeder, four half ionizator bars in delivery
- Auto-plate loading

- Programmable Roller Wash
- Programmable Blanket Wash (Cloth System)
- Programmable Cylinder Wash (Cloth System)
- Roller wash-up device controlled by Prinect Press Center
- Blanket and impression cylinders automatic washing devices by Prinect Press Center
- Prinect Press Center Compact with remote ink control
- Combi Star Compact with Ink Temp Control
- Combi Star pro inking unit temperature control, water cooled, with AlcoSmart
- Autoplate XL: simultaneous plate changer
- Filter Star: filtration System of the dampening solution
- CombiStar CANopen: Technotrans ink temp control combined with damping refrigeration + Alcosmart
- Axis Control for colour measurement
- High performance gripper system with low maintenance requirement
- Triple-sized transfer drum for sheet transfer between the printing and coating units
- Sheet travel sensor for monitoring the sheet transport through the press
- Sheet transfer with Venturi nozzles between the printing units for paper printing
- High-performance inking unit with 20 rollers
- Automatic program-controlled ink roller wash-up with central solvent and water supply
- Digital Alcolor continuous film dampening system
- Combi Star Compact (air-cooled)
- Exhaust air hood for combination unit Combistar/ CombiStar compact air-cooled
- Alcolor Vario
- Preset Plus Delivery (X2) with Non-Stop Device
- Preset Plus Delivery: a lot of preset functions and memorization, aerodynamic grippers system, slow down system by Prinect, panel in delivery

- Delivery extension with two extension modules
- Delivery control panel
- Non-stop delivery with rack
- UV ready
- Powder star Weko AP110 Spray
- Chambered Blade Coating System with Anilox Roller
- Air star Pro
- Stream Control
- Static Star Compact Antistatic for Feeder and Delivery
- Steel Plate in Feeder and Delivery
- Patented sheet guide plates with blast air system
- Sheet decurler integrated into the sheet guide plates
- Powder Star AP110
- Airstar Pro
- Exhaust air hood for central air supply cabinet Air Star Pro
- Static Star compact
- Clean Star: powder suction device in delivery
- AirStar Pro: central air box water cooled
- SCROLLSTAR: Atlas Copco compressor
- Intercom system: Microphone communication

Specific features of the Machine two (M-II), with medium level of press automation are as follows;

- CP2000 Control Center with Master Level, Instant Start, Instant Gate & Color Assistant. CP 2000 console touch screen, axial, circumferential and diagonal register remote control, ink ductors rotation control, job memorization
- CIP-Link
- Image Control Color Measurement device

- Auto plate loading
- Preset plus feeder (automatic paper size and thickness setting)
- Head feeder with three more suctions for paper transport
- Front sensor on flap of the feeder
- Ultrasonic sensor double-sheet control (double sheet detector)
- Electro mechanic shingle control
- Pneumatic side register control with integrated auto cleaning and double sheet control with direct system
- Slow down: system to slow the sheet down then 65% on feeder
- Eltex ion blowers on feeder
- Eltex antistatic on feeder
- ALCOLOR Vario dampening system
- Technotrans CombiStar Central Refrigeration (for dampening and ink temperature control) water cooled
- CP 2000 Tandem Wash. All Automatic washers (blanket, rollers and impression cylinders)
- Steel Plate in feeder and delivery
- Chromed plate, blanket and impression cylinders
- Combi Star: Technotrans ink temp control combined with damping refrigeration + Alcosmart
- Inking unit with remote distributor-roller adjustment
- Air Venturi System
- Air supply Air Star Pro, water-cooled
- Wash Star - for Wash-up Device Self-Cleaning
- Antistatic device, feeder and delivery
- Coting unit with Chambered Doctor Blade and Anilox Roller
- Ink Agitators Technotrans

- Dry-Star 3000 IR and Hot-air in delivery
- 2 UV lamp dryer for delivery available
- Prepared in all units mechanical for UV Interdeck dryer
- Preset Plus Delivery X2
- Weko AP262 powder sprayer
- Powder Star Duo Plus: Grafix Exactronic Duo Plus
- S-MODUL on delivery
- Clean Star: filter for powder spray suction
- Air Star: central air box water cooled
- Intercom system: microphone communication system

Specific features of the Machine three (M-III), with low level of press automation are as follows;

- Steel plate on feeder and delivery with ramp (for plastic or wooden pallets)
- Stream feeder with belt
- Electronic double sheet detection
- Electromechanical double sheet detection
- Photoelectronic side lay control
- Alcolor continuous dampening system with Technotrans's alcohol metering; cooling and re-circulation unit system
- Preset (automatic paper size and thickness setting)
- CP2000 Centre with touch screen control and diagnosis; self-diagnostic; Remote inking; dampening; axial, circumferential and diagonal register control with light pen; day light illuminator and cassette or memory card for job memories
- Programmable automatic blanket cylinders wash up via CP2000
- Programmable automatic impression cylinders wash up via CP2000
- Programmable automatic rollers wash up via CP2000
- Auto-plate (semi-automatic plate loader) with Bacher Control 2000 register system

- Plate cocking (diagonal register control)
- Central lubrication with automatic central service interval control via CP2000
- Centralized air supply system cabinet (vacuum and compressors)
- Venturi air transfer sheet guide system
- Grafix IR Dryer with hot air knives
- Grafix Powder Spray
- Automatic sheet de-curler

This chapter has underlined in detail of the four phases being followed to carry out the research work; in the first phase three prominent six colour sheet fed offset presses with varying levels of press automation was selected and the detailed technical specifications of these three presses are mentioned for better clarity. In the second phase; production related data of the above selected presses was collected in day-wise and month-wise into suitable tabular forms by taking various parameters related to print productivity for one complete year. In the third phase; paper wastage related data of the three presses were collected for the same period by selecting hundred printing jobs with variable job order quantities, which was aimed at corelating the cost of the particular press and the paper wastage being observed for various printing jobs. The major portion of any printed output is due to the paper and this phase is aimed at taking care of the wastage percentage for the three selected presses. Fourth phase indicates the detailed analysis of the above collected data for finding the importance and role of technological advancements in multi colour sheet fed offset presses in relation to the enhanced press productivity.

CHAPTER-6 DATA COLLECTION AND ANALYSIS

This chapter takes care of the data collection and analysis components of the research work. Print production performance of three selected multi colour sheet fed offset presses for one year were presented on various tables and graphs with their average, maximum, minimum and standard deviation values. Various factors that are taken into account includes; Number of make-readies, Make-ready Time, Press Speed, Press print output, Time for press production, Press Performance, Capacity and Real printing rate of production. Likewise the paper wastage percentage of all the three presses with variable job order quantities were presented and analysed for indicating the suitability of the press for particular length job order.

Table 6.1: Print Production Performance of Machine-I (Month-1)

	No. of MR	MR Time(min)	Avg. MR Time(min)	Total Printed Sheets	Total Production Time(h)	Avg. Press Speed(SPH)
Avg.	5	302	60.70	83917	10.58	7988
Max.	11	565	131.25	182010	16.58	12913
Min.	1	25	25	21110	4.08	4951
S.D.	2	149.15	22.28	34166	3.42	1895

Table 6.1 represents the print production performance data of Machine-I, month one. The table indicates that maximum of 131.25 minutes and minimum of 25 minutes of average make-ready time are used for preparing the press to be ready for printing operation with standard deviation of 22.28 and average of 60.70 minutes. The number of make-readies is varying between one to eleven with average of 5, with 2 standard deviations. One make-ready indicates the job in press was of high print run length. Total production time for the machine was varying in between 4.08 hours to 16.58 hours with an average of 10.58 hours. In this month, the number of printed sheets varies from 21110 to 182010 with a standard deviation of 34166. In this month, the average press speed varies from 4951 to 12913 sheets per hour with a standard deviation of 1895.

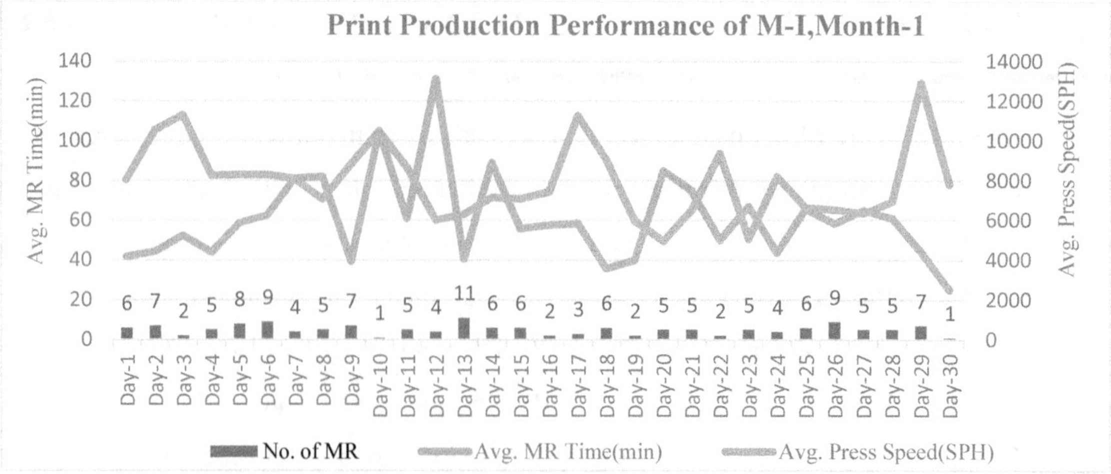

Fig. 6.1: Print Production Performance of M-I, (Month-1)

Fig.6.1 represents the average press speed in sheets per hour, average make-ready time in minutes day-wise in month-1 of Machine-I, which is equipped with high level of automation. The number of make-readies is varying from one to eleven; average make-ready time varies is in-between 25 minutes to 131.25 minutes and the average press speed is in-between 4951 to 12913 sheets per hour.

Table 6.2: P Print Production Performance of Machine-I (Month-2)

	No. of MR	MR Time(min)	Avg. MR Time(min)	Total Printed Sheets	Total Production Time(h)	Avg. Press Speed(SPH)
Avg.	5	325.18	62.38	72647	10.54	7243
Max.	9	580	121.25	131550	16.50	12980
Min.	2	75	37.50	19470	1.50	3807
S.D.	2	134.47	19.84	33555	4.32	2151

Table 6.2 represents the print production performance data of Machine-I, month two. The table indicates that maximum of 121.25 minutes and minimum of 37.50 minutes of average make ready time are used for preparing the press to be ready for printing operation with standard deviation of 19.84 and average of 62.38 minutes. The number of make-readies is varying between two to nine with average of 5, with 2 standard deviations. Total production time for the machine was varying in between 1.50 hours to 16.50 hours with an average of 10.54 hours.

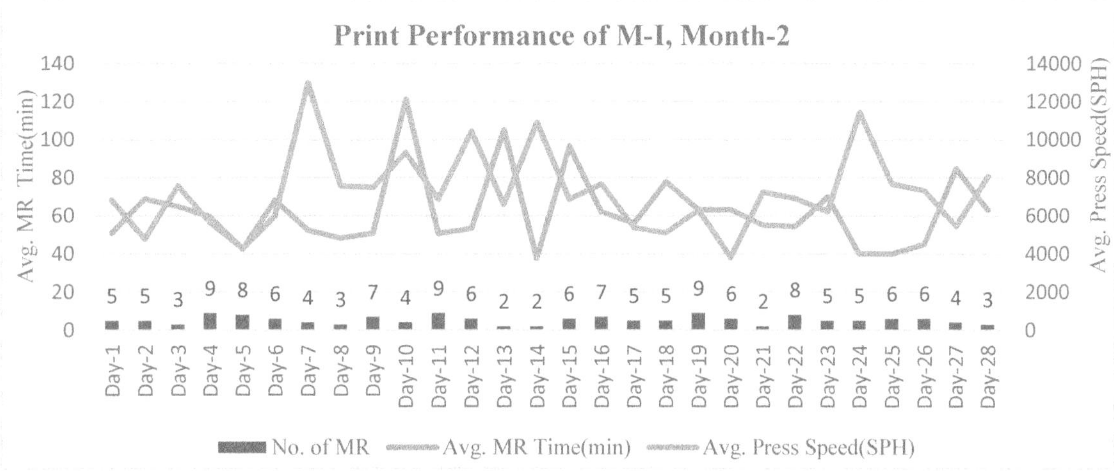

Fig. 6.2: Print Production Performance of M-I, (Month-2)

Fig.6.2 represents the average press speed in sheets per hour, average make-ready time in minutes day-wise in month-2 of Machine-I, which is equipped with high level of automation. The number of make-readies varies from two to nine; average make-ready time is in-between 37.50 minutes to 121.25 minutes and the press speed is in-between 3807 to 12980 sheets per hour.

Table 6.3: Print Production Performance of Machine-I (Month-3)

	No. of MR	MR Time(min)	Avg. MR Time(min)	Total Printed Sheets	Total Production Time(h)	Avg. Press Speed(SPH)
Avg.	5	325.56	65.43	64003	8.82	7332
Max.	10	600	120	122700	15	11936
Min.	1	40	40	10000	1.42	4013
S.D.	2	130.54	16	30006	3.82	1635

Table 6.3 represents the print production performance data of Machine-I, month three. The table indicates that maximum of 120 minutes and minimum of 40 minutes of average make ready time are used for preparing the press to be ready for printing operation with standard deviation of 16 and average of 65.43 minutes. The number of make-readies is varying between one to ten with average of 5, with 2 standard deviations. Total production time for the machine was varying in between 1.42 hours to 15 hours with an average of 8.82 hours. In this month, the number of printed sheets varies from 10000 to 122700 with an average of 64003.

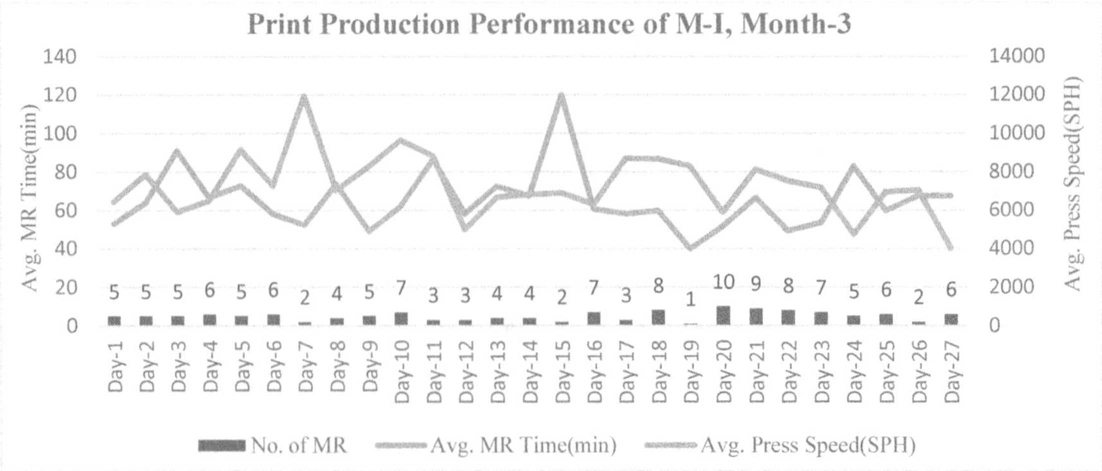

Fig. 6.3: Print Production Performance of M-I, (Month-3)

Fig.6.3 represents the average press speed in sheets per hour, average make-ready time in minutes day-wise in month-3 of Machine-I, which is equipped with high level of automation. The number of make-readies varies from one to ten; the average make-ready time is in-between 40 minutes to 120 minutes and the press speed is in-between 4013 to 11936 sheets per hour.

Table 6.4: Print Production Performance of Machine-I (Month-4)

	No. of MR	MR Time(min)	Avg. MR Time(min)	Total Printed Sheets	Total Production Time(h)	Avg. Press Speed(SPH)
Avg.	6	321.54	57.85	67976	9.32	7424
Max.	11	565	95	122080	15.33	10578
Min.	0	0	0	19350	2.25	4923
S.D.	3	143.68	19.58	28324	3.65	1235

Table 6.4 represents the print production performance data of Machine-I, month four. The table indicates that maximum of 95 minutes and minimum of 0 minutes of average make ready time are used for preparing the press to be ready for printing operation with standard deviation of 19.58 and average of 57.85 minutes. The number of make-readies is varying between zero to eleven with average of 6, with 3 standard deviations. Zero make-ready indicates the job in press was of high print run length and continued from the previous day. Total production time for the machine was varying in-between 2.25 hours to 15.33 hours with an average of 9.32 hours. In this month, the number of printed sheets varies from 19350 to

122080 with an average of 67976. In this month, the average press speed varies from 4923 to 10578 with an average of 7424 sheets per hour.

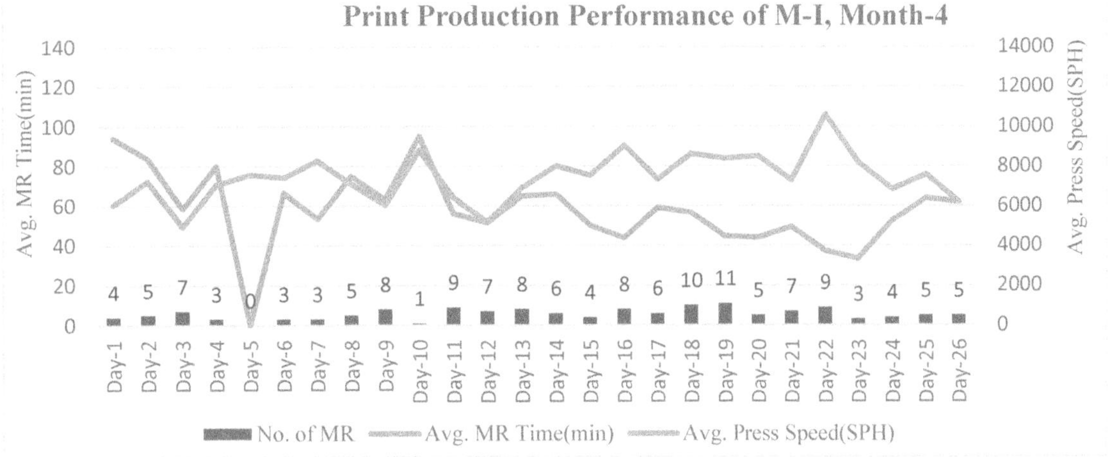

Fig. 6.4: Print Production Performance of M-I, (Month-4)

Fig.6.4 represents the average press speed in sheets per hour, average make-ready time in minutes day-wise in month-4 of Machine-I, which is equipped with high level of automation. The number of make-readies varies from zero to eleven; the average make-ready time is in-between 0 minutes to 95 minutes and the press speed is in-between 4923 to 10578 sheets per hour.

Table 6.5: Print Production Performance of Machine-I (Month-5)

	No. of MR	MR Time(min)	Avg. MR Time(min)	Total Printed Sheets	Total Production Time(h)	Avg. Press Speed(SPH)
Avg.	5	301.96	65.05	67143	8.91	7653
Max.	9	530	120	106970	14.17	10360
Min.	1	35	31.67	22290	2.75	4458
S.D.	2	142.73	20.15	26920	3.50	1280

Table 6.5 represents the print production performance data of Machine-I, month five. The table indicates that maximum of 120 minutes and minimum of 31.67 minutes of average make ready time are used for preparing the press to be ready for printing operation with standard deviation of 20.15 and average of 65.05 minutes. The number of make-readies is varying between one to nine with average of 5, with 2 standard deviations. One make-ready indicates the job in press was of high print run length. Total production time for the machine

was varying in-between 2.75 hours to 14.17 hours with an average of 8.91 hours. In this month, the number of printed sheets varies from 22290 to 106970 with an average of 67143. In this month, the average press speed varies from 4458 to 10360 with an average of 7653 sheets per hour.

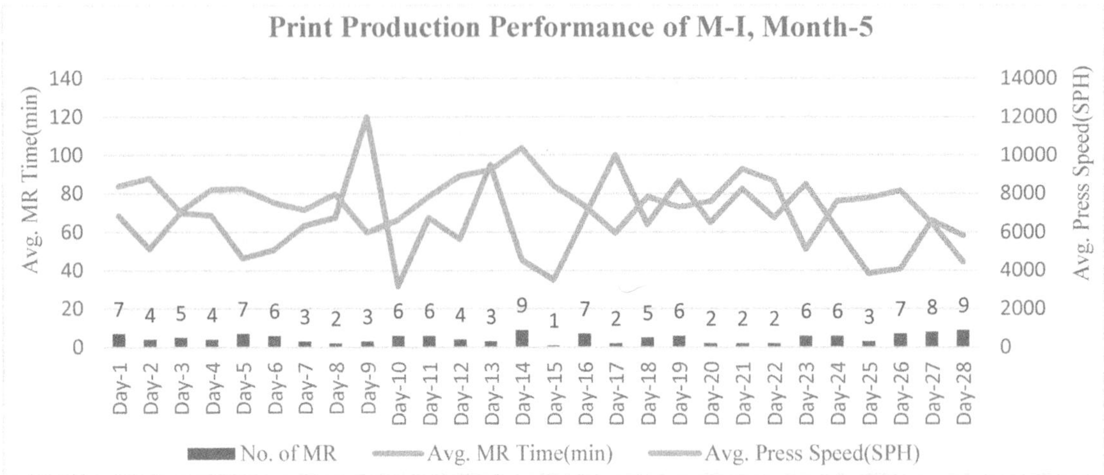

Fig. 6.5: Print Production Performance of M-I, (Month-5)

Fig.6.5 represents the average press speed in sheets per hour, average make-ready time in minutes day-wise in month-5 of Machine-I, which is equipped with high level of automation. The number of make-readies varies from one to nine; the average make-ready time is in-between 31.67 minutes to 120 minutes and the press speed is in-between 4458 to 10360 sheets per hour.

Table 6.6: Print Production Performance of Machine-I (Month-6)

	No. of MR	MR Time(min)	Avg. MR Time(min)	Total Printed Sheets	Total Production Time(h)	Avg. Press Speed(SPH)
Avg.	5	271.35	59.91	69021	9.32	7515
Max.	9	490	92.50	157430	14.17	13119
Min.	0	0	0	3050	0.33	4868
S.D.	2	120.91	19.16	33363	3.63	2008

Table 6.6 represents the print production performance data of Machine-I, month six. The table indicates that maximum of 92.50 minutes and minimum of 0 minute of average make ready time are used for preparing the press to be ready for printing operation with standard deviation of 19.16 and average of 59.91 minutes. The number of make-readies is varying

between zero to nine with average of 5, with 2 standard deviations. Zero make-ready indicates the job in press was of high print run length and continued from the previous day. Total production time for the machine was varying in between 0.33 hours to 14.17 hours with an average of 9.32 hours. In this month, the number of printed sheets varies from 3050 to 157430 with an average of 69021. In this month, the average press speed varies from 4868 to 13119.

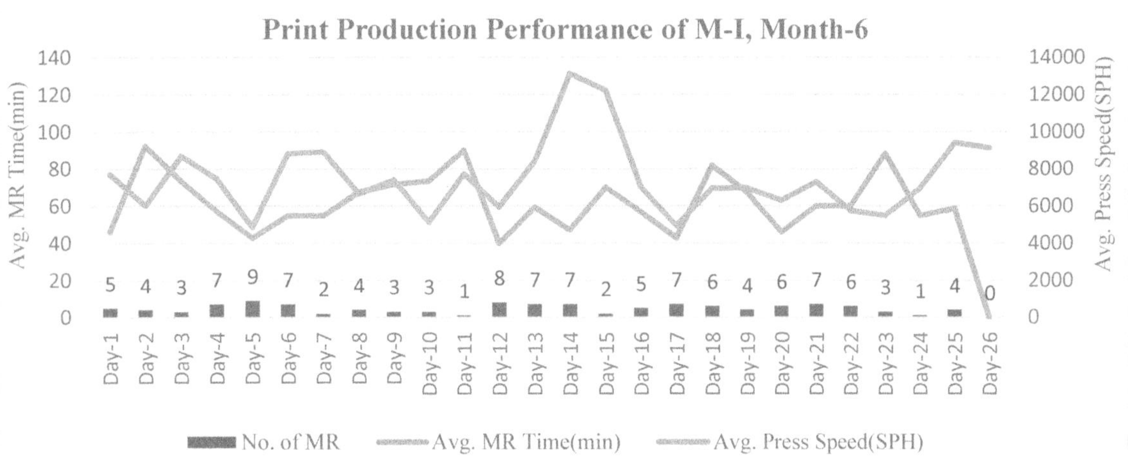

Fig. 6.6: Print Production Performance of M-I, (Month-6)

Fig.6.6 represents the average press speed in sheets per hour, average make-ready time in minutes day-wise in month-6 of Machine-I, which is equipped with high level of automation. The number of make-readies varies from zero to nine; the average make-ready time is in-between 0 minute to 92.50 minutes and the press speed is in-between 4868 to 13119 sheets per hour.

Table 6.7: Print Production Performance of Machine-I (Month-7)

	No. of MR	MR Time(min)	Avg. MR Time(min)	Total Printed Sheets	Total Production Time(h)	Avg. Press Speed(SPH)
Avg.	6	337.96	61.29	54574	8.35	6646
Max.	9	515	120	89840	12.75	10335
Min.	1	120	35	13400	3.08	3092
S.D.	2	105.84	15.52	20754	2.71	1720

Table 6.7 represents the print production performance data of Machine-I, month seven. The table indicates that maximum of 120 minutes and minimum of 35 minutes of average make

ready time are used for preparing the press to be ready for printing operation with standard deviation of 15.52 and average of 61.29 minutes. The number of make-readies is varying between one to nine with average of 6, with 2 standard deviations. One make-ready indicates the job in press was of high print run length. Total production time for the machine was varying in between 3.08 hours to 12.75 hours with an average of 8.35 hours. In this month, the number of printed sheets varies from 13400 to 89840 with an average of 54574. In this month, the average press speed varies from 3092 to 10335 with an average of 6646 sheets per hour.

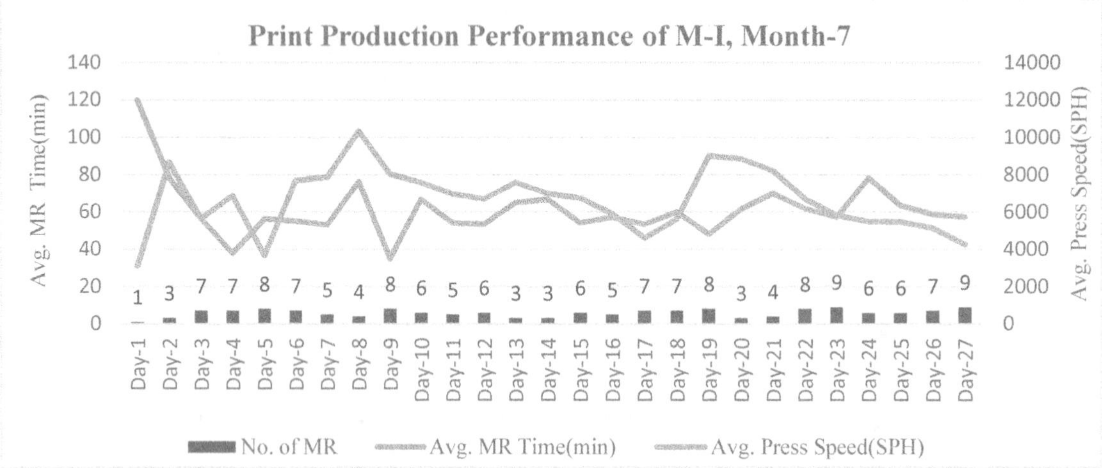

Fig. 6.7: Print Production Performance of M-I, (Month-7)

Fig.6.7 represents the average press speed in sheets per hour, average make-ready time in minutes day-wise in month-7 of Machine-I, which is equipped with high level of automation. The number of make-readies varies from one to nine; the average make-ready time is in-between 35 minutes to 120 minutes and the press speed is in-between 3092 to 10335 sheets per hour.

Table 6.8: Print Production Performance of Machine-I (Month-8)

	No. of MR	MR Time(min)	Avg. MR Time(min)	Total Printed Sheets	Total Production Time(h)	Avg. Press Speed(SPH)
Avg.	5	311.03	60.02	56251	8.49	6754
Max.	10	565	80	93630	12.83	8703
Min.	0	0	0	7970	1	4516
S.D.	2	136.84	15.08	24286	3.62	1175

Table 6.8 represents the print production performance data of Machine-I, month eight. The table indicates that maximum of 80 minutes and minimum of 0 minute of average make ready time are used for preparing the press to be ready for printing operation with standard deviation of 15.08 and average of 60.02 minutes. The number of make-readies is varying between zero to ten with average of 5, with 2 standard deviations. Zero make-ready indicates the job in press was of high print run length and continued from the previous day. Total production time for the machine was varying in between 1 hour to 12.83 hours with an average of 8.49 hours. In this month, the number of printed sheets varies from 7970 to 93630 with an average of 56251. In this month, the average press speed varies from 4516 to 8703 with an average of 6754 sheets per hour.

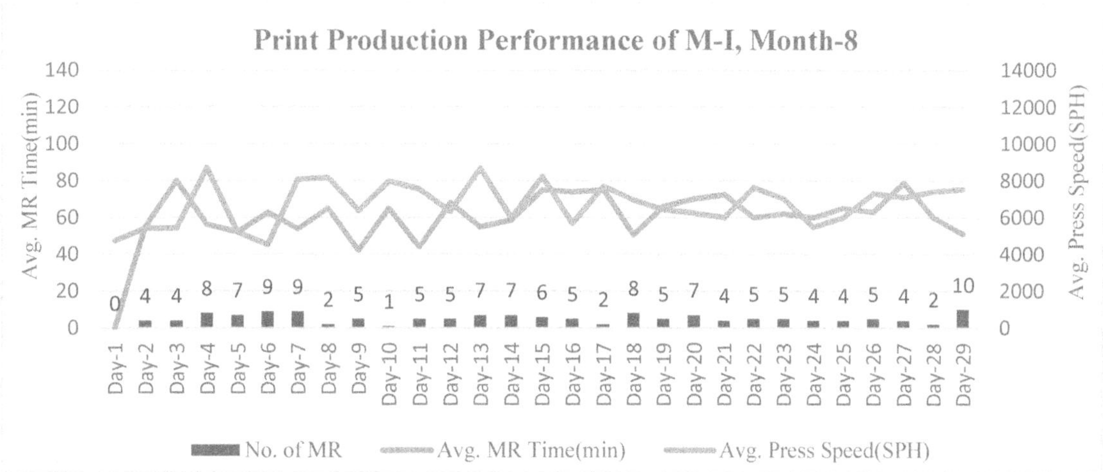

Fig. 6.8: Print Production Performance of M-I, (Month-8)

Fig.6.8 represents the average press speed in sheets per hour, average make-ready time in minutes day-wise in month-8 of Machine-I, which is equipped with high level of automation. The number of make-readies varies from zero to ten; the average make-ready time is in-between 0 minute to 80 minutes and the press speed is in-between 4516 to 8703 sheets per hour.

Table 6.9: Print Production Performance of Machine-I (Month-9)

	No. of MR	MR Time(min)	Avg. MR Time(min)	Total Printed Sheets	Total Production Time(h)	Avg. Press Speed(SPH)
Avg.	6	351.21	58.78	67229	9.80	7087
Max.	11	695	88	133170	14.58	9295
Min.	0	0	0	4240	0.50	2188
S.D.	3	149.72	16.94	26848	3.35	1759

Table 6.9 represents the print production performance data of Machine-I, month nine. The table indicates that maximum of 88 minutes and minimum of 0 minute of average make ready time are used for preparing the press to be ready for printing operation with standard deviation of 16.94 and average of 58.78 minutes. The number of make-readies is varying between zero to eleven with average of 6, with 3 standard deviations. Zero make-ready indicates the job in press was of high print run length and continued from the previous day. Total production time for the machine was varying in between 0.50 hours to 14.58 hours with an average of 9.80 hours. In this month, the number of printed sheets varies from 4240 to 133170 with an average of 67229. In this month, the average press speed varies from 2188 to 9295 with an average of 7087 sheets per hour.

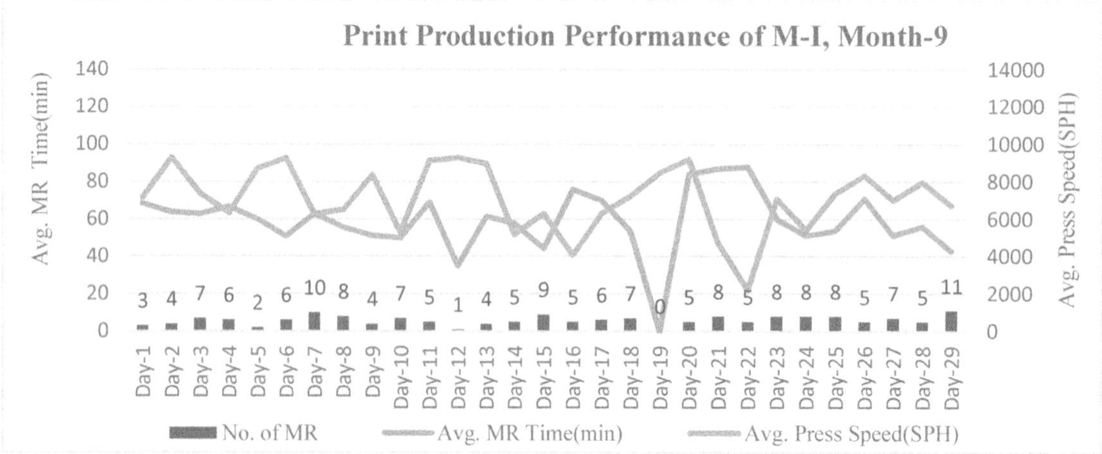

Fig. 6.9: Print Production Performance of M-I, (Month-9)

Fig.6.9 represents the average press speed in sheets per hour, average make-ready time in minutes day-wise in month-9 of Machine-I, which is equipped with high level of automation. The number of make-readies varies from zero to eleven; the average make-ready time is in-between 0 minute to 88 minutes and the press speed is in-between 2188 to 9295 sheets per hour.

Table 6.10: Print Production Performance of Machine-I (Month-10)

	No. of MR	MR Time(min)	Avg. MR Time(min)	Total Printed Sheets	Total Production Time(h)	Avg. Press Speed(SPH)
Avg.	6	349.67	60.51	66399	9.48	7093
Max.	13	590	108	118910	15.08	9513
Min.	0	0	0	5730	0.83	4108
S.D.	3	154.95	18.39	28243	3.68	1332

Table 6.10 represents the print production performance data of Machine-I, month ten. The table indicates that maximum of 108 minutes and minimum of 0 minutes of average make ready time are used for preparing the press to be ready for printing operation with standard deviation of 18.39 and average of 60.51 minutes. The number of make-readies is varying between zero to thirteen with average of 6, with 3 standard deviations. Zero make-ready indicates the job in press was of high print run length and continued from the previous day. Total production time for the machine was varying in between 0.83 hours to 15.08 hours with an average of 9.48 hours. In this month, the number of printed sheets varies from 5730 to 118910 with an average of 66399. In this month, the average press speed varies from 4108 to 9513 with an average of 7093 sheets per hour.

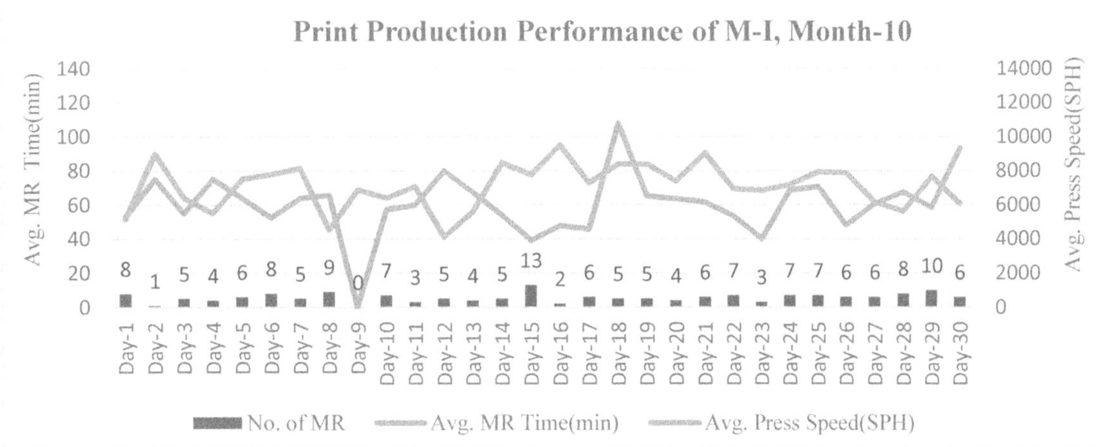

Fig. 6.10: Print Production Performance of M-I, (Month-10)

Fig.6.10 represents the average press speed in sheets per hour, average make-ready time in minutes day-wise in month-10 of Machine-I, which is equipped with high level of automation. The number of make-readies varies from zero to thirteen; the average make-ready time is in-between 0 minute to 108 minutes and the press speed is in-between 4108 to 9513 sheets per hour.

Table 6.11: Print Production Performance of Machine-I (Month-11)

	No. of MR	MR Time(min)	Avg. MR Time(min)	Total Printed Sheets	Total Production Time(h)	Avg. Press Speed(SPH)
Avg.	5	293.23	55.52	71846	9.93	7295
Max.	9	505	85	111120	14.83	10480
Min.	1	35	35	24100	2.92	4623
S.D.	2	130.89	10.04	24373	3.10	1209

Table 6.11 represents the print production performance data of Machine-I, month eleven. The table indicates that maximum of 85 minutes and minimum of 35 minutes of average make ready time are used for preparing the press to be ready for printing operation with standard deviation of 10.04 and average of 55.52 minutes. The number of make-readies is varying between one to nine with average of 5, with 2 standard deviations. One make-ready indicates the job in press was of high print run length. Total production time for the machine was varying in between 2.92 hours to 14.83 hours with an average of 9.93 hours. In this month, the number of printed sheets varies from 24100 to 111120 with an average of 71846. In this month, the average press speed varies from 4623 to 10480 with an average of 7295 sheets per hour.

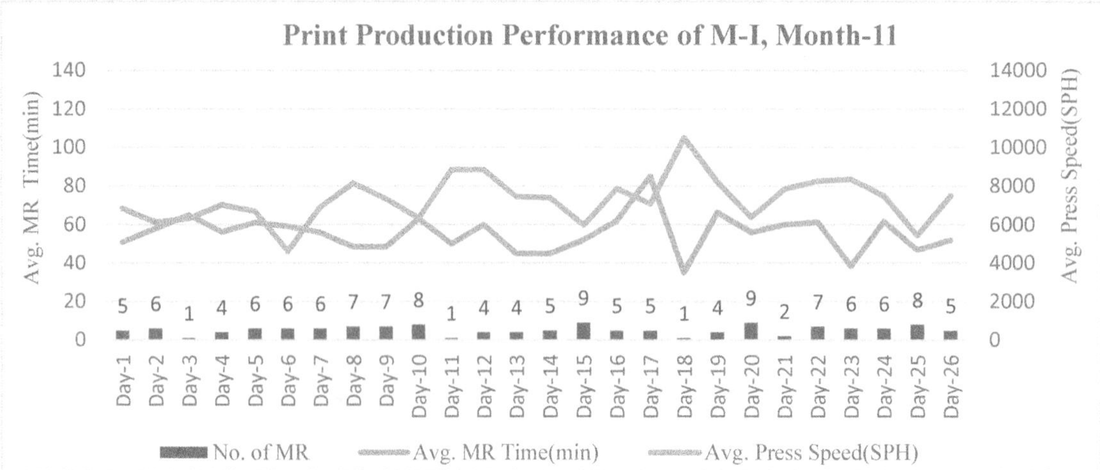

Fig. 6.11: Print Production Performance of M-I, (Month-11)

Fig.6.11 represents the average press speed in sheets per hour, average make-ready time in minutes day-wise in month-11 of Machine-I, which is equipped with high level of automation. The number of make-readies varies from one to nine; the average make-ready time is in-between 35 minutes to 85 minutes and the press speed is in-between 4623 to 10480 sheets per hour.

Table 6.12: Print Production Performance of Machine-I (Month-12)

	No. of MR	MR Time(min)	Avg. MR Time(min)	Total Printed Sheets	Total Production Time(h)	Avg. Press Speed(SPH)
Avg.	5	277.83	60.26	81686	10.89	7466
Max.	9	435	130	142440	16.42	9580
Min.	0	0	0	14750	2.42	4503
S.D.	2	91.96	20.16	30785	3.76	1056

Table 6.12 represents the print production performance data of Machine-I, month twelve. The table indicates that maximum of 130 minutes and minimum of 0 minute of average make ready time are used for preparing the press to be ready for printing operation with standard deviation of 20.16 and average of 60.26 minutes. The number of make-readies is varying between zero to nine with average of 5, with 2 standard deviations. Zero make-ready indicates the job in press was of high print run length and continued from the previous day. Total production time for the machine was varying in between 2.42 hours to 16.42 hours with an average of 10.89 hours. In this month, the number of printed sheets varies from 14750 to 142440 with an average of 81686. In this month, the average press speed varies from 4503 to 9580 with an average of 7466 sheets per hour.

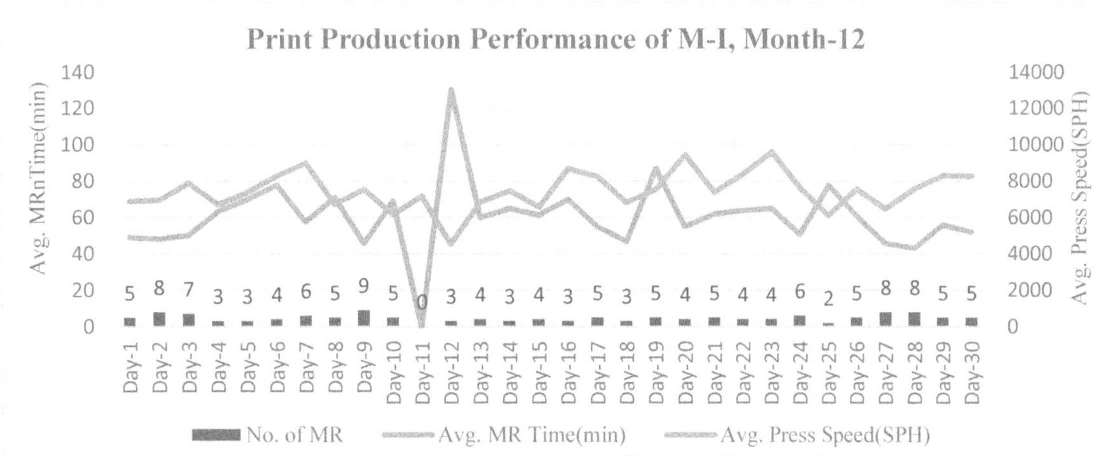

Fig. 6.12: Print Production Performance of M-I, (Month-12)

Fig.6.12 represents the average press speed in sheets per hour, average make-ready time in minutes day-wise in month-12 of Machine-I, which is equipped with high level of automation. The number of make-readies varies from zero to nine; the average make-ready time is in-between 0 minute to 130 minutes and the press speed is in-between 4503 to 9580 sheets per hour.

Table 6.13: Print Production Performance of Machine-II (Month-1)

	No. of MR	MR Time(min)	Avg. MR Time(min)	Total Printed Sheets	Total Production Time(h)	Avg. Press Speed(SPH)
Avg.	6	360.33	56.63	79626	12.85	6065
Max.	12	601	69.33	179246	20.15	8896
Min.	2	131	43.83	32610	5.82	5456
S.D.	3	132.51	6.14	34167	4.10	713

Table 6.13 represents the print production performance data of Machine-II, month one. The table indicates that maximum of 69.33 minutes and minimum of 43.83 minutes of average make ready time are used for preparing the press to be ready for printing operation with standard deviation of 6.14 and average of 56.63 minutes. The number of make-ready is varying between two to twelve with average of 6, with 3 standard deviations. Total production time for the machine was varying in between 5.82 hours to 20.15 hours with an average of 12.85 hours. In this month, the number of printed sheets varies from 32610 to 179246 with an average of 79626. In this month, the average press speed varies from 5456 to 8896 with an average of 6065 sheets per hour.

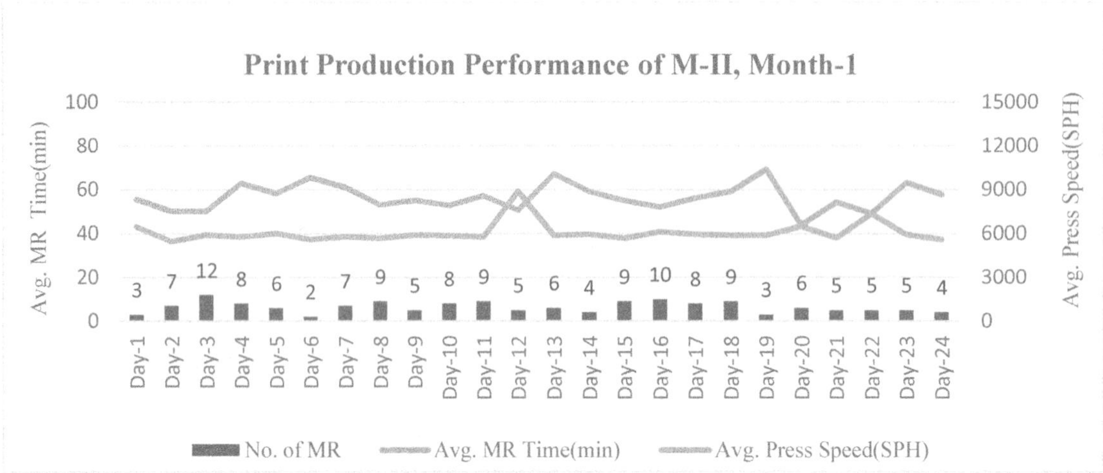

Fig. 6.13: Print Production Performance of M-II, (Month-1)

Fig.6.13 represents the average press speed in sheets per hour, average make-ready time in minutes day-wise in month-1 of Machine-II, which is equipped with medium level of automation. The number of make-readies varies from two to twelve; the average make-ready time is in-between 43.83 minutes to 69.33 minutes and the press speed is in-between 5456 to 8896 sheets per hour.

Table 6.14: Print Production Performance of Machine-II (Month-2)

	No. of MR	MR Time(min)	Avg. MR Time(min)	Total Printed Sheets	Total Production Time(h)	Avg. Press Speed(SPH)
Avg.	7	389.15	58.75	69676	10.97	6317
Max.	19	768	84.50	130390	18.12	11981
Min.	0	0	0	8780	1.43	5168
S.D.	4	177.69	16.37	33934	4.83	1283

Table 6.14 represents the print production performance data of Machine-II, month two. The table indicates that maximum of 84.50 minutes and minimum of 0 minute of average make ready time are used for preparing the press to be ready for printing operation with standard deviation of 16.37 and average of 58.75 minutes. The number of make-readies is varying between zero to nineteen with average of 7, with 4 standard deviations. Zero make-ready indicates the job in press was of high print run length and continued from the previous day. Total production time for the machine was varying in between 1.43 hours to 18.12 hours with an average of 10.97 hours. In this month, the number of printed sheets varies from 8780 to 130390 with an average of 69676. In this month, the average press speed varies from 5168 to 11981 with an average of 6317 sheets per hour.

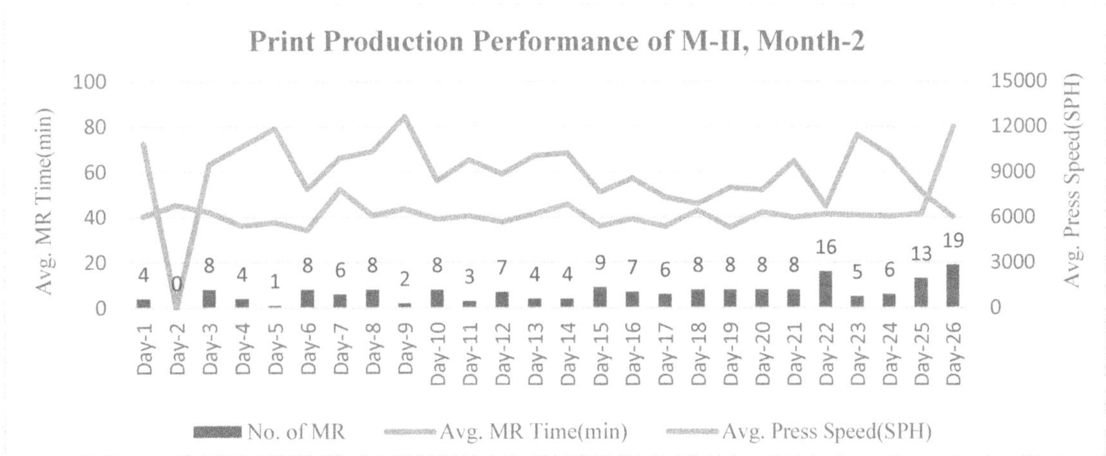

Fig. 6.14: Print Production Performance of M-II, (Month-2)

Fig.6.14 represents the average press speed in sheets per hour, average make-ready time in minutes day-wise in month-2 of Machine-II, which is equipped with medium level of automation. The number of make-readies varies from zero to nineteen; the average make-ready time is in-between 0 minute to 84.50 minutes and the press speed is in-between 5168 to 11981 sheets per hour.

Table 6.15: Print Production Performance of Machine-II (Month-3)

	No. of MR	MR Time(min)	Avg. MR Time(min)	Total Printed Sheets	Total Production Time(h)	Avg. Press Speed(SPH)
Avg.	6	334	60.24	67442	10.32	6428
Max.	15	694	73.75	122775	15.12	8122
Min.	2	117	46.27	22800	3.87	5693
S.D.	3	135.70	7.37	27444	3.64	609

Table 6.15 represents the print production performance data of Machine-II, month three. The table indicates that maximum of 73.75 minutes and minimum of 46.27 minute of average make ready time are used for preparing the press to be ready for printing operation with standard deviation of 7.37 and average of 60.24 minutes. The number of make-readies is varying between two to fifteen with average of 6, with 3 standard deviations. Total production time for the machine was varying in between 3.87 hours to 15.12 hours with an average of 10.32 hours. In this month, the number of printed sheets varies from 22800 to 122775 with an average of 67442. In this month, the average press speed varies from 5693 to 8122 with an average of 6428 sheets per hour.

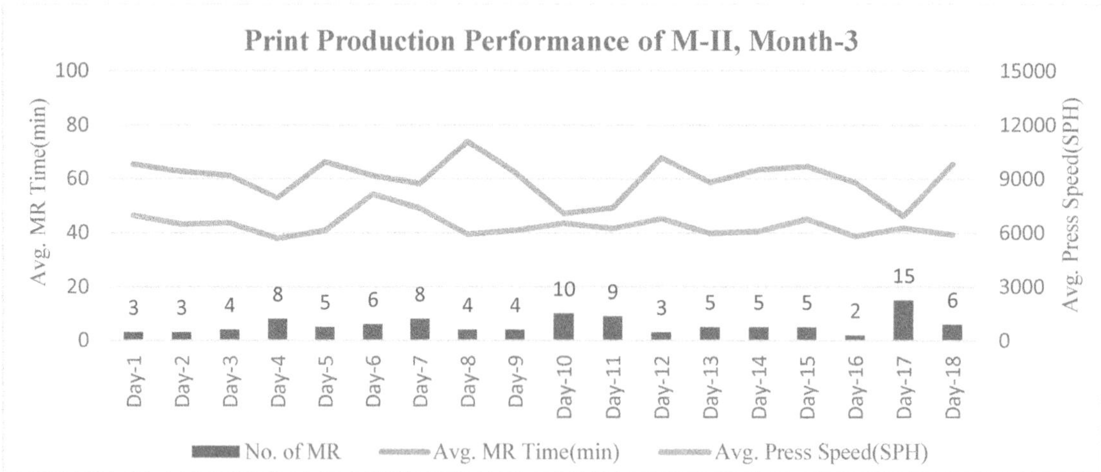

Fig. 6.15: Print Production Performance of M-II, (Month-3)

Fig.6.15 represents the average press speed in sheets per hour, average make-ready time in minutes day-wise in month-3 of Machine-II, which is equipped with medium level of automation. The number of make-readies varies from two to fifteen; the average make-ready time is in-between 46.27 minutes to 73.75 minutes and the press speed is in-between 5693 to 8122 sheets per hour.

Table 6.16: Print Production Performance of Machine-II (Month-4)

	No. of MR	MR Time(min)	Avg. MR Time(min)	Total Printed Sheets	Total Production Time(h)	Avg. Press Speed(SPH)
Avg.	2	144.57	76.62	39429	5.66	6814
Max.	3	238	91.50	75600	8.63	8757
Min.	1	69	63.50	14010	2.07	5973
S.D.	1	61.68	10.59	19594	2.20	909

Table 6.16 represents the print production performance data of Machine-II, month four. The table indicates that maximum of 91.50 minutes and minimum of 63.50 minutes of average make ready time are used for preparing the press to be ready for printing operation with standard deviation of 10.59 and average of 76.62 minutes. The number of make-readies is varying between one to three with average of 2, with 1 standard deviation. Total production time for the machine was varying in between 2.07 hours to 8.63 hours with an average of 5.66 hours. In this month, the number of printed sheets varies from 14010 to 75600 with an average of 39429. In this month, the average press speed varies from 5973 to 8757 with an average of 6814 sheets per hour.

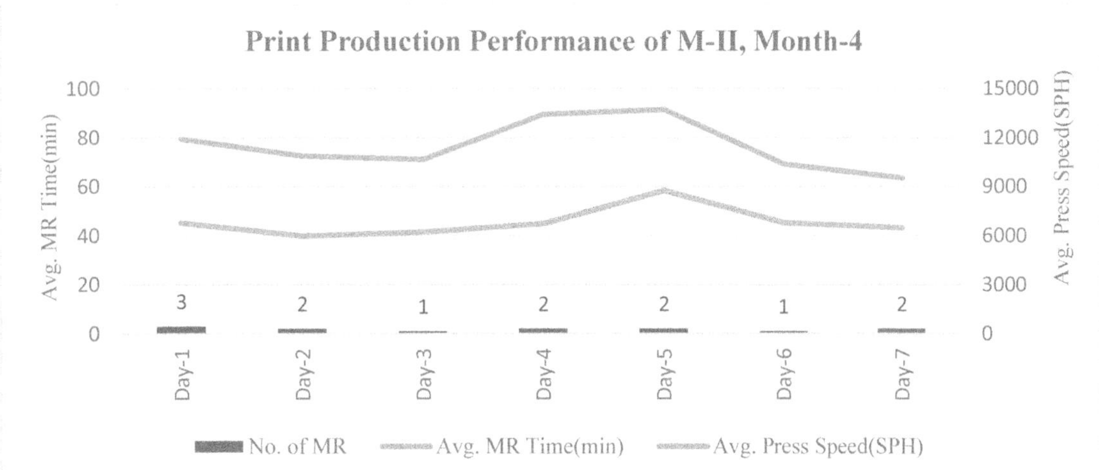

Fig. 6.16: Print Production Performance of M-II, (Month-4)

Fig.6.16 represents the average press speed in sheets per hour, average make-ready time in minutes day-wise in month-4 of Machine-II, which is equipped with medium level of automation. The number of make-readies varies from one to three; the average make-ready time is in-between 63.50 minutes to 91.50 minutes and the press speed is in-between 5973 to 8757 sheets per hour.

Table 6.17: Print Production Performance of Machine-II (Month-5)

	No. of MR	MR Time(min)	Avg. MR Time(min)	Total Printed Sheets	Total Production Time(h)	Avg. Press Speed(SPH)
Avg.	3	162.92	64.66	46159	7.62	6108
Max.	5	336	79	101012	17.20	6793
Min.	1	58	51.25	21250	3.38	5485
S.D.	2	92.08	6.52	23496	4	356

Table 6.17 represents the print production performance data of Machine-II, month five. The table indicates that maximum of 79 minutes and minimum of 51.25 minutes of average make ready time are used for preparing the press to be ready for printing operation with standard deviation of 6.52 and average of 64.66 minutes. The number of make-readies is varying between one to five with average of 3, with 2 standard deviations. Total production time for the machine was varying in between 3.38 hours to 17.20 hours with an average of 7.62 hours. In this month, the number of printed sheets varies from 21250 to 101012 with an average of 46159. In this month, the average press speed varies from 5485 to 6793 with an average of 6108 sheets per hour.

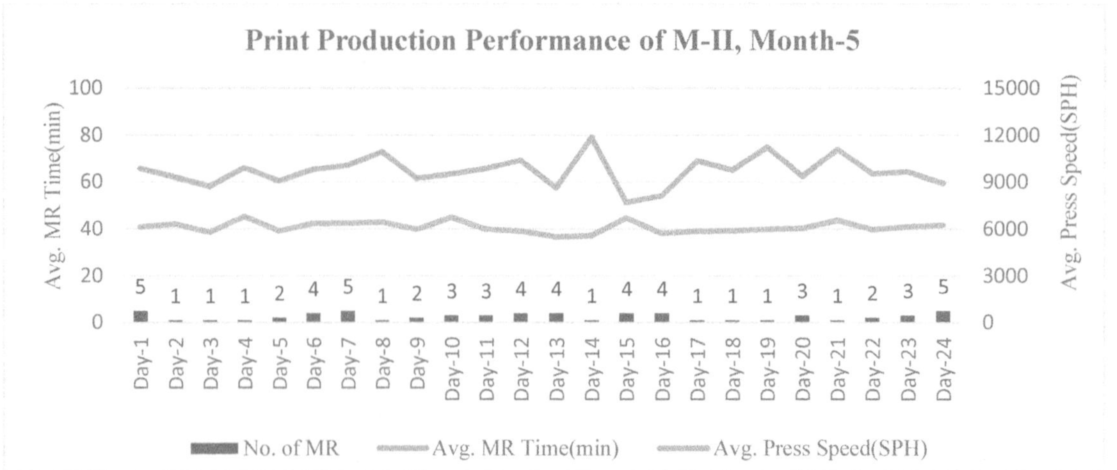

Fig. 6.17: Print Production Performance of M-II, (Month-5)

Fig.6.17 represents the average press speed in sheets per hour, average make-ready time in minutes day-wise in month-5 of Machine-II, which is equipped with medium level of automation. The number of make-readies varies from one to five; the average make-ready time is in-between 51.25 minutes to 79 minutes and the press speed is in-between 5485 to 6793 sheets per hour.

Table 6.18: Print Production Performance of Machine-II (Month-6)

	No. of MR	MR Time(min)	Avg. MR Time(min)	Total Printed Sheets	Total Production Time(h)	Avg. Press Speed(SPH)
Avg.	4	236.83	58.96	83933	12.08	6690
Max.	8	471	69.50	200100	20.40	9870
Min.	2	113	46.20	18300	2.78	5778
S.D.	2	102.82	6.54	49471	5.57	1091

Table 6.18 represents the print production performance data of Machine-II, month six. The table indicates that maximum of 69.50 minutes and minimum of 46.20 minutes of average make ready time are used for preparing the press to be ready for printing operation with standard deviation of 6.54 and average of 58.96 minutes. The number of make-readies is varying between two to eight with average of 4, with 2 standard deviations. Total production time for the machine was varying in between 2.78 hours to 20.40 hours with an average of 12.08 hours. In this month, the number of printed sheets varies from 18300 to 200100 with an average of 83933. In this month, the average press speed varies from 5778 to 9870 with an average of 6690 sheets per hour.

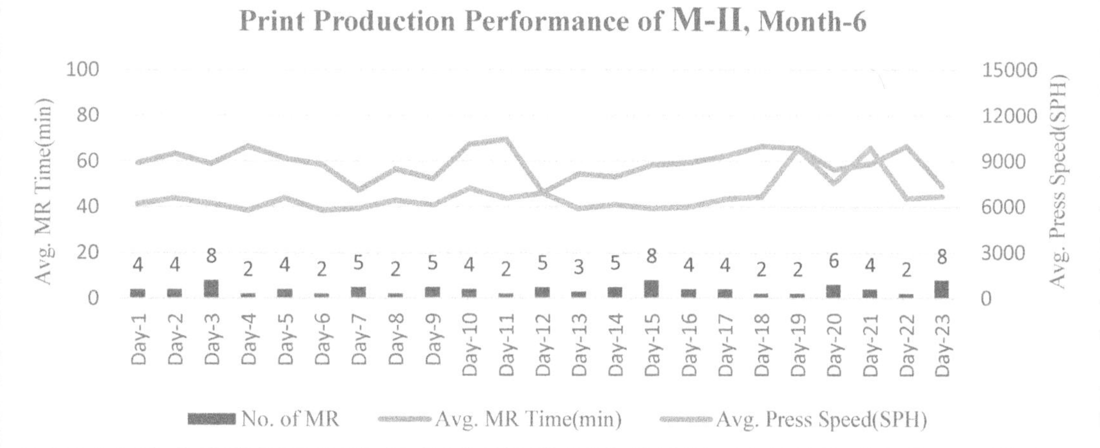

Fig. 6.18: Print Production Performance of M-II, (Month-6

Fig.6.18 represents the average press speed in sheets per hour, average make-ready time in minutes day-wise in month-6 of Machine-II, which is equipped with medium level of automation. The number of make-readies varies from two to eight; the average make-ready time is in-between 46.20 minutes to 69.50 minutes and the press speed is in-between 5778 to 9870 sheets per hour.

Table 6.19: Print Production Performance of Machine-II (Month-7)

	No. of MR	MR Time(min)	Avg. MR Time(min)	Total Printed Sheets	Total Production Time(h)	Avg. Press Speed(SPH)
Avg.	5	296.77	58.20	68913	9.60	6932
Max.	10	581	70	144650	17.10	9874
Min.	0	0	0	16300	2.48	5473
S.D.	3	140.16	12.82	35432	3.67	1135

Table 6.19 represents the print production performance data of Machine-II, month seven. The table indicates that maximum of 70 minutes and minimum of 0 minute of average make ready time are used for preparing the press to be ready for printing operation with standard deviation of 12.82 and average of 58.20 minutes. The number of make-readies is varying between zero to ten with average of 5, with 3 standard deviations. Zero make-ready indicates the job in press was of high print run length and continued from the previous day. Total production time for the machine was varying in between 2.48 hours to 17.10 hours with an average of 9.60 hours. In this month, the number of printed sheets varies from 16300 to 144650 with an average of 68913. In this month, the average press speed varies from 5473 to 9874 with an average of 6932 sheets per hour.

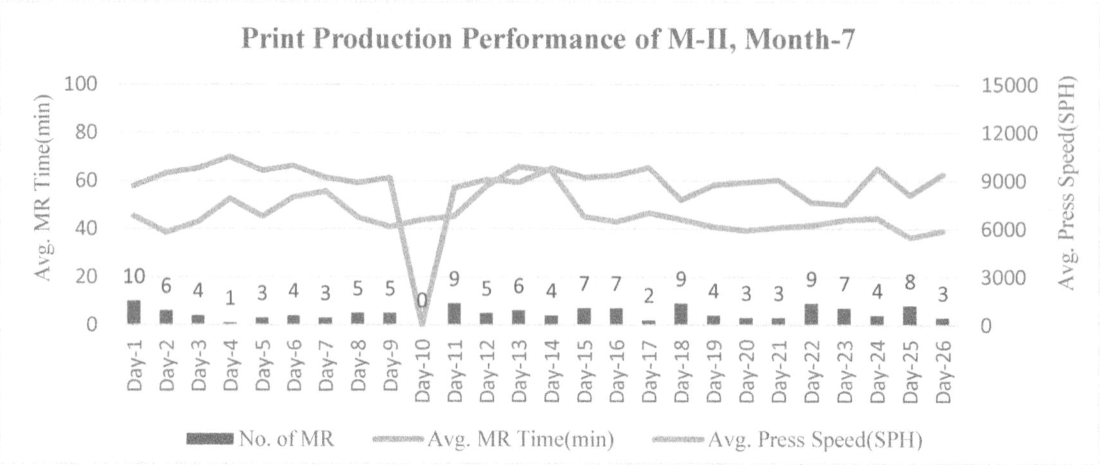

Fig. 6.19: Print Production Performance of M-II, (Month-7)

Fig.6.19 represents the average press speed in sheets per hour, average make-ready time in minutes day-wise in month-7 of Machine-II, which is equipped with medium level of automation. The number of make-readies varies from zero to ten; the average make-ready time is in-between 0 minutes to 70 minutes and the press speed is in-between 5473 to 9874 sheets per hour.

Table 6.20: Print Production Performance of Machine-II (Month-8)

	No. of MR	MR Time(min)	Avg. MR Time(min)	Total Printed Sheets	Total Production Time(h)	Avg. Press Speed(SPH)
Avg.	5	301.31	65.20	75830	10.72	6782
Max.	9	532	94	182100	20.30	9482
Min.	1	83	48.88	17200	2.50	5292
S.D.	2	138.05	9.17	41679	4.31	1149

Table 6.20 represents the print production performance data of Machine-II, month eight. The table indicates that maximum of 94 minutes and minimum of 48.88 minutes of average make ready time are used for preparing the press to be ready for printing operation with standard deviation of 9.17 and average of 65.20 minutes. The number of make-readies is varying between one to nine with average of 5, with 2 standard deviations. Total production time for the machine was varying in between 2.50 hours to 20.30 hours with an average of 10.72 hours. In this month, the number of printed sheets varies from 17200 to 182100 with an average of 75830. In this month, the average press speed varies from 5292 to 9482 with an average of 6782 sheets per hour.

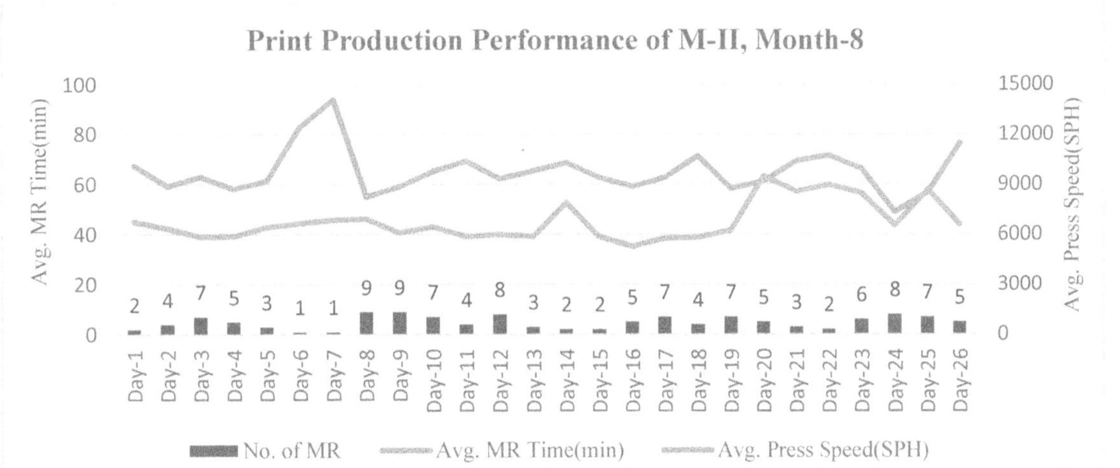

Fig. 6.20: Print Production Performance of M-II, (Month-8)

Fig.6.20 represents the average press speed in sheets per hour, average make-ready time in minutes day-wise in month-8 of Machine-II, which is equipped with medium level of automation. The number of make-readies varies from one to nine; The average make-ready time is in-between 48.88 minutes to 94 minutes and the press speed is in-between 5292 to 9482 sheets per hour.

Table 6.21: Print Production Performance of Machine-II (Month-9)

	No. of MR	MR Time(min)	Avg. MR Time(min)	Total Printed Sheets	Total Production Time(h)	Avg. Press Speed(SPH)
Avg.	6	351.64	58.67	80262	11.10	7101
Max.	11	585	69.20	134800	17.87	8564
Min.	0	0	0	15950	2.45	5874
S.D.	3	160.51	12.40	34370	4.17	805

Table 6.21 represents the print production performance data of Machine-II, month nine. The table indicates that maximum of 69.20 minutes and minimum of 0 minute of average make ready time are used for preparing the press to be ready for printing operation with standard deviation of 12.40 and average of 58.67 minutes. The number of make-readies is varying between zero to eleven with average of 6, with 3 standard deviations. Zero make-ready indicates the job in press was of high print run length and continued from the previous day. Total production time for the machine was varying in between 2.45 hours to 17.87 hours with an average of 11.10 hours. In this month, the number of printed sheets varies from 15950 to 134800 with an average of 80262. In this month, the average press speed varies from 5874 to 8564 with an average of 7101 sheets per hour.

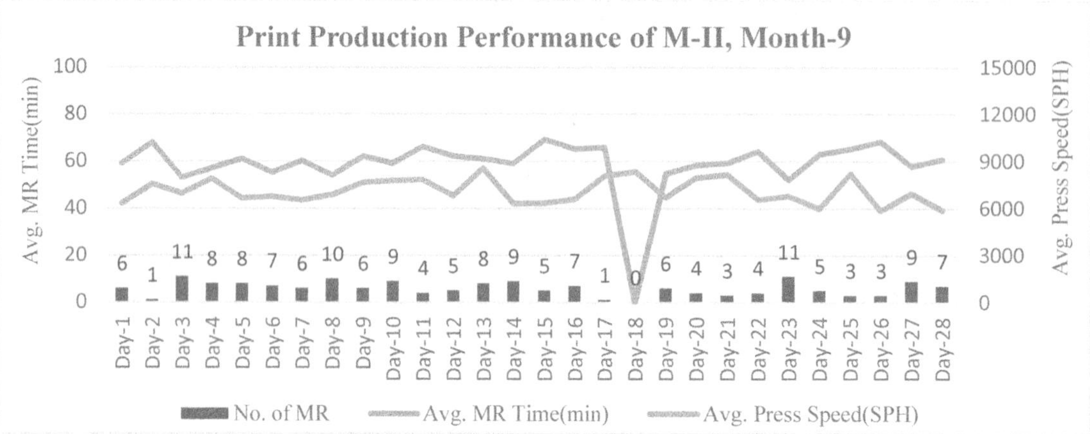

Fig. 6.21: Print Production Performance of M-II, (Month-9)

Fig.6.21 represents the average press speed in sheets per hour, average make-ready time in minutes day-wise in month-9 of Machine-II, which is equipped with medium level of automation. The number of make-readies varies from zero to eleven; the average make-ready time is in-between 0 minutes to 69.20 minutes and the press speed is in-between 5874 to 8564 sheets per hour.

Table 6.22: Print Production Performance of Machine-II (Month-10)

	No. of MR	MR Time(min)	Avg. MR Time(min)	Total Printed Sheets	Total Production Time(h)	Avg. Press Speed(SPH)
Avg.	6	384.56	62.85	70957	10.24	6876
Max.	16	865	69.63	131480	17.10	10923
Min.	2	131	52.06	16770	2.90	5783
S.D.	4	187.12	4.52	26453	3.39	1092

Table 6.22 represents the print production performance data of Machine-II, month ten. The table indicates that maximum of 69.63 minutes and minimum of 52.06 minutes of average make ready time are used for preparing the press to be ready for printing operation with standard deviation of 4.52 and average of 62.85 minutes. The number of make-readies is varying between two to sixteen with average of 6, with 4 standard deviations. Total production time for the machine was varying in between 2.90 hours to 17.10 hours with an average of 10.24 hours. In this month, the number of printed sheets varies from 16770 to 131480 with an average of 70957. In this month, the average press speed varies from 5783 to 10923 with an average of 6876 sheets per hour.

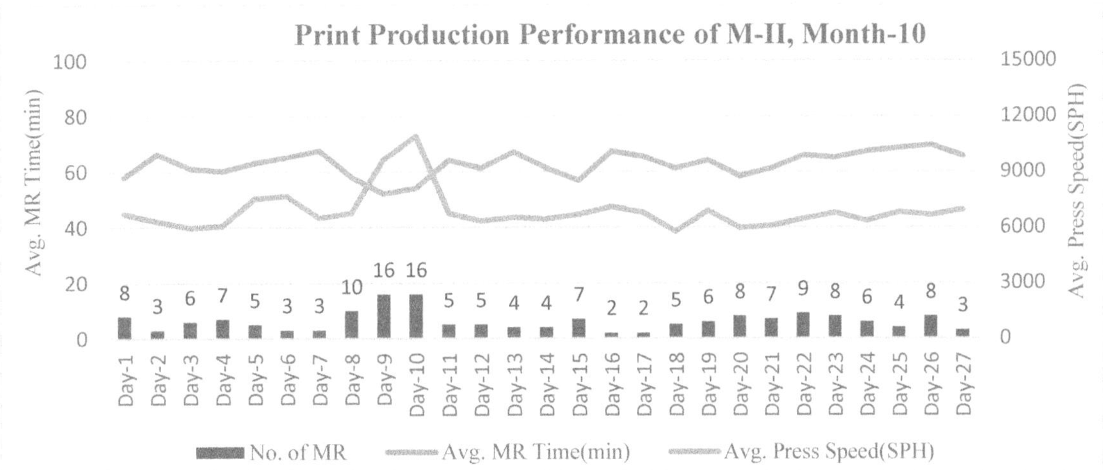

Fig. 6.22: Print Production Performance of M-II, (Month-10)

Fig.6.22 represents the average press speed in sheets per hour, average make-ready time in minutes day-wise in month-10 of Machine-II, which is equipped with medium level of automation. The number of make-readies varies from two to sixteen; the average make-ready time is in-between 52.06 minutes to 69.63 minutes and the press speed is in-between 5783 to 10923 sheets per hour.

Table 6.23: Print Production Performance of Machine-II (Month-11)

	No. of MR	MR Time(min)	Avg. MR Time(min)	Total Printed Sheets	Total Production Time(h)	Avg. Press Speed(SPH)
Avg.	5	327.09	62.36	60868	8.95	6786
Max.	12	625	69.20	117550	14.88	7898
Min.	1	66	52.08	15600	2.33	5887
S.D.	3	156.54	4.73	26062	3.60	569

Table 6.23 represents the print production performance data of Machine-II, month eleven. The table indicates that maximum of 69.20 minutes and minimum of 52.08 minutes of average make ready time are used for preparing the press to be ready for printing operation with standard deviation of 4.73 and average of 62.36 minutes. The number of make-readies is varying between one to twelve with average of 5, with 3 standard deviations. Total production time for the machine was varying in between 2.33 hours to 14.88 hours with an average of 8.95 hours. In this month, the number of printed sheets varies from 15600 to 117550 with an average of 60868. In this month, the average press speed varies from 5887 to 7898 with an average of 6786 sheets per hour.

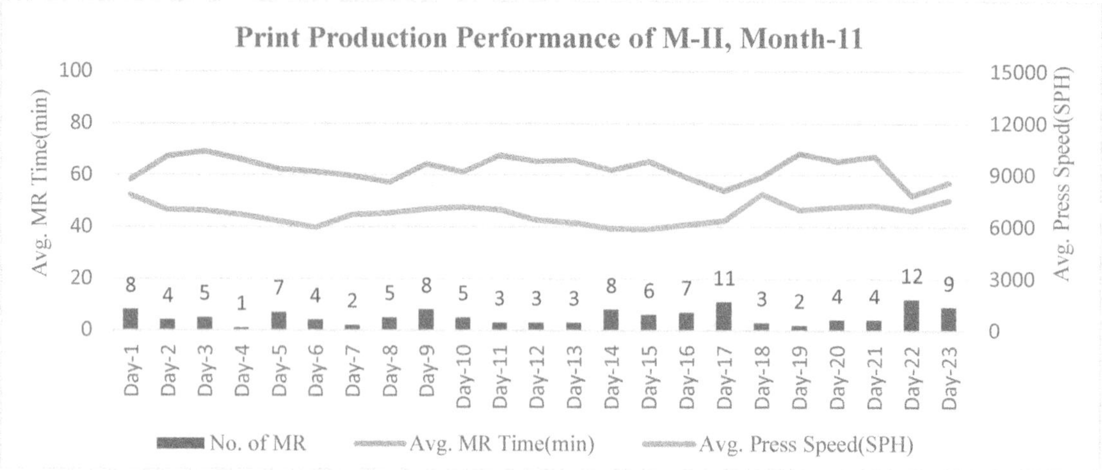

Fig. 6.23: Print Production Performance of M-II, (Month-11)

Fig.6.23 represents the average press speed in sheets per hour, average make-ready time in minutes day-wise in month-11 of Machine-II, which is equipped with medium level of automation. The number of make-readies varies from one to twelve; the average make-ready time is in-between 52.08 minutes to 69.20 minutes and the press speed is in-between 5887 to 7898 sheets per hour.

Table 6.24: Print Production Performance of Machine-II (Month-12)

	No. of MR	MR Time(min)	Avg. MR Time(min)	Total Printed Sheets	Total Production Time(h)	Avg. Press Speed(SPH)
Avg.	5	330.79	66.01	85336	10.97	7399
Max.	12	649	85.50	236700	21.72	13577
Min.	1	68	54.08	2970	0.45	5981
S.D.	3	158.10	7.99	55137	5.27	1498

Table 6.24 represents the print production performance data of Machine-II, month twelve. The table indicates that maximum of 85.50 minutes and minimum of 54.08 minute of average make ready time are used for preparing the press to be ready for printing operation with standard deviation of 7.99 and average of 66.01 minutes. The number of make-readies is varying between one to twelve with average of 5, with 3 standard deviations. Total production time for the machine was varying in between 0.45 hours to 21.72 hours with an average of 10.97 hours. In this month, the number of printed sheets varies from 2970 to 236700 with an average of 85336. In this month, the average press speed varies from 5981 to 13577 with an average of 7399 sheets per hour.

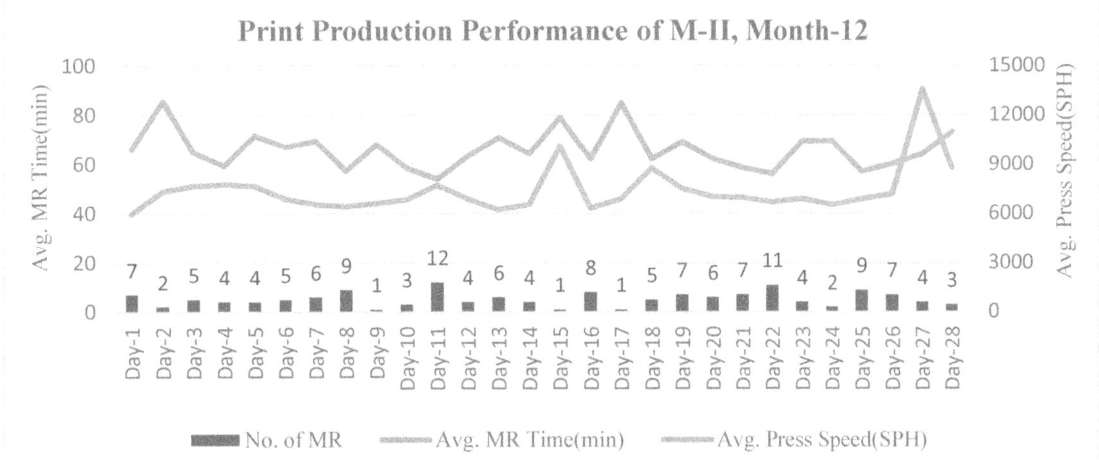

Fig. 6.24: Print Production Performance of M-II, (Month-12)

Fig.6.24 represents the average press speed in sheets per hour, average make-ready time in minutes day-wise in month-12 of Machine-II, which is equipped with medium level of automation. The number of make-readies varies from one to twelve; the average make-ready time is in-between 54.08 minutes to 85.50 minutes and the press speed is in-between 5981 to 13577 sheets per hour.

Table 6.25: Print Production Performance of Machine-III (Month-1)

	No. of MR	MR Time(min)	Avg. MR Time(min)	Total Printed Sheets	Total Production Time(h)	Avg. Press Speed(SPH)
Avg.	4	296.26	66.23	62055	11.59	5019
Max.	10	671	90	159140	21.90	7680
Min.	0	0	0	14530	3.10	3994
S.D.	3	192.64	21.75	43515	6.04	955

Table 6.25 represents the print production performance data of Machine-III, month one. The table indicates that maximum of 90 minutes and minimum of 0 minute of average make ready time are used for preparing the press to be ready for printing operation with standard deviation of 21.75 and average of 66.23 minutes. The number of make-readies is varying between zero to ten with average of 4, with 3 standard deviations. Zero make-ready indicates the job in press was of high print run length and continued from the previous day. Total production time for the machine was varying in between 3.10 hours to 21.90 hours with an average of 11.59 hours. In this month, the number of printed sheets varies from 14530 to 159140 with an average of 62055. In this month, the average press speed varies from 3994 to 7680 with an average of 5019 sheets per hour.

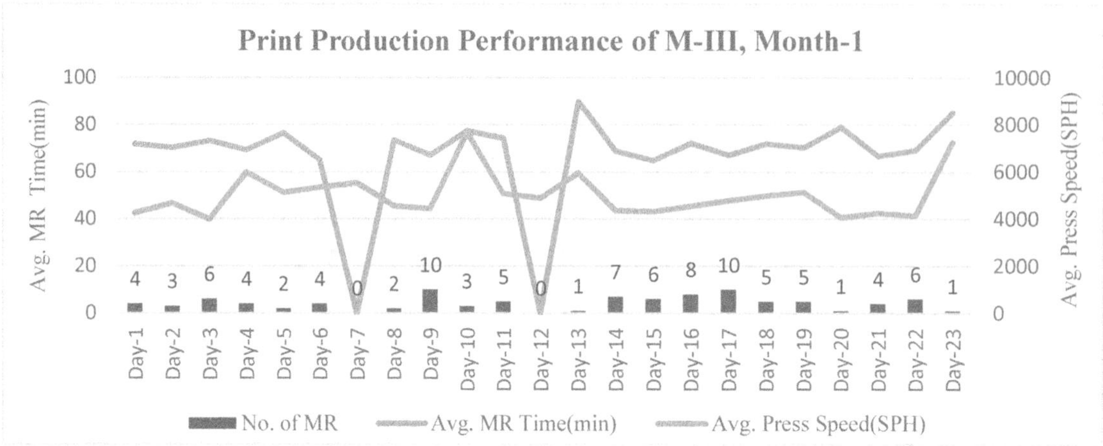

Fig. 6.25: Print Production Performance of M-III, (Month-1)

Fig.6.25 represents the average press speed in sheets per hour, average make-ready time in minutes day-wise in month-1 of Machine-III, which is equipped with low level of automation. The number of make-readies varies from zero to ten; the average make-ready time is in-between 0 minute to 90 minutes and the press speed is in-between 3994 to 7680 sheets per hour.

Table 6.26: Print Production Performance of Machine-III (Month-2)

	No. of MR	MR Time(min)	Avg. MR Time(min)	Total Printed Sheets	Total Production Time(h)	Avg. Press Speed(SPH)
Avg.	5	325.90	73.76	39410	8.35	4665
Max.	9	635	82.50	78300	15.95	5641
Min.	1	82	68.38	2490	0.62	4038
S.D.	3	173.09	4.28	20125	4.17	464

Table 6.26 represents the print production performance data of Machine-III, month two. The table indicates that maximum of 82.50 minutes and minimum of 68.38 minutes of average make ready time are used for preparing the press to be ready for printing operation with standard deviation of 4.28 and average of 73.76 minutes. The number of make-readies is varying between one to nine with average of 5, with 3 standard deviations. Total production time for the machine was varying in between 0.62 hours to 15.95 hours with an average of 8.35 hours. In this month, the number of printed sheets varies from 2490 to 78300 with an average of 39410. In this month, the average press speed varies from 4083 to 5641 with an average of 4665 sheets per hour.

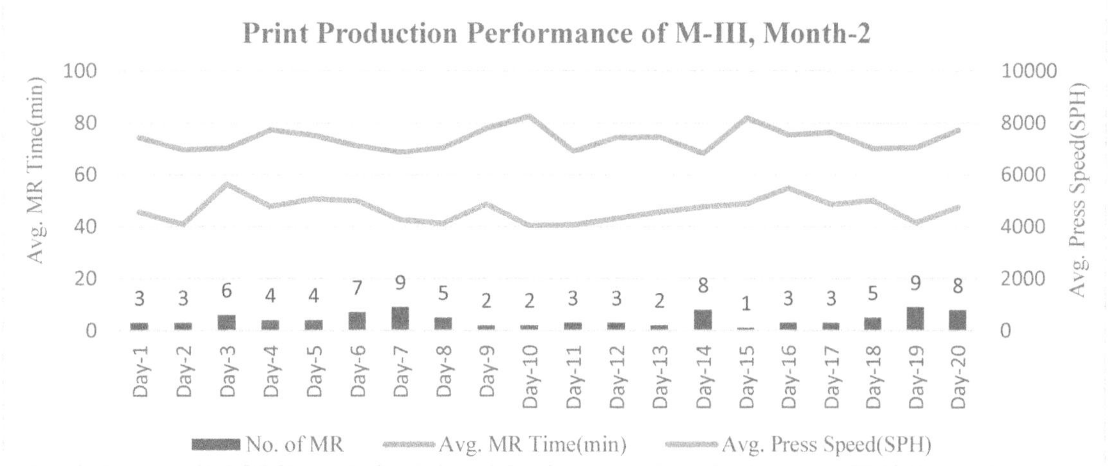

Fig. 6.26: Print Production Performance of M-III, (Month-2)

Fig.6.26 represents the average press speed in sheets per hour, average make-ready time in minutes day-wise in month-2 of Machine-III, which is equipped with low level of automation. The number of make-readies varies from one to nine; the average make-ready time is in-between 68.38 minutes to 82.50 minutes and the press speed is in-between 4038 to 5641 sheets per hour.

Table 6.27: Print Production Performance of Machine-III (Month-3)

	No. of MR	MR Time(min)	Avg. MR Time(min)	Total Printed Sheets	Total Production Time(h)	Avg. Press Speed(SPH)
Avg.	5	336.44	65.82	42556	8.77	4732
Max.	11	775	89.33	118900	20.23	5876
Min.	0	0	0	14850	2.82	4251
S.D.	3	201.05	26.28	26464	4.45	451

Table 6.27 represents the print production performance data of Machine-III, month three. The table indicates that maximum of about 89.33 minutes and minimum of 0 minute of average make ready time are used for preparing the press to be ready for printing operation with standard deviation of 26.28 and average of 65.82 minutes. The number of make-readies is varying between zero to eleven with average of 5, with 3 standard deviations. Zero make-ready indicates the job in press was of high print run length and continued from the previous day. Total production time for the machine was varying in between 2.82 hours to 20.23 hours with an average of 8.77 hours. In this month, the number of printed sheets varies from 14850 to 118900 with an average of 42556. In this month, the average press speed varies from 4251 to 5876 with an average of 4732 sheets per hour.

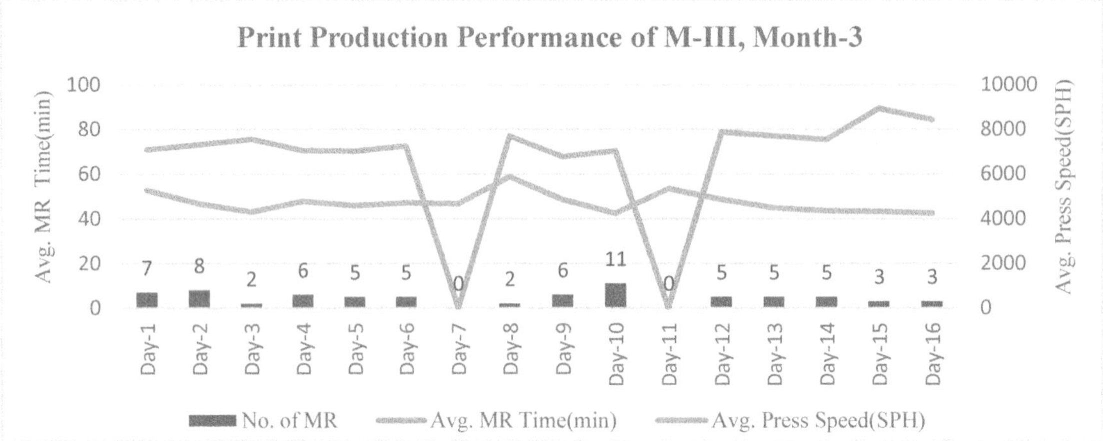

Fig. 6.27: Print Production Performance of M-III, (Month-3)

Fig.6.27 represents the average press speed in sheets per hour, average make-ready time in minutes day-wise in month-3 of Machine-III, which is equipped with low level of automation. The number of make-readies varies from zero to eleven; the average make-ready time is in-between 0 minute to 89.33 minutes and the press speed is in-between 4251 to 5876 sheets per hour.

Table 6.28: Print Production Performance of Machine-III (Month-4)

	No. of MR	MR Time(min)	Avg. MR Time(min)	Total Printed Sheets	Total Production Time(h)	Avg. Press Speed(SPH)
Avg.	4	277	79.08	23052	5.17	4446
Max.	4	318	79.50	25804	5.53	4663
Min.	3	236	78.67	20300	4.80	4229
S.D.	1	57.98	0.59	3892	0.52	307

Table 6.28 represents the print production performance data of Machine-III, month four. The table indicates that maximum of 79.50 minutes and minimum of 78.67 minutes of average make ready time are used for preparing the press to be ready for printing operation with standard deviation of 0.59 and average of 79.08 minutes. The number of make-readies is varying between three to four with average of 4, with 1 standard deviations. Total production time for the machine was varying in between 4.80 hours to 5.53 hours with an average of 5.17 hours. In this month, the number of printed sheets varies from 20300 to 25804 with an average of 23052. In this month, the average press speed varies from 4229 to 4663 with an average of 4446 sheets per hour.

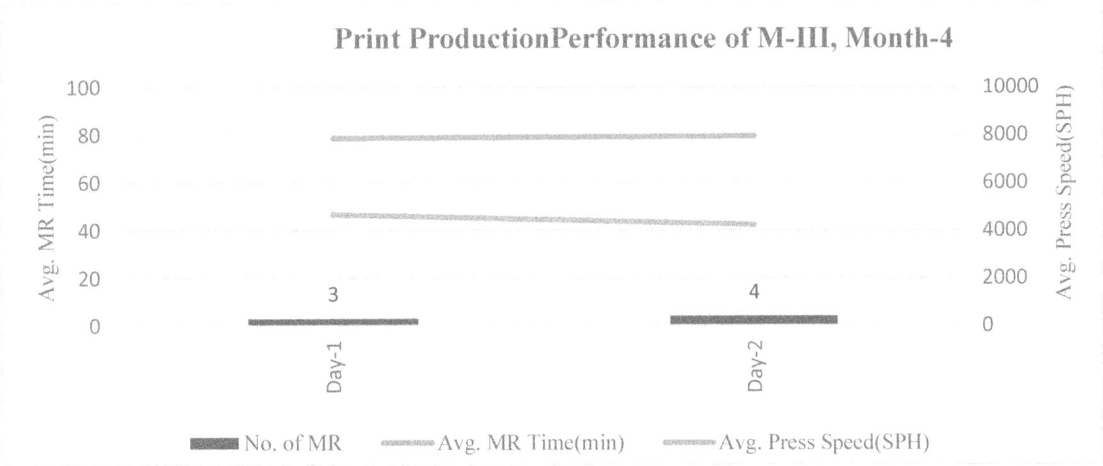

Fig. 6.28: Print Production Performance of M-III, (Month-4)

Fig.28 represents the average press speed in sheets per hour, average make-ready time in minutes day-wise in month-4 of Machine-III, which is equipped with low level of automation. The number of make-readies varies from three to four; the average make-ready time is in-between 78.67 minutes to 79.50 minutes and the press speed is in-between 4229 to 4663 sheets per hour.

Table 6.29: Print Production Performance of Machine-III (Month-5)

	No. of MR	MR Time(min)	Avg. MR Time(min)	Total Printed Sheets	Total Production Time(h)	Avg. Press Speed(SPH)
Avg.	4	298.20	69.34	35714	7.88	4483
Max.	8	577	81	79200	16.50	5237
Min.	0	0	0	7890	1.82	3854
S.D.	2	151.89	15.08	19585	4.06	380

Table 6.29 represents the print production performance data of Machine-III, month five. The table indicates that maximum of 81 minutes and minimum of 0 minute of average make ready time are used for preparing the press to be ready for printing operation with standard deviation of 15.08 and average of 69.34 minutes. The number of make-readies is varying between zero to eight with average of 4, with 2 standard deviations. Zero make-ready indicates the job in press was of high print run length and continued from the previous day. Total production time for the machine was varying in between 1.82 hours to 16.50 hours with an average of 7.88 hours. In this month, the number of printed sheets varies from 7890 to 79200 with an average of 35714. In this month, the average press speed varies from 3854 to 5237 with an average of 4483 sheets per hour.

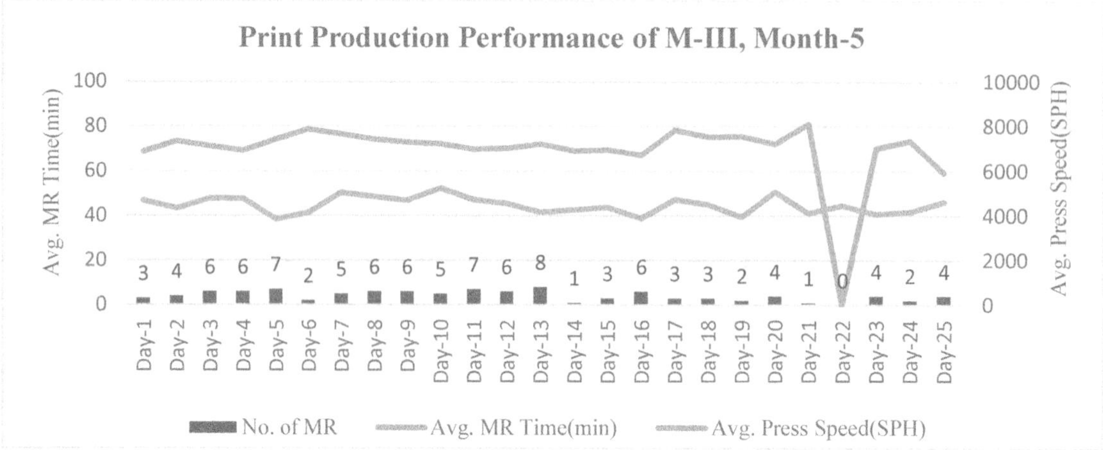

Fig. 6.29: Print Production Performance of M-III, (Month-5)

Fig.6.29 represents the average press speed in sheets per hour, average make-ready time in minutes day-wise in month-5 of Machine-III, which is equipped with low level of automation. The number of make-readies varies from zero to eight; the average make-ready time is in-between 0 minutes to 81 minutes and the press speed is in-between 3854 to 5237 sheets per hour.

Table 6.30: Print Production Performance of Machine-III (Month-6)

	No. of MR	MR Time(min)	Avg. MR Time(min)	Total Printed Sheets	Total Production Time(h)	Avg. Press Speed(SPH)
Avg.	4	273	61.51	50866	10.59	4603
Max.	9	631	95.50	146500	23.28	6292
Min.	0	0	0	10600	2.73	3878
S.D.	3	190.86	33.03	30392	5.03	593

Table 6.30 represents the print production performance data of Machine-III, month six. The table indicates that maximum of about 95.50 minutes and minimum of 0 minute of average make ready time are used for preparing the press to be ready for printing operation with standard deviation of 33.03 and average of 61.51 minutes. The number of make-readies is varying between zero to nine with average of 4, with 3 standard deviations. Zero make-ready indicates the job in press was of high print run length and continued from the previous day. Total production time for the machine was varying in between 2.73 hours to 23.28 hours with an average of 10.59 hours. In this month, the number of printed sheets varies from 10600 to 146500 with an average of 50866. In this month, the average press speed varies from 3878 to 6292 with an average of 4603 sheets per hour.

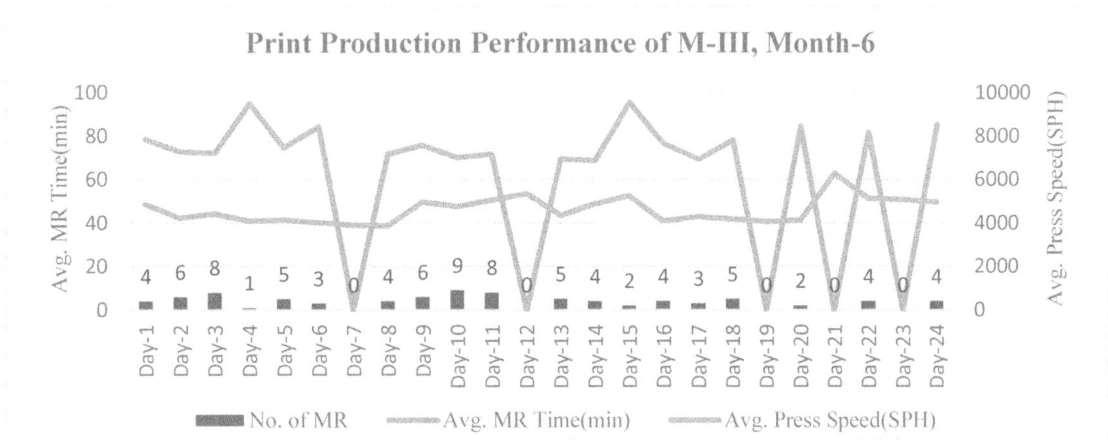

Fig. 6.30: Print Production Performance of M-III, (Month-6)

Fig.6.30 represents the average press speed in sheets per hour, average make-ready time in minutes day-wise in month-6 of Machine-III, which is equipped with low level of automation. The number of make-readies varies from zero to nine; the average make-ready time is in-between 0 minutes to 95.50 minutes and the press speed is in-between 3878 to 6292 sheets per hour.

Table 6.31: Print Production Performance of Machine-III (Month-7)

	No. of MR	MR Time(min)	Avg. MR Time(min)	Total Printed Sheets	Total Production Time(h)	Avg. Press Speed(SPH)
Avg.	4	319.35	74.77	52116	11	4727
Max.	11	694	96.50	90865	17.77	7499
Min.	0	0	0	10000	1.98	3883
S.D.	3	195.85	16.81	19518	3.60	726

Table 6.31 represents the print production performance data of Machine-III, month seven. The table indicates that maximum of 96.50 minutes and minimum of 0 minute of average make ready time are used for preparing the press to be ready for printing operation with standard deviation of 16.81 and average of 74.77 minutes. The number of make-readies is varying between zero to eleven with average of 4, with 3 standard deviations. Zero make-ready indicates the job in press was of high print run length and continued from the previous day. Total production time for the machine was varying in between 1.98 hours to 17.77 hours with an average of 11 hours. In this month, the number of printed sheets varies from 10000 to 90865 with an average of 52116. In this month, the average press speed varies from 3883 to 7499 with an average of 4727 sheets per hour.

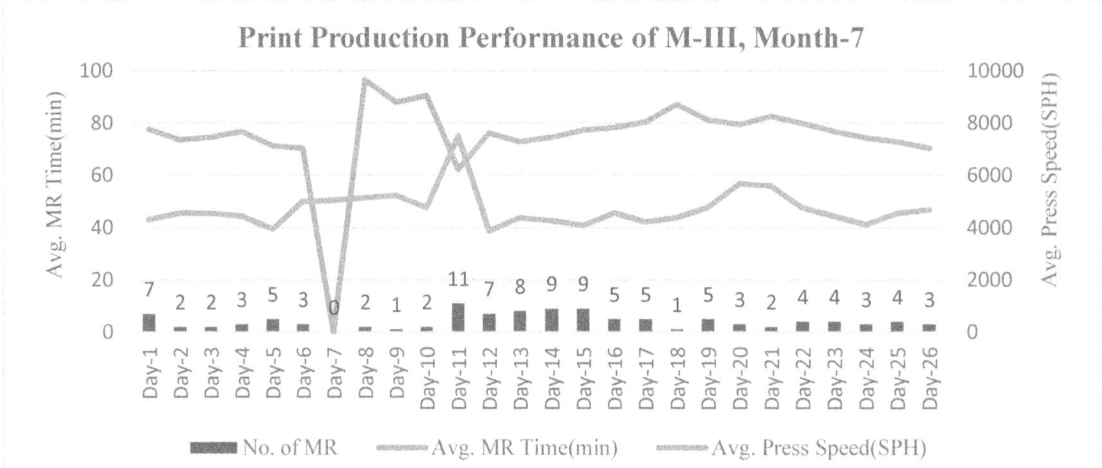

Fig. 6.31: Print Production Performance of M-III, (Month-7)

Fig.6.31 represents the average press speed in sheets per hour, average make-ready time in minutes day-wise in month-7 of Machine-III, which is equipped with low level of automation. The number of make-readies varies from zero to eleven; the average make-ready time is in-between 0 minutes to 96.50 minutes and the press speed is in-between 3883 to 7499 sheets per hour.

Table 6.32: Print Production Performance of Machine-III (Month-8)

	No. of MR	MR Time(min)	Avg. MR Time(min)	Total Printed Sheets	Total Production Time(h)	Avg. Press Speed(SPH)
Avg.	5	357.09	78.37	52843	10.12	5029
Max.	9	663	94.50	111638	17.62	6337
Min.	1	93	67.33	13270	2.72	3982
S.D.	2	160.91	9.15	27473	4.01	683

Table 6.32 represents the print production performance data of Machine-III, month eight. The table indicates that maximum of 94.50 minutes and minimum of 67.33 minutes of average make ready time are used for preparing the press to be ready for printing operation with standard deviation of 9.15 and average of 78.37 minutes. The number of make-readies is varying between one to nine with average of 5, with 2 standard deviations. Total production time for the machine was varying in between 2.72 hours to 17.62 hours with an average of 10.12 hours. In this month, the number of printed sheets varies from 13270 to 111638 with an average of 52843. In this month, the average press speed varies from 3982 to 6337 with an average of 5029 sheets per hour.

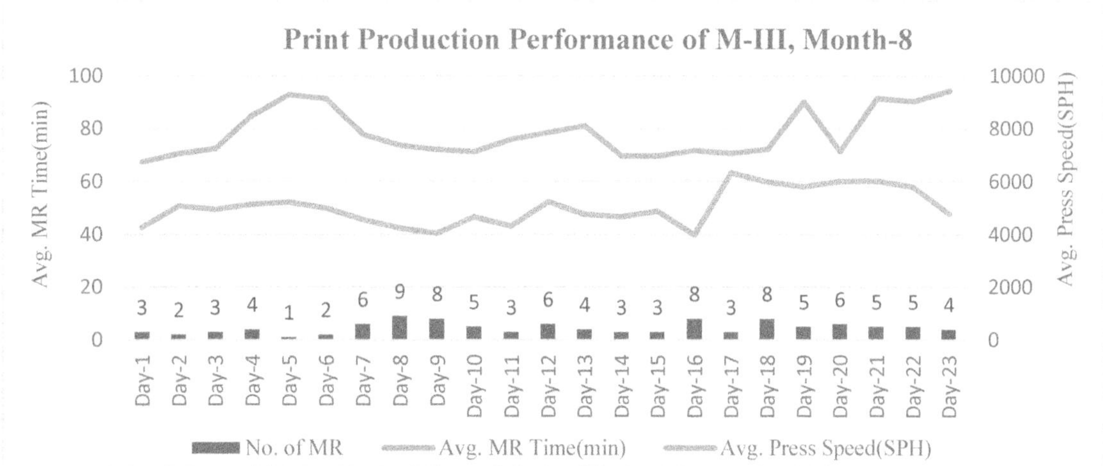

Fig. 6.32: Print Production Performance of M-III, (Month-8)

Fig.6.32 represents the average press speed in sheets per hour, average make-ready time in minutes day-wise in month-8 of Machine-III, which is equipped with low level of automation. The number of make-readies varies from one to nine; the average make-ready time is in-between 67.33 minutes to 94.50 minutes and the press speed is in-between 3982 to 6337 sheets per hour.

Table 6.33: Print Production Performance of Machine-III (Month-9)

	No. of MR	MR Time(min)	Avg. MR Time(min)	Total Printed Sheets	Total Production Time(h)	Avg. Press Speed(SPH)
Avg.	5	376.38	73.95	55033	11.05	4863
Max.	10	631	87.67	134360	22.28	7094
Min.	1	65	63.10	2200	0.55	3823
S.D.	2	121.52	5.57	26470	4.28	759

Table 6.33 represents the print production performance data of Machine-III, month nine. The table indicates that maximum of 87.67 minutes and minimum of 63.10 minutes of average make ready time are used for preparing the press to be ready for printing operation with standard deviation of 5.57 and average of 73.95 minutes. The number of make-readies is varying between one to ten with average of 5, with 2 standard deviations. Total production time for the machine was varying in between 0.55 hours to 22.28 hours with an average of 11.05 hours. In this month, the number of printed sheets varies from 2200 to 134360 with an average of 55033. In this month, the average press speed varies from 3823 to 7094 with an average of 4863 sheets per hour.

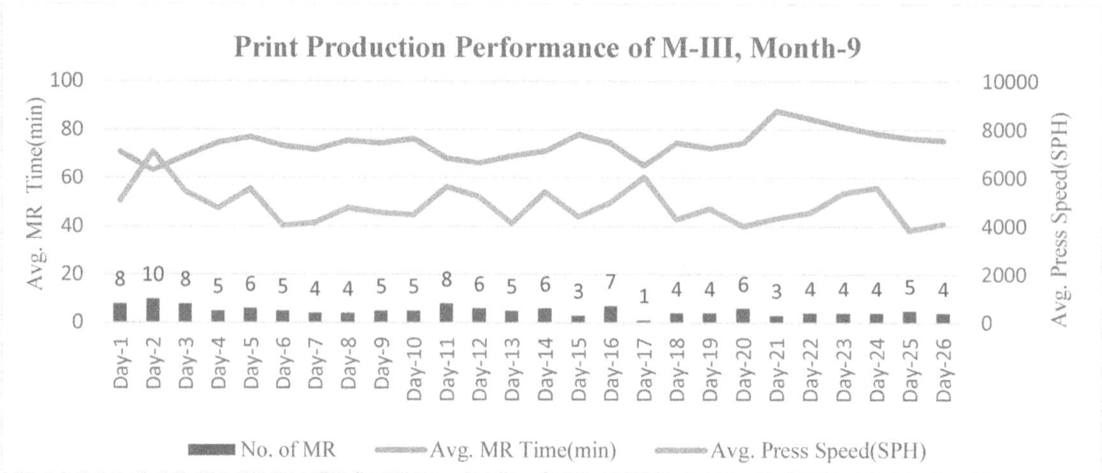

Fig. 6.33: Print Production Performance of M-III, (Month-9)

Fig.6.33 represents the average press speed in sheets per hour, average make-ready time in minutes day-wise in month-9 of Machine-III, which is equipped with low level of automation. The number of make-readies varies from one to ten; the average make-ready time is in-between 63.10 minutes to 87.67 minutes and the press speed is in-between 3823 to 7094 sheets per hour.

Table 6.34: Print Production Performance of Machine-III (Month-10)

	No. of MR	MR Time(min)	Avg. MR Time(min)	Total Printed Sheets	Total Production Time(h)	Avg. Press Speed(SPH)
Avg.	6	443.92	72.39	60778	11.88	5047
Max.	17	815	87.50	108250	18.38	8695
Min.	2	139	47.94	14720	3.68	3888
S.D.	3	179.70	7.28	23701	3.80	1021

Table 6.34 represents the print production performance data of Machine-III, month ten. The table indicates that maximum of 87.50 minutes and minimum of 47.94 minute of average make ready time are used for preparing the press to be ready for printing operation with standard deviation of 7.28 and average of 72.39 minutes. The number of make-readies is varying between two to seventeen with average of 6, with 3 standard deviations. Total production time for the machine was varying in between 3.68 hours to 18.38 hours with an average of 11.88 hours. In this month, the number of printed sheets varies from 14720 to 108250 with an average of 60778. In this month, the average press speed varies from 3888 to 8695 with an average of 5047 sheets per hour.

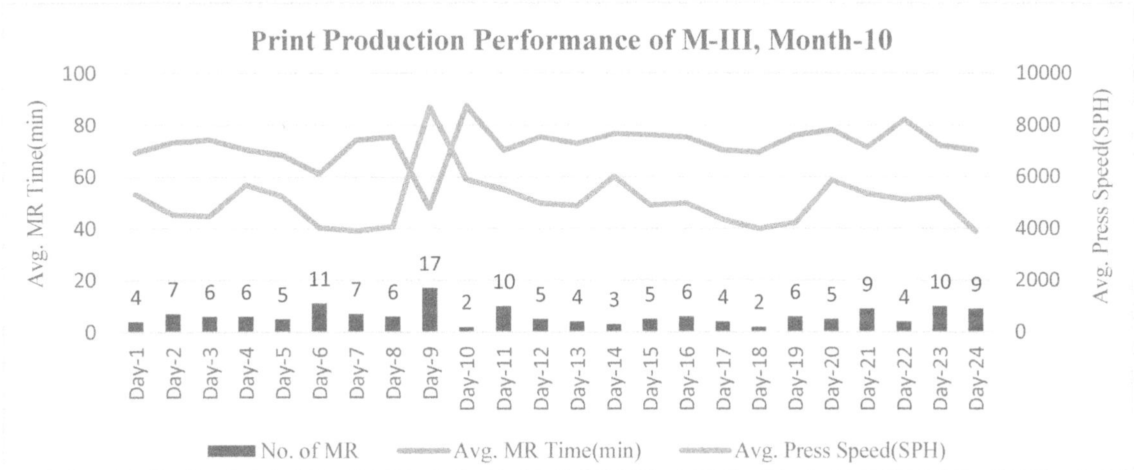

Fig. 6.34: Print Production Performance of M-III, (Month-10)

Fig.6.34 represents the average press speed in sheets per hour, average make-ready time in minutes day-wise in month-10 of Machine-III, which is equipped with low level of automation. The number of make-readies varies from two to seventeen; the average make-ready time is in-between 47.94 minutes to 87.50 minutes and the press speed is in-between 3888 to 8695 sheets per hour.

Table 6.35: Print Production Performance of Machine-III (Month-11)

	No. of MR	MR Time(min)	Avg. MR Time(min)	Total Printed Sheets	Total Production Time(h)	Avg. Press Speed(SPH)
Avg.	4	326.65	70.92	35087	7.52	4618
Max.	8	656	82.50	69183	16.33	5810
Min.	0	0	0	3900	0.98	3889
S.D.	2	157.42	15	18147	3.71	539

Table 6.35 represents the print production performance data of Machine-III, month eleven. The table indicates that of about 82.50 minutes and minimum of 0 minute of average make ready time are used for preparing the press to be ready for printing operation with standard deviation of 15 and average of 70.92 minutes. The number of make-readies is varying between zero to eight with average of 4, with 2 standard deviations. Zero make-ready indicates the job in press was of high print run length and continued from the previous day. Total production time for the machine was varying in between 0.98 hours to 16.33 hours with an average of 7.52 hours. In this month, the number of printed sheets varies from 3900 to 69183 with an average of 35087. In this month, the average press speed varies from 3889 to 5810 with an average of 4618 sheets per hour.

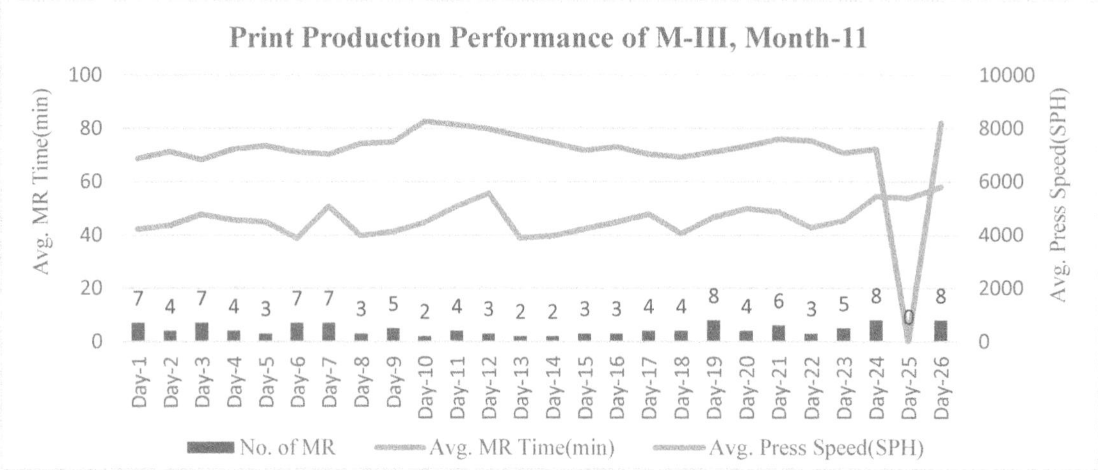

Fig. 6.35: Print Production Performance of M-III, (Month-11)

Fig.6.35 represents the average press speed in sheets per hour, average make-ready time in minutes day-wise in month-11 of Machine-III, which is equipped with low level of automation. The number of make-readies varies from zero to eight; the average make-ready time is in-between 0 minutes to 82.50 minutes and the press speed is in-between 3889 to 5810 sheets per hour.

Table 6.36: Print Production Performance of Machine-III (Month-12)

	No. of MR	MR Time(min)	Avg. MR Time(min)	Total Printed Sheets	Total Production Time(h)	Avg. Press Speed(SPH)
Avg.	4	281.65	73.38	35901	7.55	4736
Max.	7	527	90.33	75240	13.03	6092
Min.	0	0	0	11480	2.20	3804
S.D.	2	141.14	16.33	16720	3.19	595

Table 6.36 represents the print production performance data of Machine-III, month twelve. The table indicates that maximum of 90.33 minutes and minimum of 0 minute of average make ready time are used for preparing the press to be ready for printing operation with standard deviation of 16.33 and average of 73.38 minutes. The number of make-readies is varying between zero to seven with average of 4, with 2 standard deviations. Zero make-ready indicates the job in press was of high print run length and continued from the previous day. Total production time for the machine was varying in between 2.20 hours to 13.03 hours with an average of 7.55 hours. In this month, the number of printed sheets varies from 11480 to 75240 with an average of 35901. In this month, the average press speed varies from 3804 to 6092 with an average of 4736 sheets per hour.

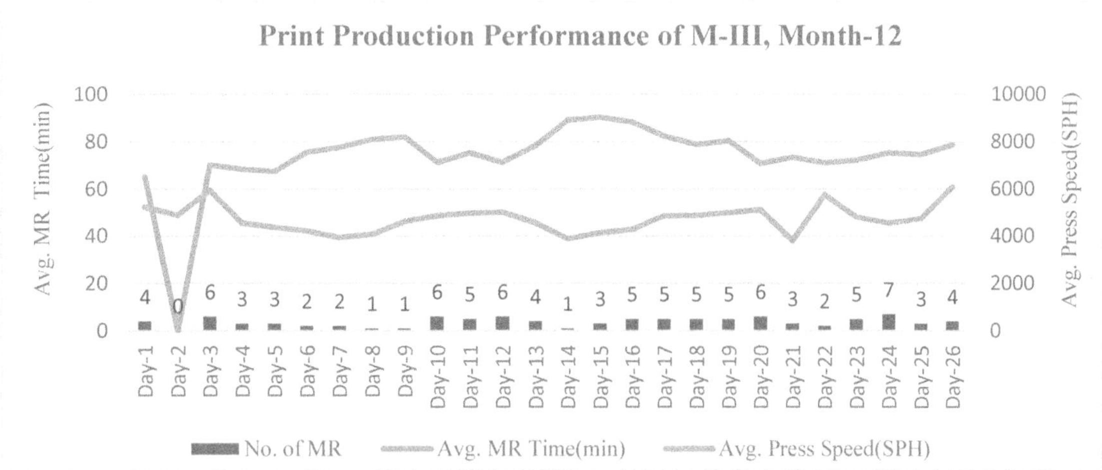

Fig. 6.36: Print Production Performance of M-III, (Month-12)

Fig.6.36 represents the average press speed in sheets per hour, average make-ready time in minutes day-wise in month-12 of Machine-III, which is equipped with low level of automation. The number of make-readies varies from zero to seven; the average make-ready time is in-between 0 minutes to 90.33 minutes and the press speed is in-between 3804 to 6092 sheets per hour. Average makeready time zero indicates, there was no makeready being carried out in that particular day.

Table 6.37, indicates the month wise average make-ready (MR) time in minutes (min.), average press speed, sheets per hour (SPH) of the three machines; Machine-I, Machine-II and Machine-III, respectively, for the whole one year. This table indicates the press with high level technology results into low make-ready time and high level of average press speed, followed by Machine-II and Machine-III, respectively; mentioning that automation in multi-colour sheet fed offset press has certainly a bigger role to play when it comes to the make-ready time and average press speed.

Table 6.37: Avg. MR Time & Avg. Press Speed of M-I, M-II & M-III

	M-I		M-II		M-III	
Month	Avg. MR Time(min)	Avg. Press Speed(SPH)	Avg. MR Time(min)	Avg. Press Speed(SPH)	Avg. MR Time(min)	Avg. Press Speed(SPH)
Month-1	60.70	7988	56.63	6065	66.23	5019
Month-2	62.38	7243	58.75	6317	73.76	4665
Month-3	65.43	7332	60.24	6428	65.82	4732
Month-4	57.85	7424	76.62	6814	79.08	4446
Month-5	65.05	7653	64.66	6108	69.34	4483
Month-6	59.91	7515	58.96	6690	61.51	4603
Month-7	61.29	6646	58.20	6932	74.77	4727
Month-8	60.02	6754	65.20	6782	78.37	5029
Month-9	58.78	7087	58.67	7101	73.95	4863
Month-10	60.51	7093	62.85	6876	72.39	5047
Month-11	55.52	7295	62.36	6786	70.92	4618
Month-12	60.26	7466	66.01	7399	73.38	4736

Table 6.38: Print Production Performance of M-I, M-II & M-III

	M-I		M-II		M-III	
	Avg. MR Time(min)	Avg. Press Speed(SPH)	Avg. MR Time(min)	Avg. Press Speed(SPH)	Avg. MR Time(min)	Avg. Press Speed(SPH)
Avg.	60.64	7291	62.43	6691	71.63	4747
Max.	65.43	7988	76.62	7399	79.08	5047
Min.	55.52	6646	56.63	6065	61.51	4446
S.D.	2.65	354	5.19	380	4.96	196

Table 6.38, represents the average, minimum, maximum and standard deviation of average make-ready (MR) time in minutes (min.); average press speed in sheets per hour (SPH) of the three machines; Machine-I, Machine-II and Machine-III, respectively. For the Machine-I, the minimum average make-ready time, maximum average make-ready time and average make-ready time in minutes is low in-comparison to the other two presses and for the Machine-II, it is low than the third press. Likewise, for the Machine-I, the minimum average press speed and maximum average press speed are high in-comparison to the other two presses (M-I and M-II) and for the Machine-II, it is higher than the third press (M-III).

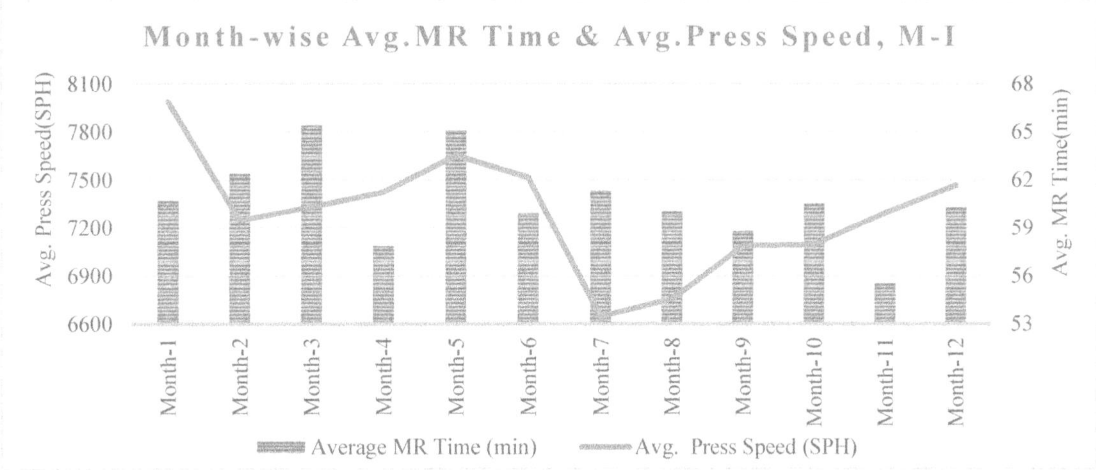

Fig. 6.37: Month-wise Avg. MR Time & Avg. Press Speed, M-I

Figure 6.37, represents the average press speed in sheets per hour, average make-ready time in minutes of Machine-I, which is equipped with high level of automation. The average make-ready time is in-between 55.52 minutes to 65.43 minutes and the press speed is in-between 6646 to 7988 sheets per hour. The machine with high level of press automation generally leads to less time for makeready operation and hence also high press speed.

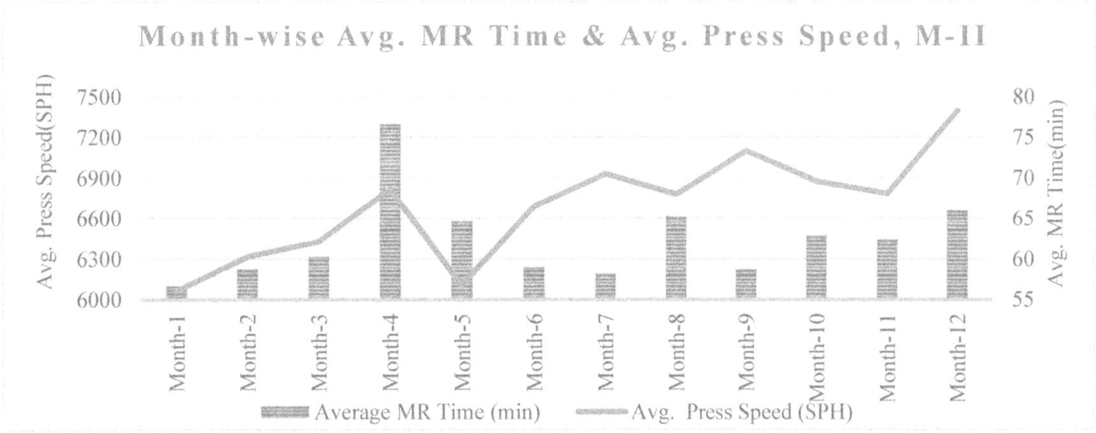

Fig. 6.38: Month-wise Avg. MR Time & Avg. Press Speed, M-II

Figure 6.38, represents the average press speed in sheets per hour, average make-ready time in minutes of Machine-II, which is equipped with medium level of automation. The average make-ready time is in-between 56.63 minutes to 76.62 minutes and the press speed is in-between 6065 to 7399 sheets per hour.

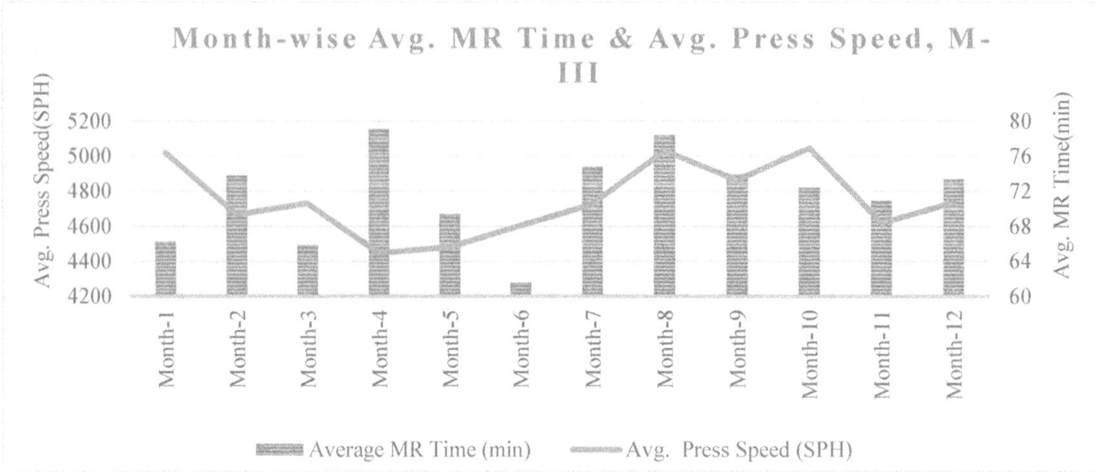

Fig. 6.39: Month-wise Avg. MR Time & Avg. Press Speed, M-III

Figure 6.39, represents the average press speed, in sheets per hour, average make-ready time in minutes of Machine-III, which is equipped with low level of automation. The average make-ready time is in-between 61.51 minutes to 79.08 minutes and the press speed is in-between 4446 to 5047 sheets per hour.

Three machines; M-I, M-II, & M-III with varying degrees of press automation results into varying average makeready time and average press speed. It is very much clear that, press with highest level of press automation contributes to low average makeready time and high average press speed in comparison to machine with medium and low level of press automation.

Table 6.39: Comparative values of Avg. MR Time & Avg. Press Speed of M-I, M-II & M-III

Machine	Avg. MR Time (min)	Avg. Press Speed (SPH)
M-I	60.64	7291
M-II	62.43	6691
M-III	71.63	4747

Table 6.39, represents the average make-ready (MR) time in minutes (min), average press speed, sheets per hour (SPH) of the three machines; Machine-I, Machine-II and Machine-III, respectively. Machine-I, shows lowest make-ready time than the other two machines, Machine-II shows lower average make-ready time than the third machine and higher than the first machine and Machine-III indicates higher average make-ready time than the first two machines. When it comes to average press speed in sheets per hour; Machine-I, shows highest SPH than the other two machines, Machine-II shows higher SPH than the third machine and lower than the first machine and Machine-III indicates lowest SPH than the first two machines.

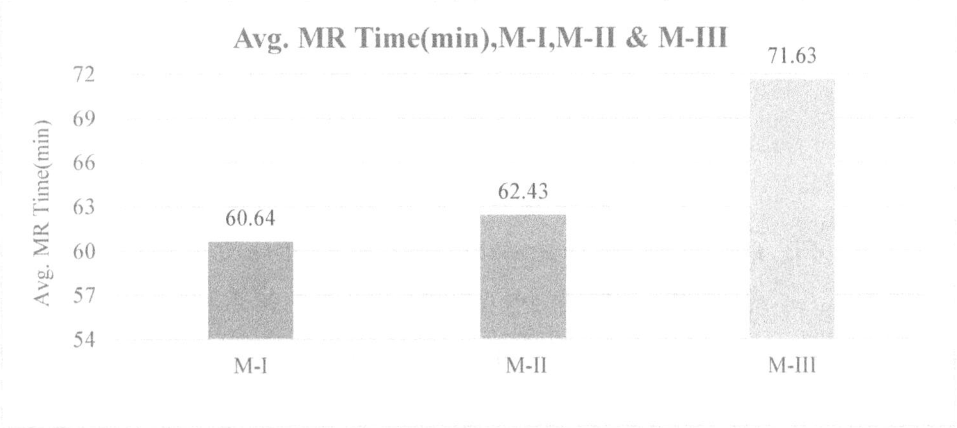

Fig. 6.40: Avg. MR Time (min), M-I, M-II & M-III

Figure 6.40, represents the average make-ready times in minutes of Machine-I, Machine-II and Machine-III. Machine-I is having 60.64 minutes average make-ready followed by Machine-II is having 62.43 minutes and Machine-III is having 71.63 minutes. This indicates machines with high level automation results into low make-ready time and vice-versa. Figure 6.41, represents the average press speed in sheets per hour of Machine-I, Machine-II and Machine-III. Machine-I is having 7291 sheets per hour average press speed followed by Machine-II is having 6691 sheets per hour average press speed and Machine-III is having 4747 sheets per hour average press speed. This indicates machines with high level automation results into high press speed and vice-versa.

Real printing rate of production of any printing machine is an important factor. Multi- colour sheet fed offset presses are designed and manufactured to handle complex multi-colour printing jobs with greater accuracy and higher speed of press operation. Moreover, multi-colour sheet fed offset presses with automation needs to justify its cost in relation with higher print output also. Here it comes to calculate the real rate of print production of the three multi-colour sheet fed offset presses selected for the research work with different levels of press automation, so that a comparison can be made the impact of press automation on real rate of print production of the particular offset press.

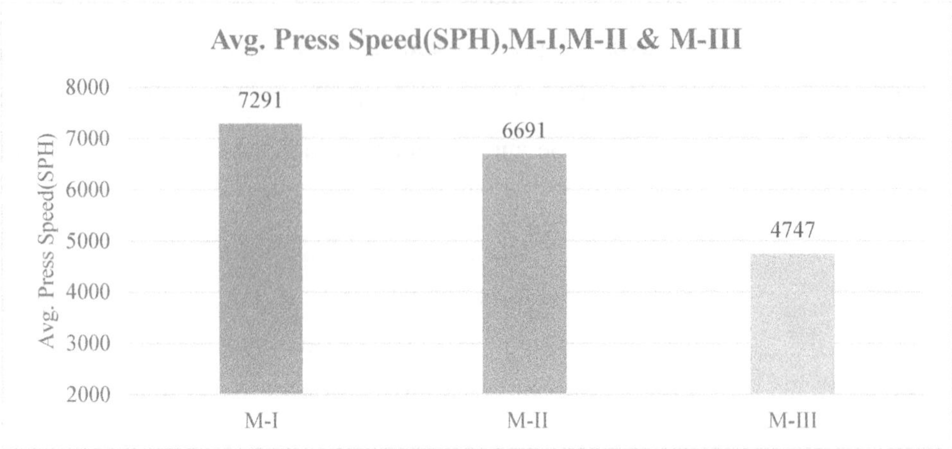

Fig. 6.41: Avg. Press Speed (SPH), M-I, M-II & M-III

Real printing rate of production of a press is calculated by multiplication of availability, performance and capacity of the particular offset press. Where, availability is the percentage of run time of the planned time and performance is the percentage of the average run speed of the maximum press speed indicated by press manufacturer, and capacity is the maximum number of sheets per unit of time rated by the press manufacturer (Uribe, 2008). There are three machines; Machine-I, Machine-II, and Machine-III, varying from highest level of press automation to medium level press automation and ending with lowest level of press automation, when they are compared with each other, the data pertaining to real rate of production is presented in Table 6.40, Table 6.41, and Table 6.42. these tables contain date pertaining to these three presses for all the twelve months for analysis purpose.

Table 6.40, indicates the real printing rate of production of Machine-I. Machine-I is equipped with high level of press automation, in comparison with Machine-II and Machine-III. Real printing rate of production of Machine-I from 3904 sheets per hour to 5375 sheets per hour, when considered in month wise print production data of the particular multi- colour sheet fed offset presses. This table essentially point out the availability, performance, and capacity of this particular sheet fed offset press and as the capacity of the press is the maximum speed of the machine, which is certainly constant, other two factors are very close without much variations.

Table 6.40: Real Printing Rate of Production of Machine-I

Month	Availability(A)	Performance(P)	Capacity (C)	Real Printing Rate of Production=(A x P x C)
Month-1	0.677580	0.528891	15000	5375
Month-2	0.660388	0.459557	15000	4552
Month-3	0.619068	0.483891	15000	4493
Month-4	0.634934	0.486211	15000	4631
Month-5	0.638984	0.502510	15000	4816
Month-6	0.673228	0.493856	15000	4987
Month-7	0.597023	0.435978	15000	3904
Month-8	0.621008	0.441486	15000	4112
Month-9	0.626170	0.457125	15000	4294
Month-10	0.619376	0.466777	15000	4337
Month-11	0.670242	0.482188	15000	4848
Month-12	0.701736	0.499862	15000	5262

Table 6.41, indicates the real printing rate of production of Machine-II. Machine-II is equipped with medium level of press automation, in comparison with Machine-I and Machine-III. Real printing rate of production of Machine-II from 3992 sheets per hour to 5238 sheets per hour, when considered in month wise print production data of the particular multi- colour sheet fed offset presses. This value is lower than the Machine-I, as because of the press automation level of this press is low than the Machine-I.

Table 6.42, indicates the real printing rate of production of Machine-III. Machine-III is equipped with low level of press automation, in comparison with Machine-I and Machine-II. Real printing rate of production of Machine-III from 2356 sheets per hour to 3754 sheets per hour, when considered in month wise print production data of the particular multi-colour sheet fed offset presses.

Table 6.41: Real Printing Rate of Production of Machine-II

Month	Availability(A)	Performance(P)	Capacity (C)	Real Printing Rate of Production=(A x P x C)
Month-1	0.681555	0.412991	15000	4222
Month-2	0.628397	0.423516	15000	3992
Month-3	0.649671	0.435536	15000	4244
Month-4	0.701475	0.464256	15000	4885
Month-5	0.737196	0.404019	15000	4468
Month-6	0.753663	0.463358	15000	5238
Month-7	0.659938	0.478623	15000	4738
Month-8	0.681013	0.471528	15000	4817
Month-9	0.654454	0.482056	15000	4732
Month-10	0.615088	0.461873	15000	4261
Month-11	0.621389	0.453537	15000	4227
Month-12	0.665620	0.518394	15000	5176

Table 6.42: Real Printing Rate of Production of Machine-III

Month	Availability(A)	Performance(P)	Capacity (C)	Real Printing Rate of Production=(A x P x C)
Month-1	0.701298	0.4117637	13000	3754
Month-2	0.605877	0.3630580	13000	2860
Month-3	0.610097	0.3730955	13000	2959
Month-4	0.528109	0.3432060	13000	2356
Month-5	0.613210	0.3486593	13000	2779
Month-6	0.699477	0.3694665	13000	3360
Month-7	0.673842	0.3645780	13000	3194
Month-8	0.629695	0.4016541	13000	3288
Month-9	0.637944	0.3829934	13000	3176
Month-10	0.616141	0.3936777	13000	3153
Month-11	0.579950	0.3590636	13000	2707
Month-12	0.616537	0.3658964	13000	2933

Table 6.43: MR, Avg. Press Speed & Real Printing Rate of Production details of M-I

Month	No. of MR	Total MR Time(min)	Avg.MR Time(min)	Total Printed Sheets	Total Production Time(h)	Real Printing Rate of Production
Month-1	153	9060	59.22	2517523	317.33	5375
Month-2	150	9105	60.70	2034115	295.08	4552
Month-3	138	8790	63.70	1728094	238.08	4493
Month-4	146	8360	57.26	1767377	242.33	4631
Month-5	135	8455	62.63	1880015	249.42	4816
Month-6	121	7055	58.31	1794551	242.25	4987
Month-7	158	9125	57.75	1473495	225.32	3904
Month-8	149	9020	60.54	1631290	246.33	4112
Month-9	169	10185	60.27	1949640	284.33	4294
Month-10	171	10490	61.35	1991970	284.50	4337
Month-11	137	7624	55.65	1867998	258.27	4848
Month-12	141	8335	59.11	2450575	326.83	5262

Table 6.43 explains the total number of make-readies, total make-ready time consumed in minutes, average make-ready time in minutes, total printed sheets, total production hour consumed for print production, and real printing rate of production details of machine-I, month wise, which is equipped with high level of press automation in-comparison with other two machines taken into research work.

Number of make-readies varies from 121 to 171 for the month wise data, which clearly shows average of 4 to 6 make-readies are being done by this machine, which is certainly a good sign for better print productivity. Being a six-colour press, and mostly complex jobs, the average make-ready time is varying in-between 55.65 minutes to 63.70 minutes. Real printing rate of production of Machine-I vary from 3904 sheets per hour to 5375 sheets per hour.

Figure 6.42 explains the total number of make-readies, total production time in hour & real printing rate of production of Machine-I, for one year with month wise data. Machine-I with high level of press automation in comparison to Machine-II and Machine-III. Number of make-readies are nearly same for all the months, which indicates the consistency of the press operation and the same is true for total production time in hours and real printing rate of production.

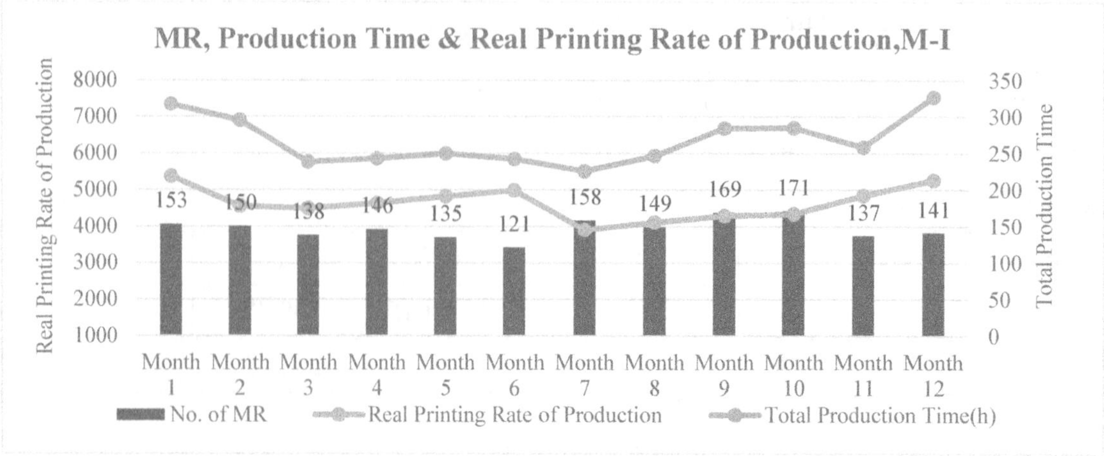

Fig. 6.42: MR, Production Time & Real Printing Rate of Production, M-I

Table 6.44: MR, Avg. Press Speed & Real Printing Rate of Production details of M-II

Month	No. of MR	Total MR Time(min)	Avg.MR Time(min)	Total Printed Sheets	Total Production Time(h)	Real Printing Rate of Production
Month-1	155	8648	55.79	1911013	308.48	4222
Month-2	180	10118	56.21	1811588	285.17	3992
Month-3	105	6012	57.26	1213947	185.82	4244
Month-4	13	1012	77.85	276000	39.63	4885
Month-5	62	3910	63.06	1107819	182.80	4468
Month-6	95	5447	57.34	1930466	277.75	5238
Month-7	131	7716	58.90	1791725	249.57	4738
Month-8	126	7834	62.17	1971577	278.75	4817
Month-9	166	9846	59.31	2247347	310.80	4732
Month-10	170	10383	61.08	1915848	276.53	4261
Month-11	124	7523	60.67	1399956	205.78	4227
Month-12	147	9262	63.01	2389409	307.28	5176

Table 6.44 explains the total number of make-readies, total make-ready time consumed in minutes, average make-ready time in minutes, total printed sheets, total production hour consumed for print production, and real printing rate of production details of machine-II,

month wise, which is equipped with medium level of press automation in-comparison with other two machines taken into research work. Number of make-readies varies from 13 to 180 for the month wise data. In month four, a very smaller number of make-readies was due to the overall maintenance of the press. Being a six-colour press, and mostly complex jobs, the average make-ready time is varying in-between 55.79 minutes to 77.85 minutes. Real printing rate of production of Machine-II varies from 3992 sheets per hour to 5238 sheets per hour.

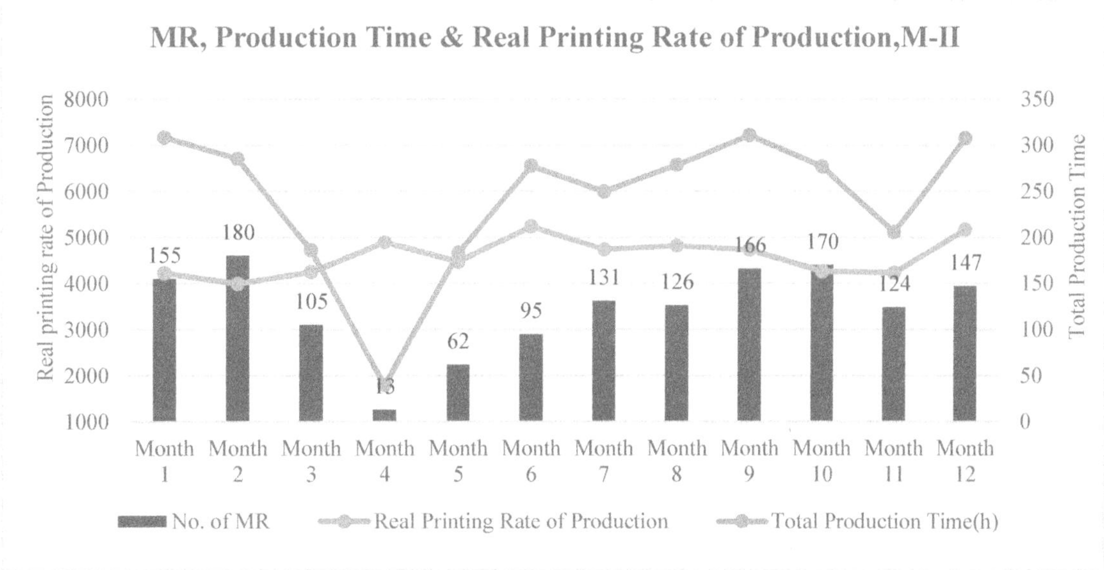

Fig. 6.43: MR, Production Time & Real Printing Rate of Production, M-II

Figure 6.43 explains the total number of make-readies, total production time in hours & real printing rate of production of Machine-II, for one year with month wise data. Machine-II with medium level of press automation in comparison to Machine-I and Machine-III. Number of make-readies are nearly same for all the months except three months, especially in month four, machine was under maintenance for a longer period of time, which indicates the consistency of the press operation and the same is true for total production time in hours and real printing rate of production.

This data indicates, press automation has certainly a bigger role to play while considering the total production time available for actual printing operation and thereby the real rate of production. Machine-II, gives the indication of the both the factors as mentioned above are little below than the values obtained for the Machine-I, which is equipped with higher press automation when compared with this machine, Machine-II.

Table 6.45: MR, Avg. Press Speed & Real Printing Rate of Production details of M-III

Month	No. of MR	MR Time(min)	Avg. MR Time(min)	Total Printed Sheets	Total Production Time(h)	Real Printing Rate of Production
Month-1	97	6814	70.25	1427269	266.63	3754
Month-2	90	6518	72.42	788199	167.00	2860
Month-3	73	5383	73.74	680893	140.38	2959
Month-4	7	554	79.14	46104	10.33	2356
Month-5	104	7455	71.68	892841	196.98	2779
Month-6	87	6552	75.31	1220779	254.17	3360
Month-7	110	8303	75.48	1355027	285.90	3194
Month-8	106	8213	77.48	1215392	232.77	3288
Month-9	134	9786	73.03	1430857	287.38	3176
Month-10	153	10654	69.63	1458661	285.02	3153
Month-11	116	8493	73.22	912249	195.43	2707
Month-12	97	7323	75.49	933414	196.23	2933

Table 6.45 explains the total number of make-readies, total make-ready time consumed in minutes, average make-ready time in minutes, total printed sheets, total production hour consumed for print production, and real printing rate of production details of machine-III, month wise, which is equipped with low level of press automation in-comparison with other two machines taken into research work. Number of make-readies varies from 7 to 153 for the month wise data. Month four, the machine was under complete maintenance for a longer period of time.

Being a six-colour press, and mostly complex jobs, the average make-ready time is varying in-between 69.63 minutes to 79.14 minutes. Real printing rate of production of Machine-III varies from 2356 sheets per hour to 3754 sheets per hour. Machine-III, gives the indication of the both the factors as mentioned above are on the lowest side than the values obtained for the Machine-I & Machine-II, which are equipped with higher press automation when compared with this machine, Machine-III.

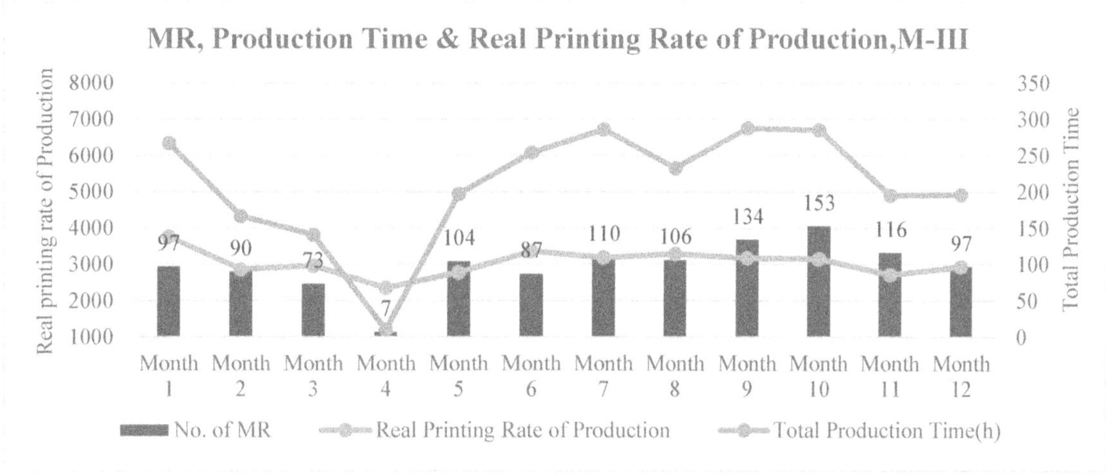

Fig. 6.44: MR, Production time & Real Printing Rate of Production, M-III

Figure 6.44 explains the total number of make-readies, total production time in hours & real printing rate of production of Machine-III, for one year with month wise data. Machine-III with low level of press automation in comparison to Machine-I and Machine-II. Number of make-readies are nearly same for all the months except three months, especially in month four, machine was under maintenance for a longer period of time, which indicates the consistency of the press operation and the same is true for total production time in hours and real printing rate of production.

Table 6.46: Print Production details of Machine-I

	No. of MR	Avg. MR Time(min)	Total Printed Sheets	Avg. Press Speed (SPH)	Real Printing Rate of Production
Avg.	147	59.71	1923887	7173	4634
Max.	171	63.70	2517523	7933	5375
Min.	121	55.65	1473495	6540	3904
S.D.	14	2.30	304560	406	445

Table 6.46, indicates the print production details of Machine-I, the make-ready per month ranges from 121 to 171 and with an average make-ready of 147. This clearly mentions that an average of 4 to 6 make-readies is carried out in this machine per day. The printed output on

this machine varies from 1473495 to 2517523 with an average of 1923887 per month. Real printing rate of production is in the range of 3904 to 5375 with an average of 4634 sheets per hour per month.

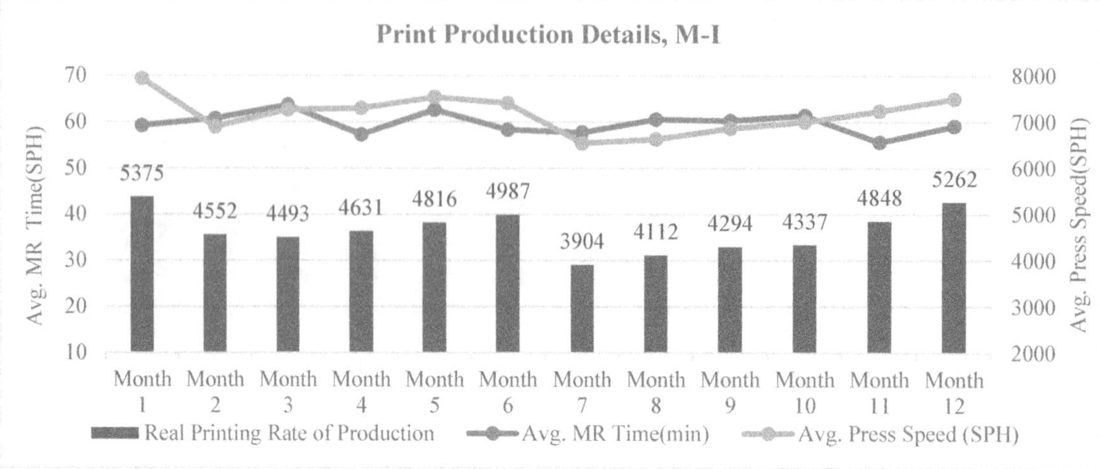

Fig. 6.45: Real Printing Rate of Production, M-I

Fig. 6.45 indicates the average make-ready time in minute, average press speed in sheets per hour and real printing rate of production of Machine-I, for the twelve months. The make-ready per month ranges from 121 to 171. Real Printing rate of production is in the range of 3904 to 5375 with an average of 4634 sheets per hour per month. The real printing rate of production of Machine-1 is showing a consistent pattern in all the three factors taken into account in this graph.

Table 6.47: Print Production details of Machine-II

	No. of MR	Avg. MR Time(min)	Total Printed Sheets	Avg. Press Speed (SPH)	Real Printing Rate of Production
Avg.	123	61.05	1663891	6837	4583
Max.	180	77.85	2389409	7776	5238
Min.	13	55.79	276000	6060	3992
S.D.	49	5.86	580189	485	406

Table 6.47, indicates the print production details of Machine-II, the make-ready per month ranges from 13 to 180 and with an average make-ready of 123. This clearly mentions that an average of 4 to 5 make-readies is carried out in this machine per day. The printed output on

this machine varies from 276000 to 2389409 with an average of 1663891 per month. Real printing rate of production is in the range of 3992 to 5238 with an average of 4583 sheets per hour per month.

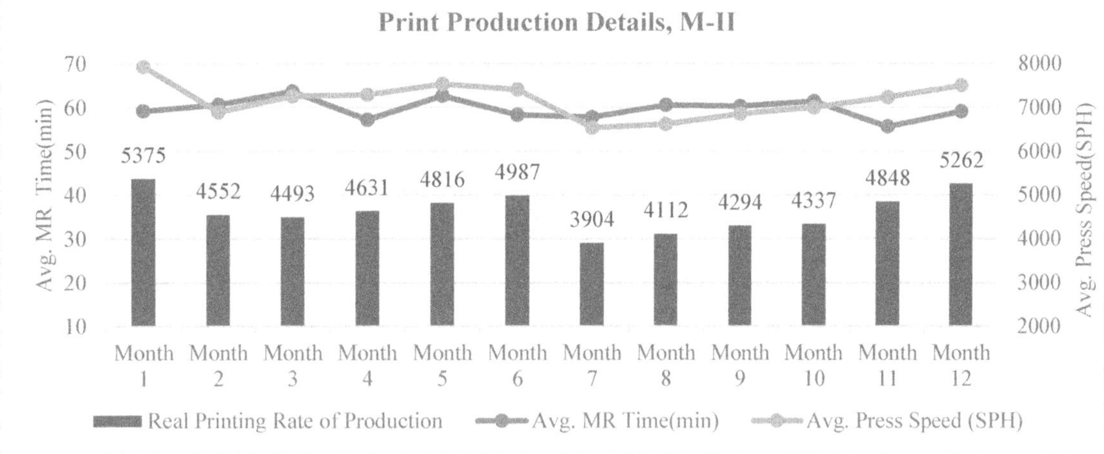

Fig. 6.46: Real Printing Rate of Production, M-II

Fig.6.46 indicates the average make-ready time in minute, average press speed in sheets per hour and real printing rate of production of Machine-II, for the twelve months. The make-ready per month ranges from 13 to 180. Real Printing rate of production is in the range of 3992 to 5238 with an average of 4583 sheets per hour per month. The real printing rate of production of Machine-II is showing a consistent pattern in all the three factors taken into account in this graph and lower in side than the values of Machine-I presented in Fig. 6.45.

Table 6.48: Print Production details of Machine-III

	No. of MR	Avg. MR Time(min)	Total Printed Sheets	Avg. Press Speed) SPH)	Real Printing Rate of Production
Avg.	98	73.91	1030140	4850	3043
Max.	153	79.14	1458661	5353	3754
Min.	7	69.63	46104	4462	2356
S.D.	36	2.82	412208	270	360

Table 6.48, indicates the print production details of Machine-III, the make-ready per month ranges from 7 to 153 and with an average make-ready of 98. This clearly mentions that an average of 3 to 4 make-readies is carried out in this machine per day. The printed output on

this machine varies from 46104 to 1458661 with an average of 1030140 per month. Real printing rate of production is in the range of 2356 to 3754 with an average of 3043 sheets per hour per month.

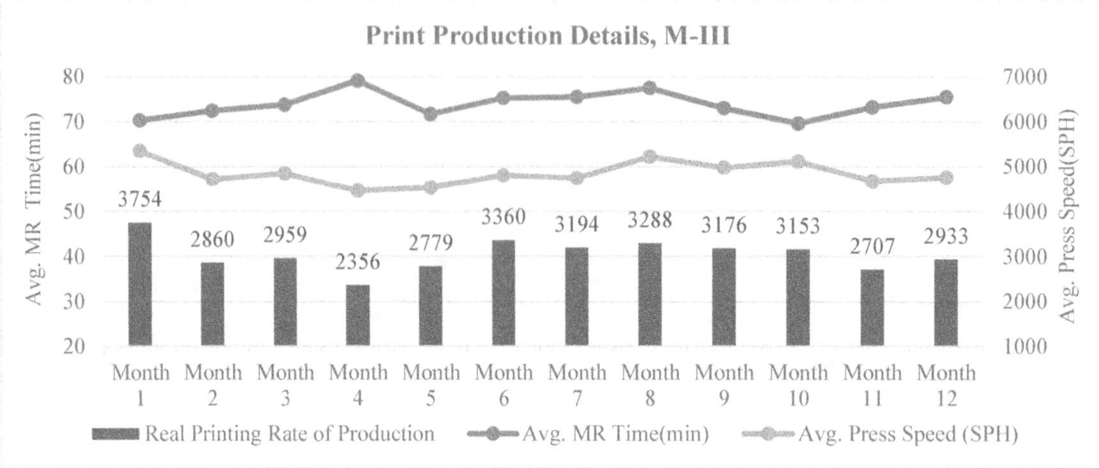

Fig. 6.47: Real Printing Rate of Production, M-III

Fig.6.47 indicates the average make-ready time in minute, average press speed in sheets per hour and real printing rate of production of Machine-III, for the twelve months. The real printing rate of production of Machine-III is showing a consistent pattern in all the three factors taken into account in this graph and lower in side than the Machine-I and Machine-II presented in Fig. 6.45 and Fig. 6.46 respectively.

Table 6.49: Comparative values of Avg. Real Printing Rate of Production of M-I, M-II & M-III

Machine	Real Printing Rate of Production (SPH)
M-I	4634
M-II	4583
M-III	3043

Table 6.49, indicates the average real printing rate of production of Machine-I, Machine-II and Machine-III, in sheets per hour in complete one year. The Machine with high level of automation has 4634 as real printing rate of production that is the highest value followed by Machine-II at 4583 with medium level of automation and Machine-III at 3043 with low level of automation. This table shows a clear-cut information relating the impact of automation in

multi colour sheet fed offset presses and their effect of press productivity; in recent times, multi colour sheet fed offset presses are designed to handle the press activities with ease and minimum human contacts for saving precious press time. It is clear from the above table that, press automation controls the real rate of production of a multi colour sheet fed offset press.

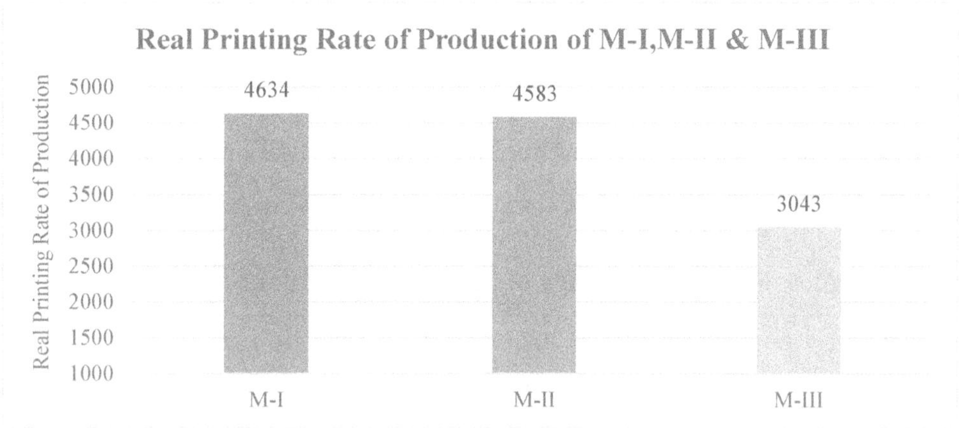

Fig. 6.48 Real Printing Rate of Production of M-I, M-II & M-III

Fig. 6.48 represents the real printing rate of production of three machine; Machine-I, Machine-II and Machine-III. These three machines are equipped with varying degree of press automation. Real printing rate of production, which is essentially a performance indicator of the printing machine, is utmost importance for any printing press. It is shown that, Machine-I equipped with high level of press automation results into high printing rate of production followed by Machine-II with medium level of press automation and Machine-III with low level of press automation, when these entire multi-colour sheet fed offset presses are evaluated in terms of level of technologies incorporated into them.

Paper is one of the most widely used substrates for the sheet fed offset presses because paper is predominantly finding its use for printing of wide range of job applications. Paper is available in a wide range of sizes, colours, textures, quality grades, surface finishes and basis weight to suit to different types of print jobs. The basic origin of paper is natural and is easily accessible. In comparison to the other substrates like; metal & plastics, paper is cost effective. Especially for the commercial printing applications for long print runs, paper is most suited. Moreover, paper offers excellent surface for achieving high printability; resulting into high colour reproduction, image sharpness and resolution.

Offset printing is basically an indirect process of printing; inked image from the plate surface is transferred onto the soft rubber surface and finally onto paper along with the hard metal impression cylinder surface. Paper essentially allows the optimal transfer of ink in offset printing technique for consistent print results because of its unique surface characteristics. Additionally, paper is renewable and recyclable, adding one more advantage to its selection as a substrate for offset applications. Wastage of paper during the print production process in a multi sheet fed offset press is a major concern and hence needs utmost care and attention, so that minimum paper wastage can be made for achieving higher level of profit. As three presses are selected with varying degree of press automation, critical study and analysis of paper wastage is very important, so that necessary suggestions can be made available to the press organizations to selecting which press is suitable in terms of paper wastage reduction.

Table 6.50: Paper Wastage of M-I with Job Quantities till 5000

Sr. No. (Job)	Date & Month	Job Quantity	Total Printed Sheets	No. of Waste Sheets	Waste Sheets (%)	Avg. Waste Sheets (%)
1	20,3	2000	2074	74	3.70	3.32
2	18,4	2000	2084	84	4.20	
3	29,8	2000	2084	84	4.20	
4	6,8	2500	2602	102	4.08	
5	11,6	2800	2912	112	4.00	
6	23, 1	3000	3086	86	2.87	
7	5,6	3500	3634	134	3.83	
8	5,7	3500	3638	138	3.94	
9	19, 2	4000	4115	115	2.88	
10	26,3	4000	4064	64	1.60	
11	7,8	4000	4125	125	3.13	
12	27,7	4500	4634	134	2.98	
13	13, 1	5000	5108	108	2.16	
14	24,7	5000	5156	156	3.12	
15	20,11	5000	5156	156	3.12	

In order to analyse and discuss the paper wastage of various job quantities of the three selected presses, the bracket for the job order quantities taken into account were; a) job order quantity up to 5000, b) job order quantity from 5001 to 10,000, c) job order quantity from 10,001 to 20,000, d) job order quantity from 20,001 to 50,000, and e) job order quantity above 50,000. These five brackets were identified in consultation with the different press organizations employing multi- colour sheet fed offset presses into their shop floors.

Randomly 100 different jobs representing the entire above five job brackets were selected from all of the three presses; altogether 300 different jobs were taken into account for data collection and analysis. They are presented in different tables and graphs subsequently for better understanding and drawing meaningful discussion to support the research work.

Table 6.50 represents paper wastage of machine-I with job quantities till 5000. In recent times low run jobs are frequently being run by sheet fed offset presses basically to compete with the digital presses. The table indicates 15 jobs were selected from the machine-I from the various months and days, representing the paper wastage for completing the particular job.

Till the job order quantity of 2000, slightly more than 4 percent paper wastage is observed, from 2001 to 4000 job order quantity it falls in-between 1.60 to 4.08 percent and from 4001 to 5000 job order quantities it is slightly less than 3 percent. For the machine-I, it indicates as the job order quantity decreases, the paper wastage percentage increases and vice-versa, with the overall average paper wastage percentage of 3.32 for this particular job order quantity.

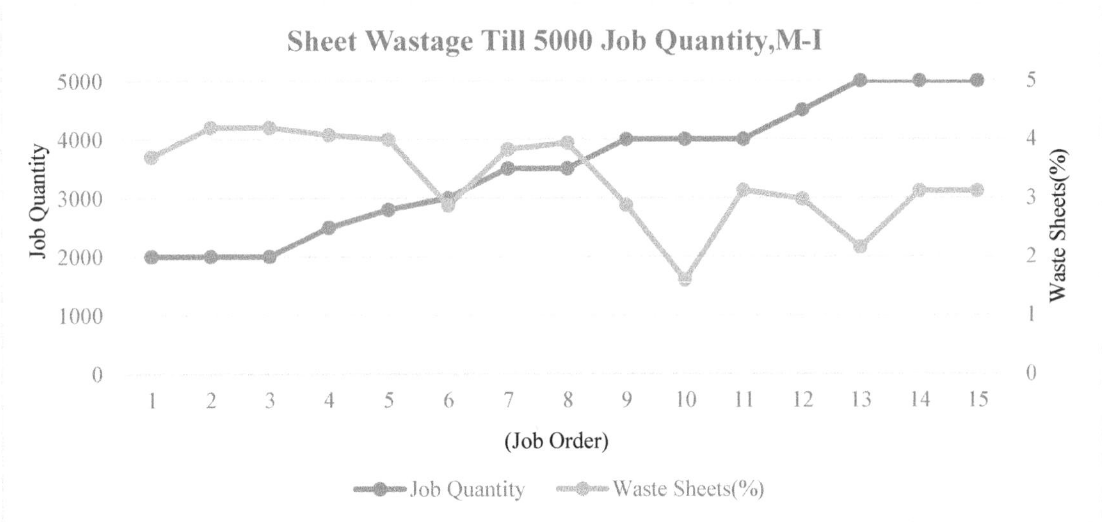

Fig. 6.49: Paper Wastage of M-I with Job Quantities till 5000

Fig. 6.49 represents the paper wastage of Machine-I for the print jobs quantities till 5000. With 15 jobs falling under this particular print bracket indicates that the percentage of paper wastage varies from 1.60 to 4.20 and the low percentage is attributed to the high level of press automation, which helps the press to save precious paper wastage during the printing cycle. With low order job quantity, more time has to be devoted for the press makeready time and vice-versa.

Table 6.51: Paper Wastage of M-I with Job Quantities from 5001 to 10,000

Sr. No. (Job)	Date & Month	Job Quantity	Total Printed Sheets	No. of Waste Sheets	Waste Sheets (%)	Avg. Waste Sheets (%)
1	11, 2	5500	5616	116	2.11	2.07
2	28,2	5500	5621	121	2.20	
3	26, 1	6000	6130	130	2.17	
4	4,2	6000	6138	138	2.30	
5	19,4	6000	6124	124	2.07	
6	15,9	6000	6134	134	2.23	
7	29,9	6000	6165	165	2.75	
8	1,5	6500	6628	128	1.97	
9	1,10	6500	6665	165	2.54	
10	11,4	7000	7132	132	1.89	
11	14,8	7000	7146	146	2.09	
12	29,10	7000	7124	124	1.77	
13	15, 1	8000	8164	164	2.05	
14	14,5	8000	8166	166	2.08	
15	19,7	8000	8145	145	1.81	
16	12,3	8500	8676	176	2.07	
17	7,9	9000	9156	156	1.73	
18	8,11	10000	10167	167	1.67	
19	9,12	10000	10178	178	1.78	
20	21,12	10000	10217	217	2.17	

Table 6.51 represents paper wastage of machine-I with job quantities from 5001 to 10,000. The table indicates 20 jobs were selected from the machine-I from the various months and days, representing the paper wastage for completing the particular job. The wastage percentage of paper for the job order quantity mentioned in this bracket falls in-between 1.67 to 2.75 percent. While comparing the previous job order quantities (till 5000) bracket, it shows with increase in job order quantity the percentage of paper wastage also reduces considerably. Overall average sheet wastage percentage for this job order quantity is 2.07.

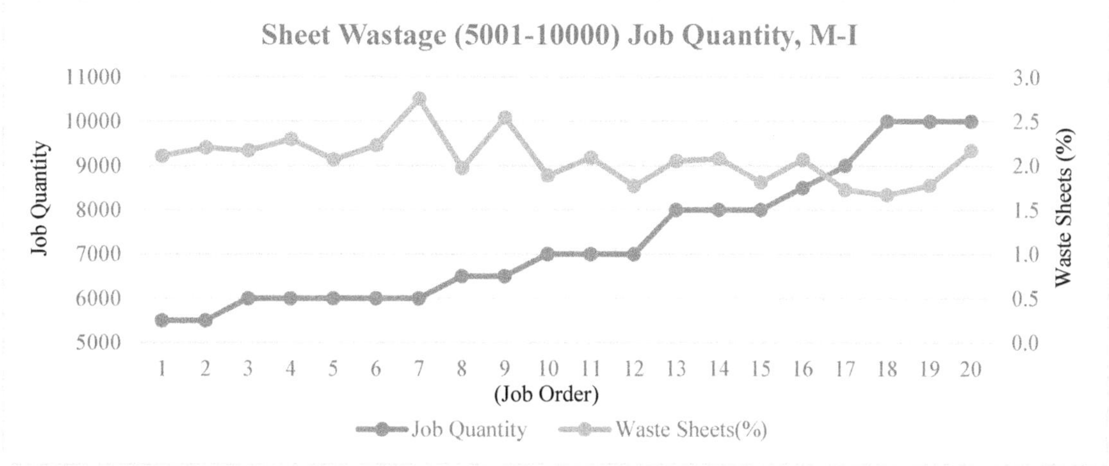

Fig. 6.50: Paper Wastage of M-I with Job Quantities from 5001 to 10,000

Fig. 6.50 represents the paper wastage of Machine-I for the print jobs quantities in-between 5001 to 10,000. With 20 jobs falling under this particular print bracket indicates that the percentage of paper wastage varies from 1.67 to 2.75 and the low percentage is attributed to the high level of press automation, which helps the press to save precious paper wastage during the printing cycle.

Fig. 6.51: Paper Wastage of M-I with Job Quantities from 10,001 to 20,000

Fig. 6.51 represents the paper wastage of Machine-I for the print jobs quantities in-between 10,001 to 20,000. With 27 jobs falling under this particular print bracket indicates that the percentage of paper wastage varies from 1.24 to 2.53 and the low percentage is attributed to the high level of press automation, which helps the press to save precious paper wastage during the printing cycle.

Table 6.52: Paper Wastage of M-I with Job Quantities from 10,001 to 20,000

Sr. No. (Job)	Date & Month	Job Quantity	Total Printed Sheets	No. of Waste Sheets	Waste Sheets (%)	Avg. Waste Sheets (%)
1	26, 4	11000	11278	278	2.53	1.89
2	16,2	12000	12262	262	2.18	
3	10,3	12000	12280	280	2.33	
4	2,4	12000	12268	268	2.23	
5	10,5	12000	12257	257	2.14	
6	1,7	12000	12258	258	2.15	
7	2,8	12000	12234	234	1.95	
8	5,9	12000	12246	246	2.05	
9	10,10	12000	12245	245	2.04	
10	25,10	12000	12168	168	1.40	
11	1,11	12000	12149	149	1.24	
12	2,12	12000	12159	159	1.33	
13	21, 1	15000	15298	298	1.99	
14	17,6	15000	15245	245	1.63	
15	24,6	15000	15267	267	1.78	
16	16,8	15000	15245	245	1.63	
17	18,9	15000	15234	234	1.56	
18	5,10	15000	15256	256	1.71	
19	17,10	15000	15258	258	1.72	
20	3,12	15000	15245	245	1.63	
21	16,7	15500	15776	276	1.78	
22	22,3	16000	16326	326	2.04	
23	1,3	17500	17806	306	1.75	
24	27, 1	18000	18424	424	2.36	
25	20,6	18000	18387	387	2.15	
26	7,7	18000	18364	364	2.02	
27	5,3	19000	19342	342	1.80	

Table 6.52 represents paper wastage of machine-I with job quantities from 10,001 to 20,000. The table indicates 27 jobs were selected from the machine-I from the various months and days, representing the paper wastage for completing the particular job. The wastage percentage of paper for the job order quantity mentioned in this bracket falls in-between 1.24 to 2.53 percent. While comparing the previous job order quantities (till 10,000) bracket, it shows with increase in job order quantity the percentage of paper wastage also reduces considerably. Overall average sheet wastage percentage for this job order quantity is 1.89.

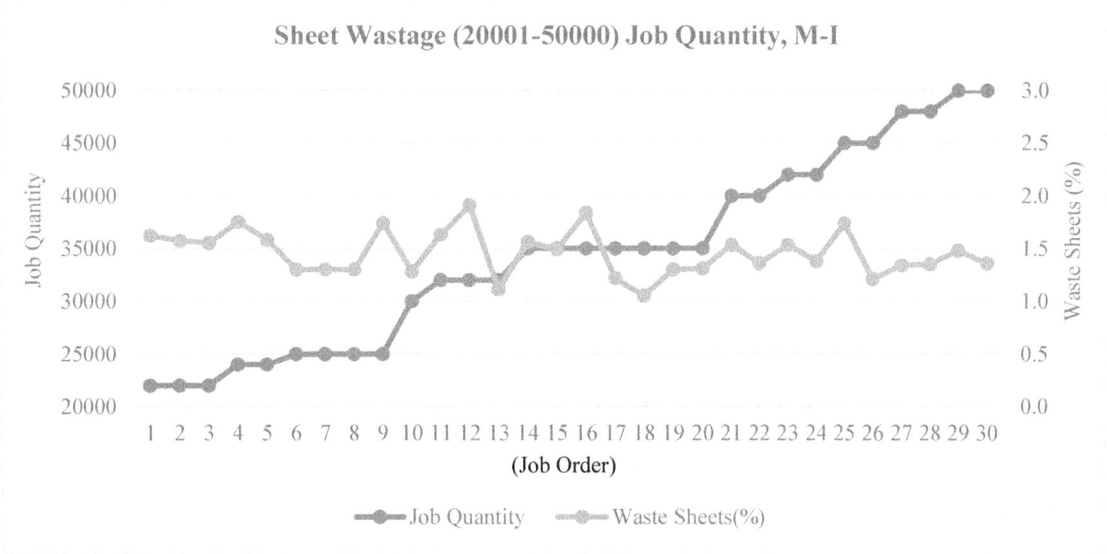

Fig. 6.52: Paper Wastage of M-I with Job Quantities from 20,001 to 50,000

Fig. 6.52 represents the paper wastage of Machine-I for the print jobs quantities in-between 20,001 to 50,000. With 30 jobs falling under this particular print bracket indicates that the percentage of paper wastage varies from 1.05 to 1.91 and the low percentage is attributed to the high level of press automation, which helps the press to save precious paper wastage during the printing cycle.

Table 6.53 represents paper wastage of machine-I with job quantities from 20,001 to 50,000. The table indicates 30 jobs were selected from the machine-I from the various months and days, representing the paper wastage for completing the particular job. The wastage percentage of paper for the job order quantity mentioned in this bracket falls in-between 1.05 to 1.91 percent. While comparing the previous job order quantities (till 20,000) bracket, it shows with increase in job order quantity the percentage of paper wastage also reduces considerably. Overall average sheet wastage percentage for this job order quantity is 1.46.

Table 6.53: Paper Wastage of M-I with Job Quantities from 20,001 to 50,000

Sr. No. (Job)	Date & Month	Job Quantity	Total Printed Sheets	No. of Waste Sheets	Waste Sheets (%)	Avg. Waste Sheets (%)
1	21,7	22000	22356	356	1.62	1.46
2	20,9	22000	22345	345	1.57	
3	20,12	22000	22342	342	1.55	
4	3,5	24000	24421	421	1.75	
5	18,5	24000	24380	380	1.58	
6	23,8	25000	25324	324	1.30	
7	19,10	25000	25326	326	1.30	
8	3,11	25000	25324	324	1.30	
9	16,11	25000	25435	435	1.74	
10	6,12	30000	30384	384	1.28	
11	14,3	32000	32520	520	1.63	
12	10,4	32000	32612	612	1.91	
13	2,9	32000	32356	356	1.11	
14	25,2	35000	35547	547	1.56	
15	19,3	35000	35523	523	1.49	
16	7,5	35000	35643	643	1.84	
17	18,8	35000	35426	426	1.22	
18	11,9	35000	35367	367	1.05	
19	16,10	35000	35456	456	1.30	
20	4,11	35000	35458	458	1.31	
21	3, 1	40000	40610	610	1.53	
22	12,11	40000	40542	542	1.36	
23	15,3	42000	42643	643	1.53	
24	25,5	42000	42578	578	1.38	
25	17,5	45000	45783	783	1.74	
26	23,12	45000	45543	543	1.21	
27	7,6	48000	48643	643	1.34	
28	12,9	48000	48647	647	1.35	
29	3,2	50000	50742	742	1.48	
30	18,11	50000	50678	678	1.36	

Table 6.54: Paper Wastage of M-I with Job Quantities above 50,000

Sr. No. (Job)	Date & Month	Job Quantity	Total Printed Sheets	No. of Waste Sheets	Waste Sheets (%)	Avg. Waste Sheets (%)
1	15,6	54000	54632	632	1.17	1.34
2	7,3	55000	55830	830	1.51	
3	14,12	55000	55683	683	1.24	
4	13,2	60000	60840	840	1.40	
5	16,12	60000	60824	824	1.37	
6	3,6	65000	65748	748	1.15	
7	16, 1	80000	81378	1378	1.72	
8	4,4	120000	121342	1342	1.12	

Table 6.54 represents paper wastage of Machine-I with job quantities above 50,000. The table indicates 8 jobs were selected from the machine-I from the various months and days, representing the paper wastage for completing the particular job. The wastage percentage of paper for the job order quantity mentioned in this bracket falls in-between 1.12 to 1.72 percent. While comparing the previous job order quantities (till 50,000) bracket, it shows with increase in job order quantity the percentage of paper wastage also reduces considerably. Overall average sheet wastage percentage for this job order quantity is 1.34.

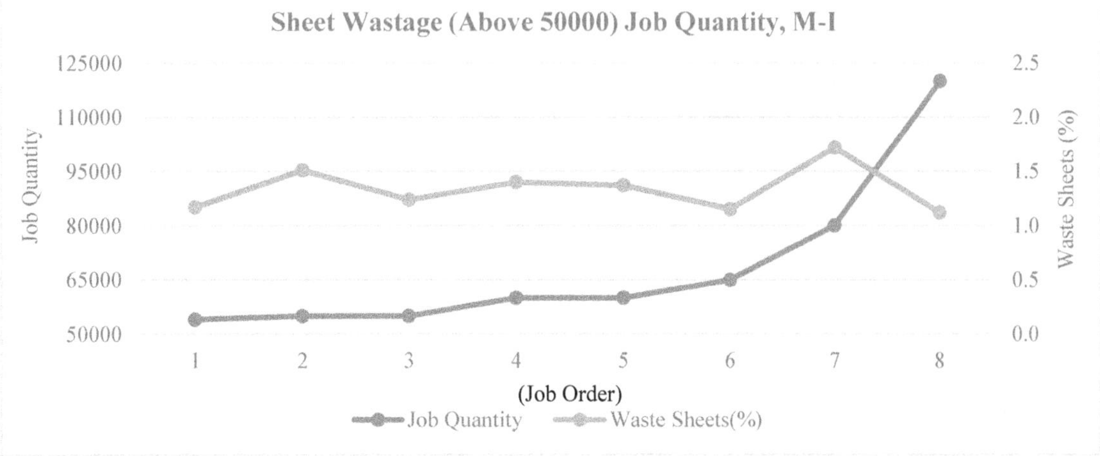

Fig. 6.53: Paper Wastage of M-I with Job Quantities above 50,000

Fig.6.53 represents the paper wastage of Machine-I for the print jobs quantities above 50,000. With 8 jobs falling under this particular print bracket indicates that the percentage of paper wastage varies from 1.12 to 1.72 and the low percentage is attributed to the high level of press automation, which helps the press to save precious paper wastage during the printing cycle.

From the five job order quantity brackets for the machine-I, it clearly indicates that job order quantity plays a major role towards the paper wastage percentage for the particular offset printing press. In the recent times, higher emphasis is given to reduce the paper wastage percentage to the lowest level possible, so that the final cost of the print job can be lowered to result into higher profit margins. This particular machine indicates the machine performs better when the job order quantity is above 10,000 and the average paper wastage is below two percent, which is certainly a very good sign.

Table 6.55: Paper Wastage of M-II with Job Quantities till 5000

Sr. No. (Job)	Date & Month	Job Quantity	Total Printed Sheets	No. of Waste Sheets	Waste Sheets (%)	Avg. Waste Sheets (%)
1	12,9	2500	2678	178	7.12	5.54
2	17,3	3500	3687	187	5.34	
3	18,7	3500	3687	187	5.34	
4	25,7	3500	3712	212	6.06	
5	19,8	3500	3667	167	4.77	
6	22 ,2	4000	4168	168	4.20	
7	18,3	4000	4321	321	8.03	
8	22,11	4000	4267	267	6.68	
9	3,1	4500	4678	178	3.96	
10	24,1	4500	4656	156	3.47	
11	15,6	4500	4776	276	6.13	
12	1,7	4500	4767	267	5.93	
13	22,7	4500	4789	289	6.42	
14	3,8	4500	4754	254	5.64	
15	8,9	4500	4778	278	6.18	
16	9,10	4500	4667	167	3.71	
17	9,11	4500	4789	289	6.42	
18	4,2	5000	5234	234	4.68	
19	1,4	5000	5192	192	3.84	
20	6,5	5000	5345	345	6.90	

Table 6.55 represents paper wastage of machine-II with job quantities till 5000. In recent times low run jobs are frequently being run by sheet fed offset presses basically to compete with the digital presses. The table indicates 20 jobs were selected from the machine-II from the various months and days, representing the paper wastage for completing the particular job. Till the job order quantity of 4000, slightly more than 4.20 to 8.03 percent paper wastage is observed and from 4001 to 5000 job order quantity it is in-between 3.47 to 6.90 percent in most of the cases. For the machine-II, it indicates as the job order quantity decreases, the paper wastage percentage increases and vice-versa, with the overall average paper wastage percentage of 5.54 for this particular job order quantity.

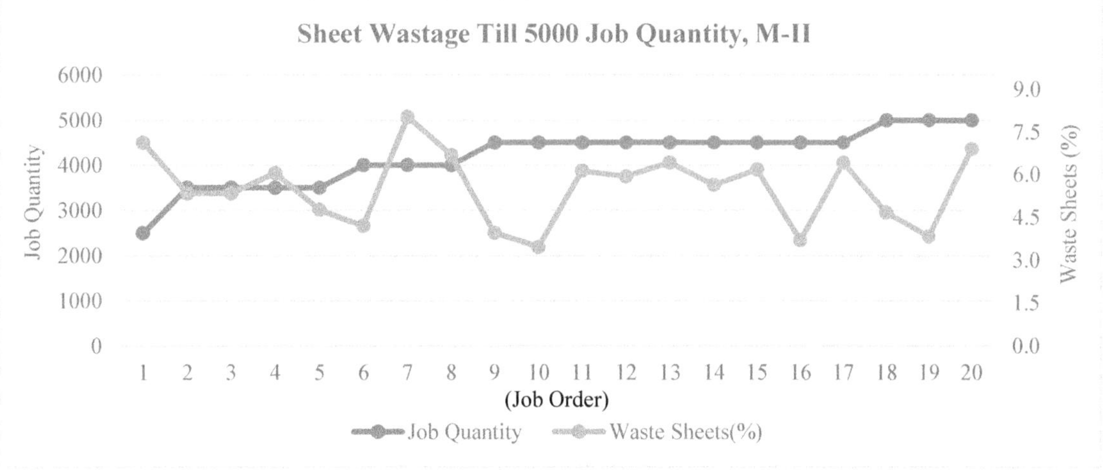

Fig. 6.54: Paper Wastage of M-II with Job Quantities till 5000

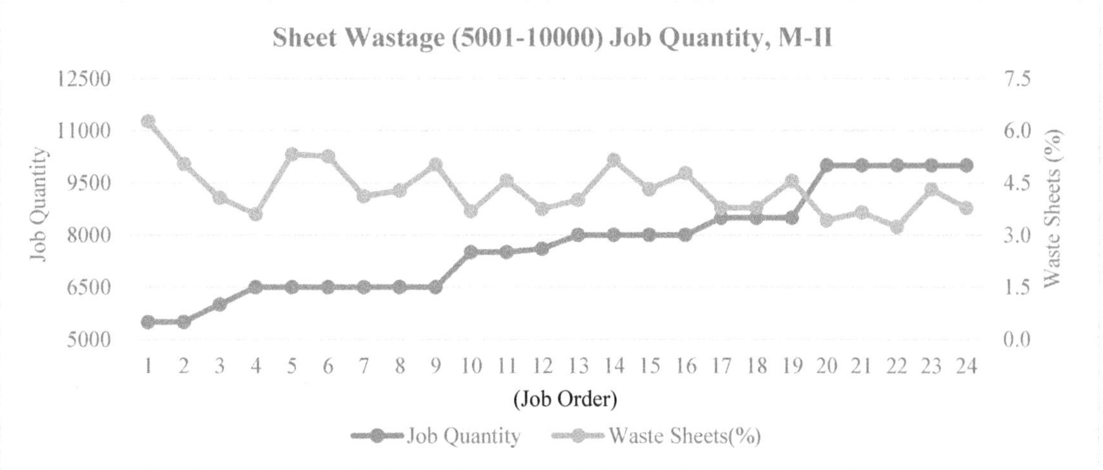

Fig. 6.55: Paper Wastage of M-II with Job Quantities from 5001 to 10,000

Fig. 6.54 represents the paper wastage of Machine-II for the print jobs quantities till 5000. With 20 jobs falling under this particular print bracket indicates that the percentage of paper wastage varies from 3.47 to 8.03 and the moderate percentage is attributed to the medium level of press automation, which helps the press to save precious paper wastage during the printing cycle.

Fig. 6.55 represents the paper wastage of Machine-II for the print jobs quantities in-between 5001 to 10,000. With 24 jobs falling under this particular print bracket indicates that the percentage of paper wastage varies from 3.24 to 6.27 and the moderate percentage is attributed to the medium level of press automation, which helps the press to save precious paper wastage during the printing cycle

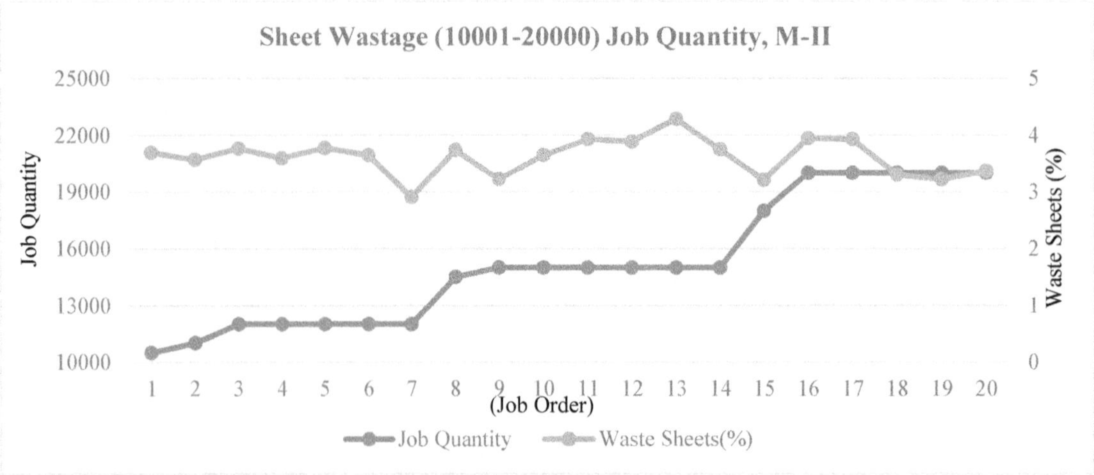

Fig. 6.56: Paper Wastage of M-II with Job Quantities from 10,001 to 20,000

Fig. 6.56 represents the paper wastage of Machine-II for the print jobs quantities in-between 10,001 to 20,000. With 20 jobs falling under this particular print bracket indicates that the percentage of paper wastage varies from 2.91 to 4.29 and the moderate percentage is attributed to the medium level of press automation, which helps the press to save precious paper wastage during the printing cycle.

Table 6.56 represents paper wastage of machine-II with job quantities in-between 5001 to 10,000. The table indicates 24 jobs were selected from the machine-II from the various months and days, representing the paper wastage for completing the particular job. The wastage percentage of paper for the job order quantity mentioned in this bracket falls in-between 3.24 to 6.27 percent. While comparing the previous job order quantities (till 5000) bracket, it shows with increase in job order quantity the percentage of paper wastage also reduces considerably. Overall average sheet wastage percentage for this job order quantity is 4.32.

Table 6.56: Paper Wastage of M-II with Job Quantities from 5001 to 10,000

Sr. No. (Job)	Date & Month	Job Quantity	Total Printed Sheets	No. of Waste Sheets	Waste Sheets (%)	Avg. Waste Sheets (%)
1	2,7	5500	5845	345	6.27	4.32
2	22,10	5500	5778	278	5.05	
3	10,3	6000	6245	245	4.08	
4	16, 1	6500	6734	234	3.60	
5	3,6	6500	6846	346	5.32	
6	12,8	6500	6842	342	5.26	
7	23,9	6500	6767	267	4.11	
8	10,10	6500	6778	278	4.28	
9	17,11	6500	6826	326	5.02	
10	11,3	7500	7776	276	3.68	
11	5,11	7500	7842	342	4.56	
12	18, 1	7600	7885	285	3.75	
13	4,3	8000	8321	321	4.01	
14	17,8	8000	8412	412	5.15	
15	3,9	8000	8345	345	4.31	
16	8,12	8000	8382	382	4.78	
17	15,7	8500	8821	321	3.78	
18	1,9	8500	8821	321	3.78	
19	7,11	8500	8887	387	4.55	
20	7, 1	10000	10342	342	3.42	
21	19 ,2	10000	10365	365	3.65	
22	12,5	10000	10324	324	3.24	
23	11,7	10000	10432	432	4.32	
24	1,12	10000	10378	378	3.78	

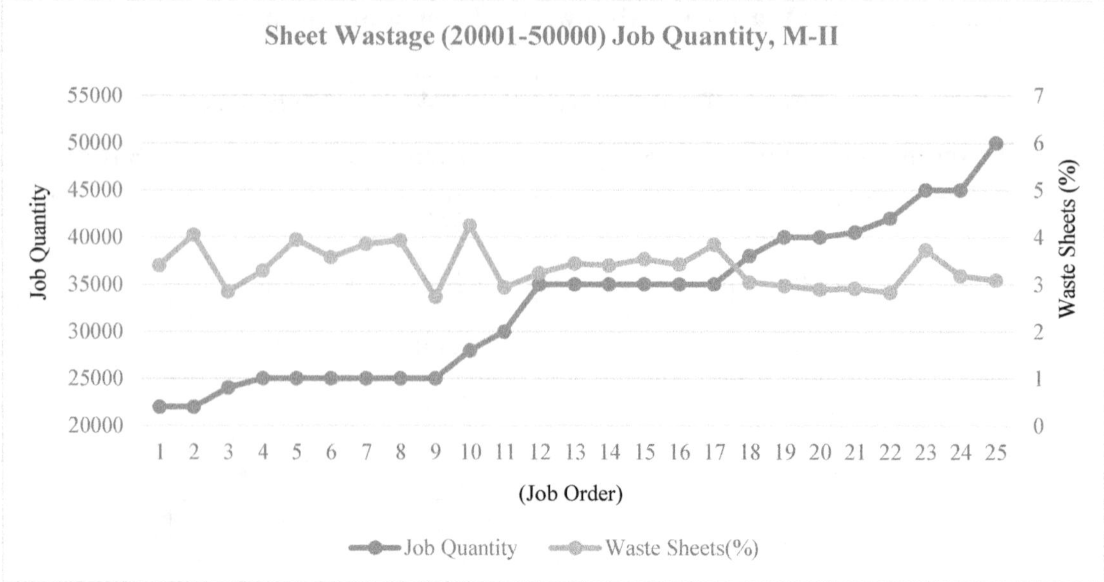

Fig. 6.57: Paper Wastage of M-II with Job Quantities from 20,001 to 50,000

Fig. 6.57 represents the paper wastage of Machine-II for the print jobs quantities in-between 20,001 to 50,000. With 25 jobs falling under this particular print bracket indicates that the percentage of paper wastage varies from 2.73 to 4.25 and the moderate percentage is attributed to the medium level of press automation, which helps the press to save precious paper wastage during the printing cycle.

Table 6.57 represents paper wastage of machine-II with job quantities in-between 10,001 to 20,000. The table indicates 20 jobs were selected from the machine-II from the various months and days, representing the paper wastage for completing the particular job. The wastage percentage of paper for the job order quantity mentioned in this bracket falls in-between 2.91 to 4.29 percent. While comparing the previous job order quantities (till 10,000) bracket, it shows with increase in job order quantity the percentage of paper wastage also reduces considerably. Overall average sheet wastage percentage for this job order quantity is 3.62.

Table 6.58 represents paper wastage of machine-II with job quantities in-between 20,001 to 50,000. The table indicates 25 jobs were selected from the machine-II from the various months and days, representing the paper wastage for completing the particular job. The wastage percentage of paper for the job order quantity mentioned in this bracket falls in-between 2.73 to 4.25 percent. While comparing the previous job order quantities (till 20,000) bracket, it shows with increase in job order quantity the percentage of paper wastage also reduces considerably. Overall average sheet wastage percentage for this job order quantity is 3.37.

Table 6.57: Paper Wastage of M-II with Job Quantities from 10,001 to 20,000

Sr. No. (Job)	Date & Month	Job Quantity	Total Printed Sheets	No. of Waste Sheets	Waste Sheets (%)	Avg. Waste Sheets (%)
1	8,8	10500	10889	389	3.70	
2	10,9	11000	11393	393	3.57	
3	10,2	12000	12452	452	3.77	
4	14,3	12000	12432	432	3.60	
5	23,6	12000	12453	453	3.78	
6	6,10	12000	12438	438	3.65	
7	7,12	12000	12349	349	2.91	
8	27,9	14500	15043	543	3.74	
9	9 ,2	15000	15483	483	3.22	
10	15,3	15000	15547	547	3.65	3.62
11	7,4	15000	15589	589	3.93	
12	5,6	15000	15583	583	3.89	
13	9,7	15000	15643	643	4.29	
14	1,10	15000	15563	563	3.75	
15	2,4	18000	18578	578	3.21	
16	5,5	20000	20789	789	3.95	
17	24,5	20000	20785	785	3.93	
18	7,6	20000	20659	659	3.30	
19	12,10	20000	20643	643	3.22	
20	12,11	20000	20673	673	3.37	

Table 6.58: Paper Wastage of M-II with Job Quantities from 20,001 to 50,000

Sr. No. (Job)	Date & Month	Job Quantity	Total Printed Sheets	No. of Waste Sheets	Waste Sheets (%)	Avg. Waste Sheets (%)
1	21, 1	22000	22749	749	3.40	3.37
2	1,6	22000	22892	892	4.05	
3	6,1	24000	24682	682	2.84	
4	20, 1	25000	25823	823	3.29	
5	4,4	25000	25984	984	3.94	
6	8,5	25000	25893	893	3.57	
7	2,8	25000	25963	963	3.85	
8	1,11	25000	25983	983	3.93	
9	6,11	25000	25683	683	2.73	
10	20,6	28000	29189	1189	4.25	
11	6,4	30000	30878	878	2.93	
12	22, 1	35000	36134	1134	3.24	
13	2,5	35000	36205	1205	3.44	
14	9,5	35000	36189	1189	3.40	
15	23,8	35000	36234	1234	3.53	
16	24,9	35000	36197	1197	3.42	
17	4,12	35000	36345	1345	3.84	
18	12,6	38000	39156	1156	3.04	
19	14, 2	40000	41189	1189	2.97	
20	16,3	40000	41156	1156	2.89	
21	1,3	40500	41678	1178	2.91	
22	7,10	42000	43189	1189	2.83	
23	3,4	45000	46678	1678	3.73	
24	10,6	45000	46432	1432	3.18	
25	12,3	50000	51543	1543	3.09	

Table 6.59: Paper Wastage of M-II with Job Quantities above 50,000

Sr. No. (Job)	Date & Month	Job Quantity	Total Printed Sheets	No. of Waste Sheets	Waste Sheets (%)	Avg. Waste Sheets (%)
1	1,1	52000	53678	1678	3.23	2.82
2	5, 2	52000	53459	1459	2.81	
3	5,4	55000	56678	1678	3.05	
4	7,7	55000	56567	1567	2.85	
5	1,8	55000	56567	1567	2.85	
6	17,10	55000	56563	1563	2.84	
7	2,12	80000	82156	2156	2.70	
8	3,5	90000	92867	2867	3.19	
9	18,5	100000	102783	2783	2.78	
10	1 ,2	130000	132856	2856	2.20	
11	2,9	130000	133216	3216	2.47	

Table 6.59 represents paper wastage of machine-II with job quantities above 50,000. The table indicates 11 jobs were selected from the machine-II from the various months and days, representing the paper wastage for completing the particular job. The wastage percentage of paper for the job order quantity mentioned in this bracket falls in-between 2.20 to 3.23 percent. While comparing the previous job order quantities (till 50,000) bracket, it shows with increase in job order quantity the percentage of paper wastage also reduces considerably. Overall average sheet wastage percentage for this job order quantity is 2.82.

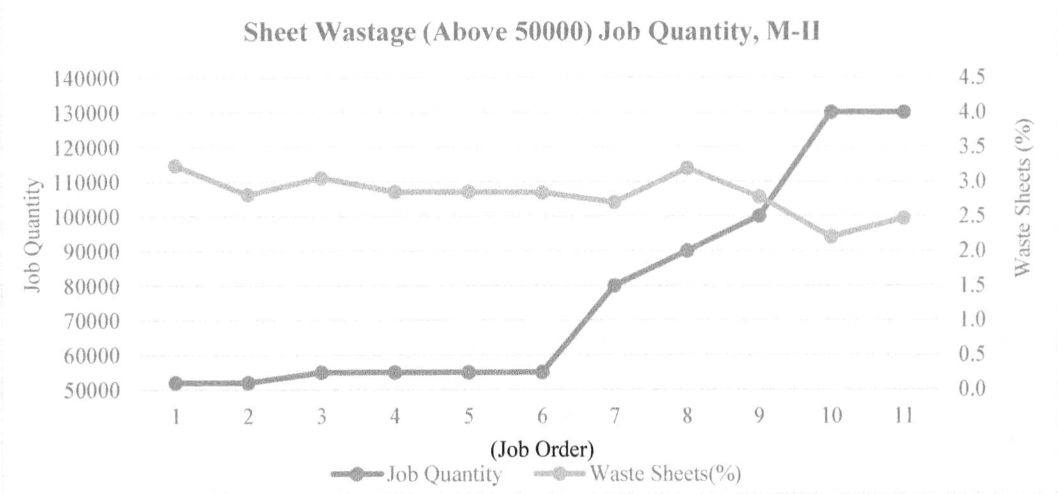

Fig. 6.58: Paper Wastage of M-II with Job Quantities above 50,000

Fig.6.58 represents the paper wastage of Machine-II for the print jobs quantities above 50,000. With 11 jobs falling under this particular print bracket indicates that the percentage of paper wastage varies from 2.20 to 3.23 and the moderate percentage is attributed to the medium level of press automation, which helps the press to save precious paper wastage during the printing cycle.

From the five job order quantity brackets for the machine-II, it clearly indicates that job order quantity plays a major role towards the paper wastage percentage for the particular offset press. Wastage reduction needs utmost attention for any printing press and in the recent times high cost associated with the multi-colour sheet fed offset presses clearly demands to save money from the possible means of minimizing paper wastage during the print production cycle. This particular machine indicates the machine performs better when the job order quantity is above 10,000 and the average paper wastage is slightly more than three percent, which is certainly a very good sign.

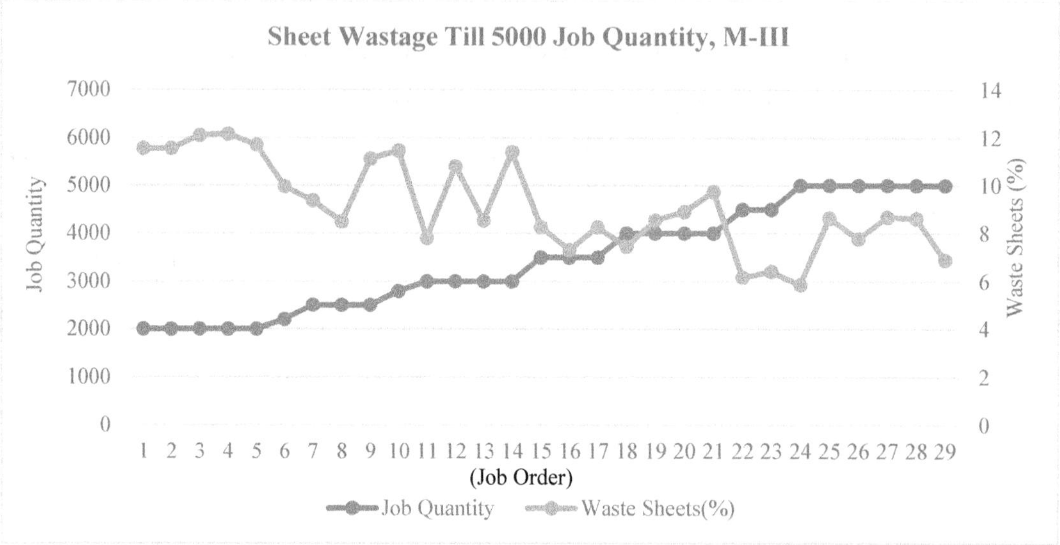

Fig. 6.59: Paper Wastage of M-III with Job Quantities till 5000

Fig. 6.59 represents the paper wastage of Machine-III for the print jobs quantities till 5000. With 29 jobs falling under this particular print bracket indicates that the percentage of paper wastage varies from 5.86 to 12.15 and the high percentage is attributed to the low level of press automation. As this particular machine is equipped with low levels of press automation in comparison to the other two presses, for small job order quantity, high time is required for carrying out the press set-up. As the machine is quite old, more time is required for make-ready steps also with high paper wastage percentage.

Table 6.60: Paper Wastage of M-III with Job Quantities till 5000

Sr. No. (Job)	Date & Month	Job Quantity	Total Printed Sheets	No. of Waste Sheets	Waste Sheets (%)	Avg. Waste Sheets (%)
1	12, 2	2000	2231	231	11.55	9.15
2	10,3	2000	2231	231	11.55	
3	13,3	2000	2242	242	12.10	
4	5,5	2000	2243	243	12.15	
5	14,11	2000	2234	234	11.70	
6	2,5	2200	2419	219	9.95	
7	7,2	2500	2734	234	9.36	
8	1,3	2500	2712	212	8.48	
9	25,5	2500	2778	278	11.12	
10	6,6	2800	3121	321	11.46	
11	19,2	3000	3234	234	7.80	
12	8,8	3000	3324	324	10.80	
13	1,9	3000	3256	256	8.53	
14	4,11	3000	3342	342	11.40	
15	14, 1	3500	3789	289	8.26	
16	3,5	3500	3756	256	7.31	
17	16,5	3500	3789	289	8.26	
18	2,3	4000	4298	298	7.45	
19	12,8	4000	4342	342	8.55	
20	6,10	4000	4356	356	8.90	
21	22,11	4000	4389	389	9.73	
22	1, 1	4500	4778	278	6.18	
23	13,5	4500	4789	289	6.42	
24	3, 1	5000	5293	293	5.86	
25	17, 1	5000	5432	432	8.64	
26	7,5	5000	5389	389	7.78	
27	10,6	5000	5434	434	8.68	
28	9,10	5000	5431	431	8.62	
29	10,12	5000	5345	345	6.90	

Table 6.60 represents paper wastage of machine-III with job quantities till 5000. In recent times low run jobs are frequently being run by sheet fed offset presses basically to compete with the digital presses. The table indicates 29 jobs were selected from the machine-III from the various months and days, representing the paper wastage for completing the particular

job. Till the job order quantity of 2000, slightly more than 11.55 to 12.15 percent paper wastage is observed, from 2001 to 4000 job order quantity it falls in-between 7.31 to 11.46 percent and from 4001 to 5000 job order quantity it is 5.86 to 8.68 percent in most of the cases. For the machine-III, it indicates as the job order quantity decreases, the paper wastage percentage increases and vice-versa, with the overall average paper wastage percentage of 9.15 for this particular job order quantity

Table 6.61: Paper Wastage of M-III with Job Quantities from 5001 to 10,000

Sr. No. (Job)	Date & Month	Job Quantity	Total Printed Sheets	No. of Waste Sheets	Waste Sheets (%)	Avg. Waste Sheets (%)
1	1,7	6000	6452	452	7.53	6.14
2	1,11	6000	6432	432	7.20	
3	9, 1	6500	6825	325	5.00	
4	1,6	7000	7452	452	6.46	
5	11,10	7000	7529	529	7.56	
6	2,4	8000	8298	298	3.73	
7	9, 5	8000	8467	467	5.84	
8	13,6	8000	8676	676	8.45	
9	11,7	8000	8453	453	5.66	
10	1,10	8000	8543	543	6.79	
11	2,11	8200	8689	489	5.96	
12	6, 2	8500	8931	431	5.07	
13	4,9	9000	9721	721	8.01	
14	10,9	9000	9538	538	5.98	
15	26,11	9600	10253	653	6.80	
16	3,2	10000	10653	653	6.53	
17	1,4	10000	10326	326	3.26	
18	1,5	10000	10389	389	3.89	
19	2,6	10000	10536	536	5.36	
20	2,9	10000	10672	672	6.72	
21	15,10	10000	10673	673	6.73	
22	23,10	10000	10653	653	6.53	

Table 6.61 represents paper wastage of machine-III with job quantities in-between 5001 to 10,000. The table indicates 22 jobs were selected from the machine-II from the various months and days, representing the paper wastage for completing the particular job. The wastage percentage of paper for the job order quantity mentioned in this bracket falls in-between 3.26 to 8.45 percent. While comparing the previous job order quantities (till 5000) bracket, it shows with increase in job order quantity the percentage of paper wastage also reduces considerably. Overall average sheet wastage percentage for this job order quantity is 6.14.

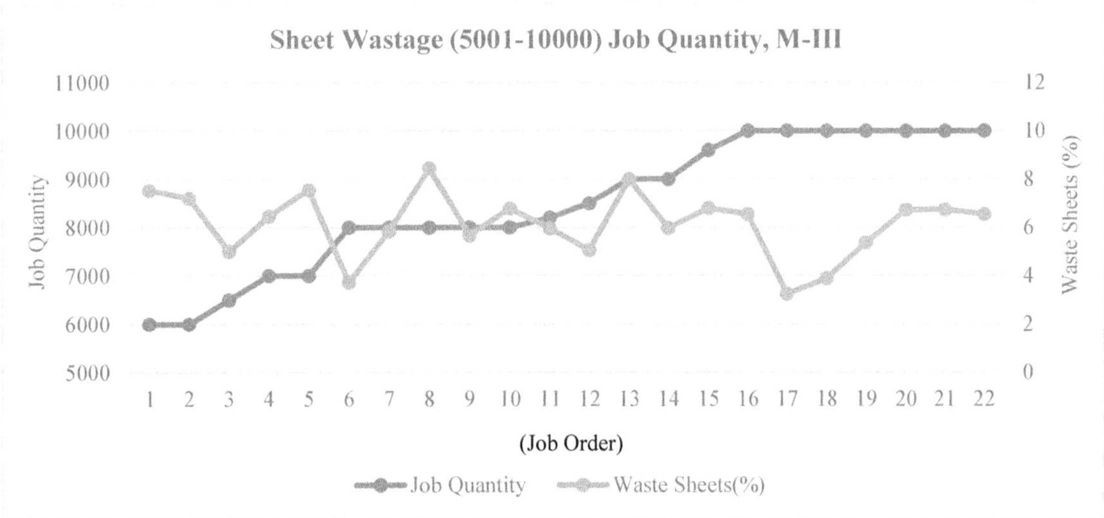

Fig. 6.60: Paper Wastage of M-III with Job Quantities from 5001 to 10,000

Fig. 6.60 represents the paper wastage of Machine-III for the print jobs quantities in-between 5001 to 10,000. With 22 jobs falling under this particular print bracket indicates that the percentage of paper wastage varies from 3.26 to 8.45 and the high percentage is attributed to the low level of press automation. Due the low level of press automation of this particular offset press and quite old machine, wastage of paper in this press is also high.

Table 6.62 represents paper wastage of machine-III with job quantities in-between 10,001 to 20,000. The table indicates 24 jobs were selected from the machine-III from the various months and days, representing the paper wastage for completing the particular job. The wastage percentage of paper for the job order quantity mentioned in this bracket falls in-between 3.87 to 6.40 percent. While comparing the previous job order quantities (till 10,000) bracket, it shows with increase in job order quantity the percentage of paper wastage also reduces considerably. Overall average sheet wastage percentage for this job order quantity is 5.16.

Table 6.62: Paper Wastage of M-III with Job Quantities from 10,001 to 20,000

Sr. No. (Job)	Date & Month	Job Quantity	Total Printed Sheets	No. of Waste Sheets	Waste Sheets (%)	Avg. Waste Sheets (%)
1	7,11	10500	11172	672	6.40	5.16
2	5,3	12000	12585	585	4.88	
3	15,3	12000	12637	637	5.31	
4	10,5	12000	12563	563	4.69	
5	19,5	12000	12657	657	5.48	
6	23,5	12000	12673	673	5.61	
7	6,9	12000	12632	632	5.27	
8	22,9	12000	12572	572	4.77	
9	9,11	12000	12721	721	6.01	
10	1,2	14000	14778	778	5.56	
11	12,9	14000	14542	542	3.87	
12	17,2	15000	15735	735	4.90	
13	12,3	15000	15678	678	4.52	
14	16,3	15000	15782	782	5.21	
15	18,5	15000	15678	678	4.52	
16	1,8	15000	15732	732	4.88	
17	11,8	15000	15672	672	4.48	
18	20,8	15000	15785	785	5.23	
19	20,10	15000	15892	892	5.95	
20	3,12	15500	16332	832	5.37	
21	4,6	16000	16878	878	5.49	
22	3,10	17000	17867	867	5.10	
23	24,6	18000	18982	982	5.46	
24	2,7	20000	20982	982	4.91	

Fig.6.61 represents the paper wastage of Machine-III for the print jobs quantities in-between 10,001 to 20,000. With 24 jobs falling under this particular print bracket indicates that the percentage of paper wastage varies from 3.87 to 6.40 and the high percentage is attributed to the low level of press automation.

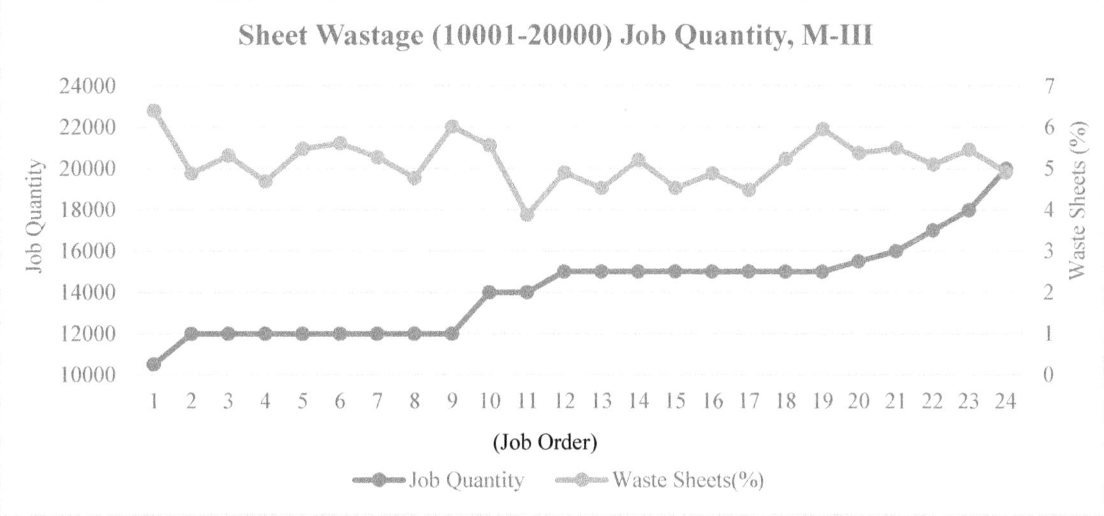

Fig. 6.61: Paper Wastage of M-III with Job Quantities from 10,001 to 20,000

Table 6.63: Paper Wastage of M-III with Job Quantities from 20,001 to 50,000

Sr. No. (Job)	Date & Month	Job Quantity	Total Printed Sheets	No. of Waste Sheets	Waste Sheets (%)	Avg. Waste Sheets (%)
1	14,12	22000	22762	762	3.46	
2	24,9	24000	25176	1176	4.90	
3	4,7	25000	26195	1195	4.78	
4	6,12	25000	26281	1281	5.12	
5	9,2	30000	31452	1452	4.84	
6	15,2	30000	31452	1452	4.84	
7	20,5	30000	31189	1189	3.96	
8	8,12	32000	33342	1342	4.19	
9	14,5	35000	36204	1204	3.44	4.14
10	11, 1	40000	41672	1672	4.18	
11	10,7	40000	41245	1245	3.11	
12	20,6	45000	46783	1783	3.96	
13	21,7	45000	46672	1672	3.72	
14	2,8	45000	46634	1634	3.63	
15	17,8	45000	46739	1739	3.86	
16	8,7	50000	52343	2343	4.69	
17	5,8	50000	51873	1873	3.75	

Table 6.63 represents paper wastage of machine-III with job quantities in-between 20,001 to 50,000. The table indicates 17 jobs were selected from the machine-III from the various months and days, representing the paper wastage for completing the particular job. The wastage percentage of paper for the job order quantity mentioned in this bracket falls in-between 3.11 to 5.12 percent. While comparing the previous job order quantities (till 20,000) bracket, it shows with increase in job order quantity the percentage of paper wastage also reduces considerably. Overall average sheet wastage percentage for this job order quantity is 4.14.

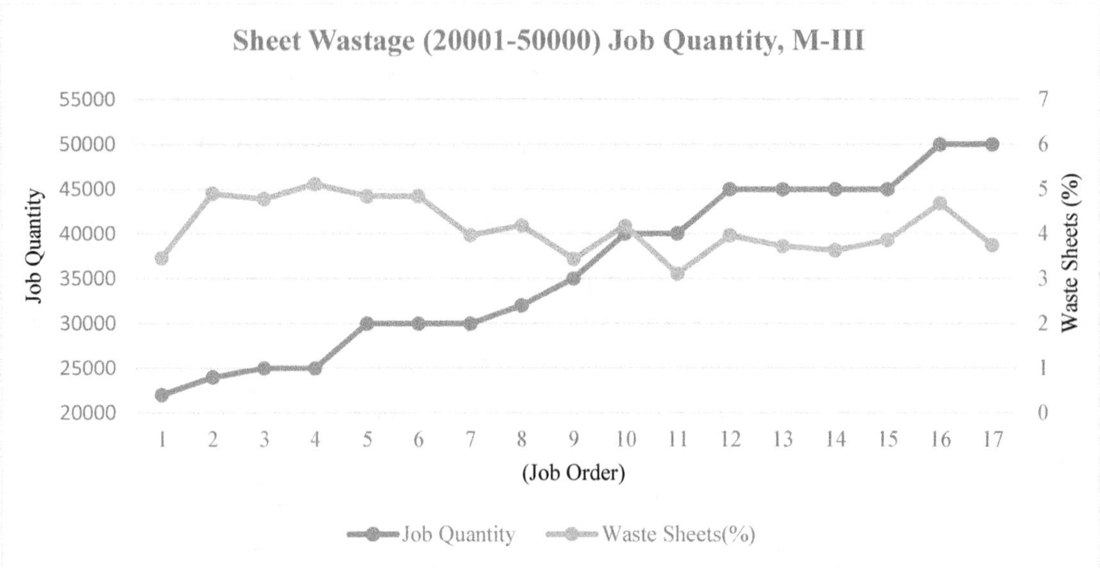

Fig. 6.62: Paper Wastage of M-III with Job Quantities from 20,001 to 50,000

Fig. 6.62 represents the paper wastage of Machine-III for the print jobs quantities in-between 20,001 to 50,000. With 17 jobs falling under this particular print bracket indicates that the percentage of paper wastage varies from 3.11 to 5.12 and the high percentage is attributed to the low level of press automation.

Table 6.64 represents paper wastage of machine-III with job quantities above 50,000. The table indicates 8 jobs were selected from the machine-III from the various months and days, representing the paper wastage for completing the particular job. The wastage percentage of paper for the job order quantity mentioned in this bracket falls in-between 3.32 to 4.43 percent. While comparing the previous job order quantities (till 50,000) bracket, it shows with increase in job order quantity the percentage of paper wastage also reduces considerably. Overall average sheet wastage percentage for this job order quantity is 3.86.

Table 6.64: Paper Wastage of M-III with Job Quantities above 50,000

Sr. No. (Job)	Date & Month	Job Quantity	Total Printed Sheets	No. of Waste Sheets	Waste Sheets (%)	Avg. Waste Sheets (%)
1	1,12	62000	64345	2345	3.78	3.86
2	10, 1	75000	77643	2643	3.52	
3	8,3	75000	77948	2948	3.93	
4	9,7	80000	83410	3410	4.26	
5	11,3	85000	88167	3167	3.73	
6	6, 1	120000	125321	5321	4.43	
7	17,9	130000	134321	4321	3.32	
8	23,1	150000	155823	5823	3.88	

Fig. 6.63 represents the paper wastage of Machine-III for the print jobs quantities above 50,000. With 8 jobs falling under this particular print bracket indicates that the percentage of paper wastage varies from 3.32 to 4.43 and the high percentage is attributed to the low level of press automation.

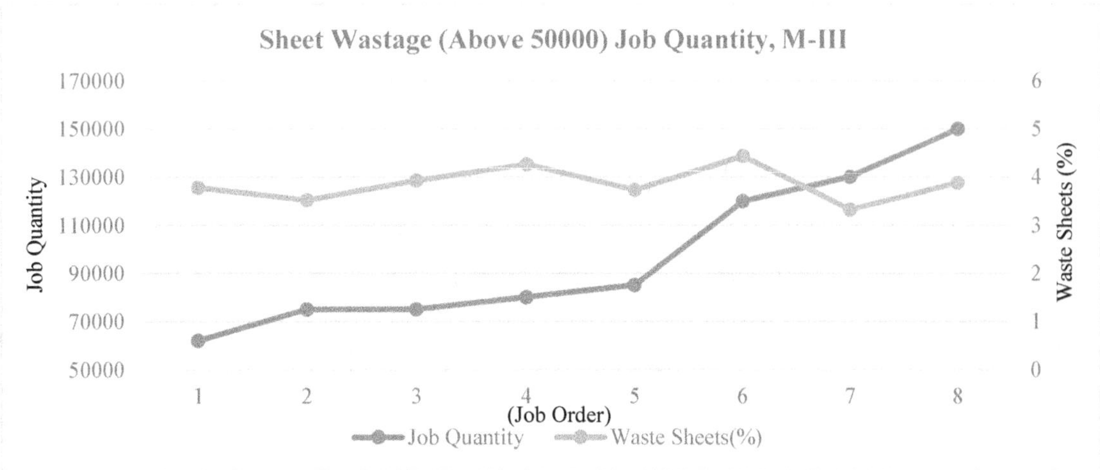

Fig. 6.63: Paper Wastage of M-III with Job Quantities above 50,000

From the five job order quantity brackets for the machine-III, it clearly indicates that job order quantity plays a major role towards the paper wastage percentage for the particular offset press. Ultimate goal of any sheet fed offset press is to print a particular job with less wastage of paper, so that more profit can be generated. This particular machine indicates the machine performs better when the job order quantity is above 20,000 and the average paper wastage is around four percent, which is certainly a very good sign.

Table 6.65: Avg. Paper Wastage of M-I, M-II & M-III

Job Order Quantity	M-I	M-II	M-III
5000	3.32	5.54	9.15
5001-10000	2.07	4.32	6.14
10001-20000	1.89	3.62	5.16
20001-50000	1.46	3.37	4.14
Above 50000	1.34	2.82	3.86

Table 6.65 represents average paper wastage of Machine-I, Machine-II and Machine-III respectively for the various print run job quantities. The table clearly indicates that, press automation has a bigger role to play when the paper wastage is concerned for the particular print job in hand.

For the Machine-I, that represent the multi-colour sheet fed offset press with high level of press automation in-comparison with the other two presses results into low paper wastage percentage in all the five print run brackets. Especially after the 5000-print run length, the average paper wastage falls in the range of 2.07 to 1.34 percent. The average paper wastage percentage is continuously getting reduced with the increase of the print run bracket.

For the Machine-II, which represents the multi-colour sheet fed offset press with medium level of press automation in-comparison with the other two presses results into moderate paper wastage percentage in all the five print run brackets. Especially after the 10,000-print run length, the average paper wastage falls in the range of 3.62 to 2.82 percent. The average paper wastage percentage is continuously getting reduced with the increase of the print run bracket.

For the Machine-III, which represents the multi-colour sheet fed offset press with low level of press automation in-comparison with the other two presses results into high paper wastage percentage in all the five print run brackets. Especially after the 20,000-print run length, the average paper wastage falls in the range of 4.14 to 3.86 percent. The average paper wastage percentage is continuously getting reduced with the increase of the print run bracket.

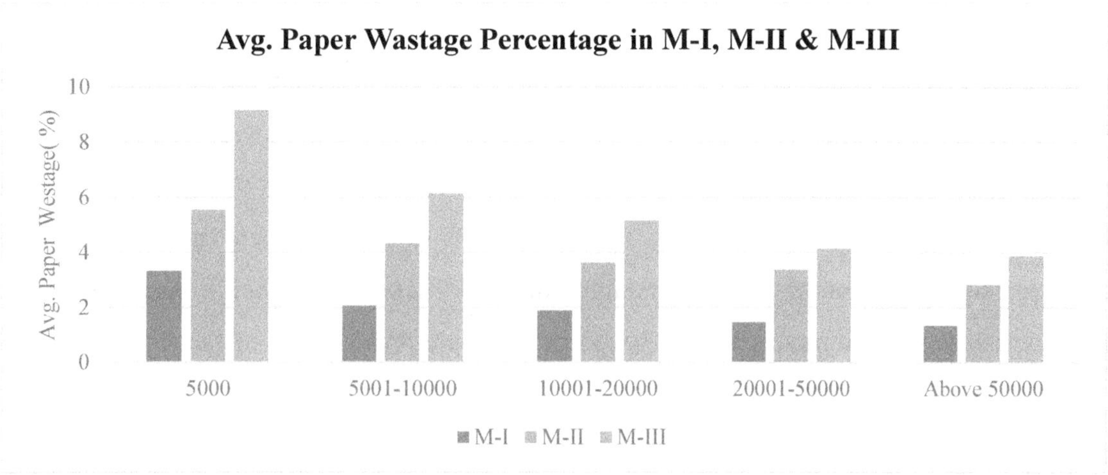

Fig. 6.64: Avg. Paper Wastage Percentage of M-I, M-II & M-III

Fig. 6.64 represents the average paper wastage of Machine-I, Machine-II and Machine-III respectively. Machine-I indicating low level of paper wastage for all the five brackets of the print job order quantity, followed by Machine-II with moderate paper wastage and Machine-III with high average paper wastage percentage. From the above graph, it is observed that press automation plays a major role towards the final average paper wastage percentage of the particular multi-colour sheet fed offset press.

This chapter essentially concludes with, print production performance data and analysis of three multi colour sheet fed offset presses for the month one to twelve, completing one year. Various tables and graphs indicate the number of makeready, makeready time in minutes, total printed sheets, total production time in hours and average press speed of the all the three presses. Average makeready time in minutes and average press speed of all the three presses are also analyzed for better understanding of the press productivity of the particular printing press. Real rate of print production of three machines for each month is also presented and analyzed in detail with suitable tables and graphs. Paper wastage of the above three presses with varying job order quantities are presented and analyzed in the subsequent parts, which clearly mentions the percentages of wastage due to the varying degree of press automation on a wide range of print run length jobs.

CHAPTER-7 RESULTS AND DISCUSSION

This chapter contains the result and discussion part of the thesis. This section addresses the implications of the findings for the broader field of study. The goal of this section is to offer a thorough and perceptive analysis of the study results. It is aimed at to provide a comprehensive understanding of the findings, their significance, and their consequences for the larger academic community, going beyond the simple presentation of facts. This section is highly crucial to the thesis's overall findings. The results are contextualized in this chapter and also explained how the findings relate to the goals or study questions.

When it comes to dissemination of information among the masses, printing press still plays a crucial role and invention of printing press is considered as one of the milestones in the history of mankind. In the present era of digital media, the relevance of print media cannot be ignored altogether. In addition to dissemination of information, print media carries a high amount of credibility and trust, and in the era of fake news and misinformation, print has created a unique place of trustworthy among the people.

Even though digital media is making inroads into our individual life very fast, but at the same time digital devices or internet are not easily accessible to everyone. This may be due to inadequate and limited network coverage and infrastructure in certain geographical areas leading to uneven access to the internet among the people residing in those areas. Moreover, internet subscription plans/tariffs, the cost of purchasing the digital devices along with the data plans are some of the possible barriers particularly with the lower income individuals. Printing also takes care of persons with reading difficulties of visual impairments, like Braille format or large print can be printed to take care of such specialized requirements.

Offset printing process is one of the major forms of printing as because of some of the unique characteristics; consistent print quality, higher range of colour printing, printing on a wide range of printing substrates and cost effective both for the short, medium to large print runs. Sheet fed offset is known for accommodating a wide range of commercial printing jobs including packaging & security printing. This may be due to that this particular printing industry is a matured printing segment with high degree of press automation embedded into these presses. Over the last three decades, sheet fed offset presses have successfully incorporated automation and digital technologies in order to streamline the press operation and thereby enhancing press efficiency.

Print productivity is a major issue especially in sheet fed offset presses, as because modern multi-colour sheet fed offset presses are costly loaded with high and advanced technology, which demands for production of more printed copies in a given time span. This essentially leads into increased and improved press efficiency and shorter print production cycles. Higher print productivity leads into improved customer satisfaction in terms of handling high printing volumes and taking care of tight print deadlines. All of the above factors ultimately contribute to higher business profitability and helps the press organization to reduce the final per unit print production cost considerably. On the other hand, with improved press productivity, more print copies can be produced in less time; the possible fixed costs that are associated with press make-ready/set-up, wastage of raw materials are also distributed effectively across the various print jobs, resulting into more cost-effective printing technique among the other available printing systems.

In the current market scenario, technologies have certainly changed the face of multi-colour sheet fed offset presses and the future of this industry essentially depends upon the level and degree of automation, adoption of sustainable print production techniques and processes and taking care of the present needs and requirements of customer demands. By successful integration and adoption of such advanced technologies into the presses, multi-colour sheet fed offset presses can certainly remain competitive, produce very high-quality print output and yet reducing the final cost of print output coupled with green and cleaner printing products.

Out of the three multi-colour sheet fed offset presses, Machine-I is equipped with high level of technology/press automation. This machine is with Prinect Press Centre, which is basically a centralized press control system and is aimed at offering a range of benefits to the press functioning. It essentially controls and monitors all the press functions, centrally. The press operator has the facility to make necessary press settings and adjustment and settings of various press parameters from a single press location. This essentially results into producing consistent print quality and simplifying press operations. Press operator can successfully access the job information (from pre-press, press and post-press) directly and the potential benefits leads to streamlining the workflow, possible reduction of human/manual intervention and improved print productivity of the press.

Further, Press Centre helps the real-time monitoring of the press and made available important parameters like; print colour density, colour registration, print colour consistency, etc. for prompt rectification of identified problems. It essentially collects and analyses the various production related data, prepares comprehensive reports, which helps the press operator to identify, monitor and optimize press production, making informed decisions for press process enhancement and identifications of press bottlenecks, so that the same can be taken care effectively. Such facilities are generally incorporated into the machine for taking care of possible deviations during the printing cycle, so that the chances of errors can be minimized and consistency in printing quality can be maintained throughout the whole printing cycle.

Machine-I is equipped with Intellistart Job Preparation, which is aimed at streamlining and simplifying the process of job preparation; ink zone setting, job colour profiling, and post-press requirements, for possible elimination of manual input and ensuring correct job set-up for improved press productivity. It is very useful for repetitive print jobs, which automatically sets the ink keys of various printing stations, plate positioning on the respective plate cylinders, setting of colour registers and other parameters being selected on the particular template. This provides step-by-step guidance to the press operator before the actual production cycle, so that possible errors can be taken care well in advance. Real-time feedback on the job preparation process helps the press operator in the forms of reports on the job details, press set-up time and process optimization.

Machine-I, production data, relating to number of make-readies, total make-ready time, average make-ready time, time available for actual printing production, total number of printed sheets, average production speed of the press, day-wise, summing up to the individual months and all the twelve months leading to the complete year data, gives a better understanding of the press functioning and thereby the press productivity. Press set-up time is a crucial factor while considering the press productivity, because in recent times, job run quantity is shrinking in the marketplace and particularly sheet fed offset presses needs to put higher importance on possible reduction of make-ready time. By reducing press make-ready time, more time can be made available to the press to focus on actual print production activities.

Machine-I is fitted with Preset plus Feeder, whose function is to enable non-stop feeding of printing substrates into the press. Continuous feeding of sheets allows for uninterrupted print production, undercutting the possibilities of press downtime and hence improves the productivity of the press. The press operator can pre-set the various parameters of the feeder unit specific to the particular print job to be printing; substrate size, thickness of the sheets, substrate alignments for precise sheet registration; which essentially eliminates the need and requirements of manual press adjustment. All the pre-setting of the feeding unit helps to reduce the make-ready time effectively. The system is designed to automatically adjust the various settings of the feeder unit, thereby eliminating the time required for manual setting and hence the make-ready time of the press is reduced considerably.

Feeder section Machine-I is equipped with air-assisted feeding technology, in which streams of air is used to separate and lift the sheets for smooth, reliable and efficient feeding. Such technology essentially reduces the possible risks of mis-feeds, paper jamming, double sheet feeding, etc., thereby leading to non-stop press production and minimizing press down time. Time and again the feeding of the multi-colour sheet fed offset presses are including latest technology, so that the various activities of the feeding unit can be smoothly and accurately managed. Machine-I is the perfect example of offset press with high degree of press automation in feeding unit also, to perform the various tasks automatically and helping to reduce press make-ready time, more systematically and effectively.

Machine-I is with the facility of Preset plus Delivery with Non-Stop Device; whose function is to run the non-stop delivery of the press printed output, even during the sheet changes also. This is certainly a welcome step towards reducing possible pile changeover time in delivery unit, so that this time can be made available for the press to print and contributing towards higher press productivity.

Delivery unit parameters like; printed stack height, printed sheet alignment on the delivery board, air blast setting in relation to the particular printing job, are adjusted automatically. Like the feeding unit, this feeder is also equipped with also with air-assisted delivery technology. Air assisted technology, with the use of air streams transfers and stacks printed sheets on the delivery board; thereby resulting into, smooth and even transfer of printed sheets, reduction of sheet jams, etc. such delivery system is especially designed to be suitable for high-speed print production.

Ink drying a major point in multi-colour sheet fed offset presses, because these presses are now manufactured with multiple printing units from four to six colours. It is not only the speed of the press that matters that most, but at the same time superimposition of different layers of printing ink on to one another and most prominently drying the printed layers ink, so that possible printing problems like, set-off can be taken care effectively.

Machine-I is equipped with Press Center DryStar Advanced, to take care of ink drying. This technology is aimed at rapid and effective drying of printed ink layers, so that higher press speed can be attained without ink drying problems, which results into sharper, defect free printed output and vibrant printed sheets. When the press is free from such problems, the time saved from this front is made available for the print production activities. From the various tables and graphs related to print production data of Machine-I, it is clearly shown that the productivity of this particular press is high than the other two presses with medium to low level of press automation.

Machine-I is also equipped with Alcolor Vario inking and dampening control systems. The basic purpose of this system is to offer precise ink distribution in each of the printing unit, accurate & controlled supply of dampening solution onto the plate surface, complete automated controls of inking and dampening for improved print quality. This particular advanced technology is aimed at increasing press efficiency, possible reduction of paper wastage, high and consistent print quality, convenience to the press operator for working on various press functions, and finally leading to high press productivity.

This system offers fast and efficient ink changes during switching between different ink colours, so the more time is saved which can be used for increasing overall productivity of the press. With minimum variations of printed ink density and dampening solution, the press is able to print sharper images and higher colour consistencies across all the printed sheets.

Ink and dampening solution are the two important raw materials for effecting printing, and for the present generation multi sheet fed offset presses are manufactured with an aim of reduction of wastage of the above two inputs, so that the final cost of print production can be lower down considerably. Alcolor Vario inking and dampening control systems helps to accurate control over the ink and dampening solution in all the printing stations in Machine-I, results into minimizing the amount of ink, fountain solution and paper also during the press set-up/make-ready operations and throughout the printing cycle. This only leads to potential cost savings but also helps to extending more sustainable printing operation.

For the Machine-I, twelve tables which represents the month-wise consolidated data and subsequent analysis of factors like; average, minimum, maximum, standard deviation of; number of make-readies, make-ready time in minutes, average make-ready time in minutes, total printed sheets, total production time in hour and average press speed in sheets per hour. Likewise, there are twelve graphs which indicate the number of make-readies, average make-ready time in minutes and average press speed in hour. On the consolidated month wise data and graph, it indicates the average make-ready time varies from 55.52 to 65.43 minutes with an average of 60.64 minutes. Likewise, the average press speed in sheets per hour ranges from 6646 to 7988 with an average of 7291.

Even though the make-ready time is high, which is mainly due to handling of complex natured print jobs, average press speed is quite good. All this supports to enhanced print productivity of the Machine-I with high level of press automation and suggests the multi-colour sheet fed offset press owners to focus on the advanced technology while going for installation of the press for increased/enhanced press productivity. In the recent years, the nature of the printing jobs is keep on changing and the potential printing customers are demanding for printing of jobs which are highly complex with intricate colours, more number of spot colours and high colour gamut jobs, hence the press set-up time is quite high also.

Machine-II is equipped with medium level of press automation in-comparison to Machine-I. This press is having CP2000 Control Centre, which is aimed at managing various functions of printing press, centrally. A touchscreen display system essentially assists the press operators to easily access and adjusts various press settings, tracking the progress of the job and monitoring the different print production parameters. With the help of CP2000 Control Centre, the press operator can upload job files, setting of various job parameters and can also access pre-press related data like; ink profiles, imposition related information, etc.

Besides the above facilities, this system also offers monitoring colour consistencies of the print output and also colour corrections during the print production. Due to the real time monitoring of various print quality parameters like, colour registration, ink densities, tonal value increase, ink & fountain solution balance. It is easy to maintain print quality standards by the press operator, leading to short make-ready time and possible increase of press productivity.

Machine-II is equipped with Instant Start, Instant Gate and Colour Assistant functions. Instant Start is aimed at quick and efficient press setup, which facilitates the press operator to load various job parameters comprising ink profiles, pre-press data and press settings directly from the CP2000 Control Center. This certainly helps to improve overall press productivity. At the same time, Instant Gate is for streamlining print job processing and thereby improves workflow efficiency. Operators have the liberty to easily prioritize and manage the incoming print jobs with ease and effective manner. Colour Assistant is loaded with advanced colour management capabilities, like, ink density control, colour matching and colour correction for producing accurate and consistent colour reproduction throughout the whole printing cycle.

Machine-II is having with auto plate loading feature, which is designed to automate and streamline the loading of plates into different printing stations, thereby making the work faster and efficient. This press is equipped with system that automatically takes care of plate changing process in the different printing units. The ultimate purpose of automatic plate loading system is to minimize press set-up time and thereby enhancing the press productivity. During the manual plate changeover system, there are some possibilities of errors or damage to the plates, whereas in automatic plate loading these points are well taken care of.

Press make-ready time of multi-colour sheet fed offset presses needs special attention, so that the steps involved in it can be streamlined and can be performed with ease and less human interference. In Machine-II, with the inbuilt automatic plate loading system, it is very much possible, as shown the data relating to press make-ready time is reduced and hence the press productivity is finally enhanced.

Machine-II is fitted with ultrasonic double sheet detection technology, whose function is to take care of issues like; sheet misregistration, ghosting & ink transfer related problems and possible damages to the rollers or the press components. This essentially helps to non-stop press run and leading to higher press productivity. This machine is fitted with Eltex Ion Blowers on Feeder, to neutralize static electrical charges on the printing substrates, before they guided into the printing unit.

There are some possibilities that static electric may be accumulated in the substrates at the feeding table, leading to various feeding problems like, misfeeding, double sheet feeding, ink picking or hickeys, etc. Press down time is reduced in Machine-II, as the data shows from the various tables and graphs; print productivity is certainly improved than the Machine-III, whose automation level is lower than the Machine-II.

Machine-II is equipped with CP 2000 Tandem Wash, which automatically washes the blanket, rollers and impression cylinders. Its main function is to streamlining the cleaning system and thereby reducing manual labor required for these activities. As per the requirements of each press component, specific cleaning solutions are used for effective and safe cleaning of the press parts. The CP 2000 Tandem Wash system automatically starts cleaning the blanket, followed by the rollers (both inking and dampening units), and finally the impression cylinder.

After washing of the press components, a drying cycle is initiated with warm air or other suitable means to accelerate the drying of the different components. Machine-II with CP 2000

Tandem Wash system, essentially reduces the time, effort and other cleaning agents for cleaning of rollers, blanket and impression cylinder, thereby leading to minimizing possible press down time between the print jobs and improving the overall print productivity of this press.

Machine-II with medium level of press automation uses, CombiStar Technotrans ink temp control combined with damping refrigeration plus Alcosmart system. This system performs dual functions; Technotrans ink temperature control and damping refrigeration, along with the Alcosmart feature. In sheet fed offset presses, for achieving accurate and consistent print quality, it is highly desired to regulate and control the ink temperature in all the printing stations throughout the particular printing cycle. Temperature of ink is very crucial in sheet fed offset presses, as because it affects the flow and viscosity of ink during the printing run. As the offset ink is in constant contact with the fountain solution, hence controlling ink temperature and damping solution refrigeration is key to the successful printing in offset press.

Possible problems like, ink-water emulsification, ink drying on the rollers and plate surface, ink viscosity variations can be addressed properly with the help of stable ink temperature. Other function is dampening refrigeration, for maintaining optimal characteristics of the fountain solution; it plays a very crucial role. By effective control of temperature of dampening solution, it is very much possible; to improve final print quality, possible waste reduction and increased press efficiency and productivity. Alcosmart in Machine-II is aimed at ensuring accurate alcohol dosage in the fountain solution for controlling the surface tension of the dampening solution and proper ink-water balance for achieving high print quality.

For the Machine-II, twelve tables which represents the month-wise consolidated data and subsequent analysis of factors like; average, minimum, maximum, standard deviation of; number of make-readies, make-ready time in minutes, average make-ready time in minutes, total printed sheets, total production time in hour and average press speed in sheets per hour. Likewise, there are twelve graphs which indicate the number of make-readies, average make-ready time in minutes and average press speed in hour. On the consolidated month wise data and graph, it indicates the average make-ready time varies from 56.63 to 76.62 minutes with an average of 62.43 minutes. Likewise, the average press speed in sheets per hour ranges from 6065 to 7399 with an average of 6691.

Even though the make-ready time is higher than the Machine-I, which is mainly due to handling of complex natured print jobs, average press speed is quite good, as because the level of press automation is low when comparing with the Machine-I. All this supports to enhanced print productivity of the Machine-II with medium level of press automation and suggests the multi-colour sheet fed offset press owners to focus on the advanced technology while going for installation of the press for increased/enhanced press productivity.

Machine-III is equipped with low level of press automation while comparing with the Machine-I and Machine-II. The stream feeder with a belt type is included in the feeding unit, whose function is to feed smoothly and accurately individual substrates into the printing station. Belt movement helps to create an even and consistent flow of printing substrates into the press for printing operation. This type of feeder offers number of advantages; uniform supply of sheets, reducing press down time, and resulting into improved press productivity. Additionally, accurate registration of substrates, handling various substrate sizes & thicknesses are some of the potential benefits derived from the stream feeder with belt, which is embedded in to Machine-III.

Machine-III is equipped with electronic double sheet detection, which essentially helps to feed one paper at a time to the printing unit for printing, thereby minimizing the risk of substrate misfeeds, paper jams, image ghosting and other related issues which may hamper the press productivity and print quality. This device is very useful when feeding thin or lightweight papers and which essentially reduces the manual intervention in sheet feeding unit. Overall press productivity gets increased due to this device in the feeding unit.

This machine is also equipped with photoelectronic side lay control system, whose function is to ensure that the sheets are aligned properly before introduced into the printing unit for printing, thereby taking care of any misalignment being caused by sheet size variations, paper skew and other factors. This device maintains accurate lateral registration of sheets and essentially takes care of image mispositioning, and finally leading to reduction of make-ready time, minimizing paper wastage and increased press productivity.

Machine-III is fitted with combined Alcolor continuous dampening system with Technotrans's alcohol metering, cooling, and re-circulation unit, which successfully replaces the traditional method of dampening (which is essentially an intermittent dampening system) with continuous applications of fountain solution on to the plate surface. This dampening system is meant for creating optimal conditions for ink transfer on to the plate and maintaining a stable ink-water balance. The cooling and re-circulation unit is designed for maintaining the fountain solution at a desired temperature for ensuring stable and consistent dampening. This unit certainly provides; sharp image reproduction, increased colour consistency and minimizing the ink drying time. All these results into, faster make-ready time, wastage reduction, improved press efficiency and minimizing the manual adjustments.

Machine-III is equipped with Preset (automatic paper size and thickness setting) facilities, whose function is to automate the paper size setting during the press make-ready operations. The press operator manually inputs the related information of the substrate and the preset automatically adjusts the gripper positions, side lays, front lays and ink zones as per the specific substrate in use. This essentially reduces the time and operator efforts for manual adjustment of the feeding section. Preset results into accurate and quicker press make-ready time, thereby minimizing press set-up time and increasing press productivity.

Machine-III is fitted with programmable automatic wash-up system via CP2000, which offer the facility of setting the various parameters like; duration of cleaning, type of cleaning solution and sequence of cleaning steps. After setting the required parameters, the system automatically starts the wash-up procedure, which successfully eliminates any kind of manual intervention by the press operator. This system is aimed at minimizing press down time and hence improving press productivity.

There are some common facilities between the three machines; Machine-I, Machine-II and Machine-III, as it is mentioned in the machine specification part. From these three machines, with different levels of press automation, it is very much clear that the make-ready time essentially depends upon the automatic functions embedded into the particular press. In recent times, multi-colour sheet fed offset presses are being manufactured with advanced technologies for reducing the press set-up time as low as possible, so that the job changeover time can be minimized for accommodating a greater number of printing jobs in a given span of production time.

For the Machine-III, twelve tables which represents the month-wise consolidated data and subsequent analysis of factors like; average, minimum, maximum, standard deviation of; number of make-readies, make-ready time in minutes, average make-ready time in minutes, total printed sheets, total production time in hour and average press speed in sheets per hour. Likewise, there are twelve graphs which indicate the number of make-readies, average make-ready time in minutes and average press speed in hour. On the consolidated month wise data and graph, it indicates the average make-ready time varies from 61.51 to 79.08 minutes with an average of 71.63 minutes. Likewise, the average press speed in sheets per hour ranges from 4446 to 5047 with an average of 4747.

For the Machine-I, Machine-II and Machine-III, the average make-ready time varies from 60.64, 62.43 and 71.63 minutes respectively and average press speed in sheets per hour varies from 7291, 6691 and 4747 respectively. All these data support to the fact that, press automation has a direct impact on the press make-ready time and press speed of the multi-colour sheet fed offset presses. Higher the level of press automation embedded into the press higher the press productivity and lowers the make-ready time and vice-versa. In the present era, the sheet fed offset press manufacturers are adding automation to the various press functions for minimizing the human interference and maximizing the press speed for higher press output.

Make-ready operation of a sheet fed offset press starts from receiving the plates for printing from the pre-press department and till the OK print sheet is produced. In between there are numerous activities which needs to be carried out for press set-up and from the various tables and graphs in the data collection and analysis chapter of the research thesis, it is very much clear that, as the level of technology increases in the multi-colour sheet fed offset press, so the reduction of make-ready time. Also, the number of make-readies increases along with reduction of average make-ready time on day basis, month basis and the same is true for the year end result of three machines being selected for the research work.

In today's competitive print market, faster make-ready time coupled with quick job changeover time will certainly help the print business an edge over its competitor in order to grow and develop. From the production data of three multi-colour sheet fed offset presses, it is clearly visible that, with high level of press automation more jobs can be printed in the stipulated time frame and thereby a greater number of print customer can be served with value based quick deliver and reliable press production capabilities. This is the main reason behind the sheet fed offset printing industry investing in advanced technology in the recent times in order to improve print quality and press productivity.

The concept of real printing rate of production of any multi-colour sheet fed offset press is very important and it essentially depends upon several factors; year of machine manufacturing, press configuration, skill of the press operator, job complexity, and the size, characteristics and type of printing substrates. Model of the particular offset press essentially offers varying capabilities and press speed also. Machine-I and Machine-II are equipped with a speed of 15,000 sheets per hour and Machine-III with a press speed of 13,000 SPH. Machine-I is the 2014 model, Machine-II is of 2005 and Machine-III is of 1999 model, and press configuration of these presses are also quite different. From the various tables and graphs of these three presses, it is very much clear that, higher-end press models are resulting into faster production rates.

All the three selected offset presses are designed to handle complex print job easily, smoothly and effectively. As complex printing jobs demands for higher press make-ready time and accordingly the speed of press is also kept slow. From the data analysis of all the machines; Machine-I, Machine-II and Machine-III, it is very much informed that, Machine-I which is equipped with high level of press automation is able to handle complex print job very easily and still the press set-up time is low while comparing with other two presses. Machine-II, whose press automation level is higher than the Machine-III and lower than the Machine-I, indicates make-ready time higher than the Machine-I and lower than the Machine-III. Machine-III with lowest level of press automation is able to manage the highest make-ready time.

From the various tables and graphs relating to average make-ready time for each of the three presses, it is clearly shown that there is a strong relationship between the level of automation being used in the particular multi-colour sheet fed offset press and make-ready time. In order to enhance print productivity, it is advised to select offset presses with greater degree of press automation, which will result into automatic control of various press activities thereby reducing manual work systems. When the make-ready time is reduced considerably, more time can be made available to the press for production and hence productivity of the press can be enhanced.

When discussing the average real printing rate of production of Machine-I, Machine-II and Machine-III, the data shows that, Machine-I which is equipped with high level of press automation in-comparison to other two presses, also having highest value, followed by Machine-II and Machine-III respectively. Machine-I results into 4634, Machine-II results into 4583 and Machine-III is having 3043 values. The gap between Machine-I and Machine-II is very low, as because press configuration wise there is a little difference.

Paper wastage a big concern when it comes to multi-colour sheet fed offset presses, especially in the current print market scenario, where it is expected to keep the production cost low, while maintain the desired quality level, so that the protentional savings from the low level of paper wastage can be converted into profits. Paper contributes to a significant cost component of the final print; hence it needs extra care and attention also. For maximizing resource utilization of multi-coloured sheet fed offset presses, it is always expected to minimize the paper wastage percentage which will result into reduced operational costs. By focussing on the reduction of paper wastage during the print production cycle, overall efficiency of the particular press can be enhanced along with reliability of the production process. Reduction of paper wastage results into smoother press operations, reduced lead times, lowering the final cost of print production and improved customer satisfaction.

For the calculation of paper wastage of three presses, according to the job quantities (till 5000, from 5001 to 10,000, from 10,001 to 20,000, from 20,001 to 50,000 and above 50,000) for each press 100 production data were analysed representing to all the above-mentioned brackets. For all the job quantity brackets, Machine-I is indicating the paper wastage percentage from 3.32 to 1.34 percent, for Machine-II it ranges from 5.54 to 2.82 percent and for the Machine-III, it varies from 9.15 to 3.86 percent. For all the three machines, as the job order quantity increases, so the average paper wastage percentage decreases and vice-versa. When co-relating with the cost of the press, the high valued press results into low wastage, but for Indian printers, it can be suggested that above 20,000 print job order quantity, Machine-III proves to be the best choice, as because it is cheaper in cost and most of the multi-colour sheet fed offset presses are strong and sturdy.

From the various tables, graphs, analysis, result and discussion it is very much clear that, multi-colour sheet fed offset presses are adopting various advanced technologies into various sections, so that most of the manual work can be automatized for improving print quality and enhancing print productivity. It indicates technology has a bigger role in reduction of make-ready time, job change over time, improving real printing rate of production, increasing number of print jobs in a given frame of time, enhancing the final print productivity along with reduction of paper wastage. Cost, press configuration and model of the press has a direct impact on the final print quality and print productivity.

This chapter conclude that, there is a strong relationship between the level of press automation to that of the press print productivity. Machine one (M-I) with highest level of press automation certainly leads to high print productivity while comparing with the other two presses Machine two (M-II) and Machine three (M-III), which gives the indication of the latest machines with higher technological advancements should be preferred over the presses with low level of automation, when considering the enhanced print productivity. Likewise, the press M-II is preferred over the press M-III, as the second press is technologically advanced than the third press. When it comes to the percentage of paper wastage of the above three sheet fed offset presses, press with highest levels of automation is indicating better result than the other two presses and thereby potential savings from the paper substrate, which is the main reason behind saving the final cost of print production. But from the point of the cost of the press, the press M-III can be taken into consideration while discussing about the paper wastage, because the low cost of the press clearly justifies the paper wastage percentage cost during the print production cycle.

CHAPTER-8 CONCLUSION & FUTURE SCOPE

This chapter is about the conclusion and future scope of the research work. A research thesis's conclusion and future scope part, which addresses the study's relevance, focuses on the insights acquired, and plots a course for further investigation, is the pinnacle of an academic journey. This essay explores the dual function of this part, looking at how it closes up the current study while also creating opportunities for further research. The conclusion is the piece that pulls all the research journey's threads together; it is more than just a recap. This chapter summarizes the main findings and goes over the original research problem and objectives. The main objective of is chapter to provide a coherent and perceptive analysis of the findings, highlighting the relevance and possible future studies to be undertaken further in this area.

8.1 Conclusion

Sheet fed offset presses are most commonly used by most of the press organizations and it essentially occupies a larger portion of the total print market also. Over the last few decades, it has evolved and undergone significant changes, be it be in the front of adoption of advanced technology, process standardization and reducing the paper wastage, all have contributed to the enhanced press productivity. Be it computer-to-plate (CTP) systems, automation and control systems, all these helped to reduced press set-up times and enhanced overall press efficiency. Subsequently sheet fed offset manufacturers started using advanced automation functions; simultaneous automatic plate loading/changing, automatic colour registration and consistency control systems, and closed loop press control system, for enhancing the press productivity and reduction of possible paper wastage.

The whole research work was carried out on three fronts; make-ready time, real printing rate of production and paper wastage in relation to the press configuration and cost of the press. With the advanced level of technology that is embedded into the press, essentially helps to reduce press make-ready time, successfully. Automatic feeder unit controls, ink and dampening unit controls, printing unit various activities and delivery unit's various activities are being automatized to take care of make-ready time, effectively.

In order to compete with the digital presses, it is always demanded that the sheet fed offset presses should successfully adopt advanced technologies into its various units, so that the activities can be performed with ease and yet producing best possible results. From the research, it is very much concluded that, level of technology has certainly an important impact of the press make-ready time. While selecting the multi-colour sheet fed offset press, technology should be given an important place.

Second point was relating to real printing rate of production of the presses with the impact of level of technology incorporated into the multi-colour sheet fed offset presses. Productivity and more precisely print productivity of any sheet fed offset press is co-related with the real rate of print production. Higher the real printing rate of production, higher is the press productivity. The relationship between the real printing rate of production and level of technology of the press is well established in this research work. It has been concluded that the multi-colour sheet fed offset press with high level of press automation leads to enhanced print productivity than the press with medium and low level of press automation. Ultimate aim of any sheet fed offset press is to produce higher number of print copies in a given time and it has been established that, the press should be selected with advanced technology for enhanced print productivity.

Third point was the percentage of paper wastage of the various multi-colour sheet fed offset presses in relation with the press configuration, speed of the press, cost of the press and moreover technological adoptions in the sheet fed offset presses. From the research work it is concluded that, as cost of paper contributes a larger portion of the final print cost of production, utmost care should be given to keep the paper wastage percentage as low as possible, so that the saving from this can be diverted towards profit making. Presses with high advanced technology and high cost, even though contributes to the lower percentage of paper wastage, but above a particular print job order quantity, the machines with low cost and low level of press automation proves to be beneficial.

8.2 Future Scope

The future scope and prospects of the research can be the identification and critical analysis of various components of press make-ready time, especially in advanced level multi-colour sheet fed offset presses. Press make-ready is a crucial component of any multi-colour sheet fed offset press, as because, in most of the cases, a considerable amount of press time is consumed for performing this activity. As number of sub-activities is involved during the make-ready operation, critical investigation of all these activities along with their degree of importance and contributions towards press set-up time can be one of the possible areas of research.

Colour matching and consistent colour reproduction is a very challenging area in multi-colour sheet fed offset presses and study on how to attain optimum value with shortest possible time is a major components of press set-up time. Press productivity also draws attention to the press personnel and the academician for the essential growth and development of any printing press. All these can be taken into account for further extension of this research in a meaningful direction.

This chapter concluded with, three factors; make-ready time, real printing rate of production and paper wastage in relation to the multi colour sheet fed offset printing press configuration and cost of the press, are the deciding factors for the print productivity of a press. In the recent times, with the changing needs and requirements of the print buyers and end-users, print productivity is a major point to consider for the effective functioning of the offset presses. In order to justify the short run printing jobs with competitive cost, press productivity needs to be enhanced for the multi colour sheet fed offset presses. Press automation is one of the areas where the press manufacturers should eye upon for increasing the print output productivity. The future scope of research for the prospective researchers in this area are also indicated with justification. It is clearly mentioned that, two prominent areas; press makeready and colour matching on the multi colour sheet fed offset presses are the two segments for the future research work.

REFERENCES

- Adams, J., Michael & Dolin, P.A. (2002). Printing Technology (5th ed.). Delmar Thomson Learning.
- Alberta. (19995). Waste Minimization Manual. Printing & Publishing Industry, ISBN 0-7732-1450-X.
- Al- Najjar, B., (1998). Improved effectiveness of vibration monitoring of rolling element bearings in paper mills. Journal of Engineering Tribology, Proceedings of Instrumental Mechanical Engineering 212(J). pp 111-120.
- Al- Najjar, B., (2002). Company's business and competitiveness enhancement: A model of integrated vibration-based maintenance impact on company's effectiveness, proceeding of 15th International Congress Comadem. The University of Birmingham, Edgbaston, UK.
- Andrade, L., (2012). Management strategy for hazardous waste from atomised SME: application to the printing industry. Journal of Cleaner Production. Pp 214-229.
- Antonio, D., Kalaw, Jr. (2015). Handbook on Productivity. Asian Productivity Organization, Philippines.
- Aph. (2019). Productivity growth and its importance. Productivity Commission (PC).pp1.
- Baral, A.K. (2010). Sheet Fed Offset Technology. Arihant Prakashan, ISBN 978-81-909828-3-2.
- Beckline, M.,Yujun, S., Eric, Z. & Kato Monono, S. (2016). Paper Consumption and Environmental Impact in an Emerging Economy. Journal of Energy, Environmental & Chemical Engineering, 1(1), 13-18.
- Bellander, M., Handberg, L., and Stenberg, J. (1997).Workflow analysis in commercial printing: methods and results. IARIGAI conference. pp 1-14.
- Boltz, William, G., (2017). Early Chinese Writing. The Worlds' Writing System. pp. 191.
- Britannica. (2007). Papermaking.
- Corning Data. (2021). How to improve Productivity & Efficiency in Manufacturing.
- Daniel, D., (2023). Lean manufacturing (lean production). Tech Target.
- Daydaynews. (2020). Bi Sheng first invented movable type printing in history, did European printing originate in China?
- Dejidas, L.P. Jr. and Destree, T. M. (2005). Sheet-fed Offset Press operating (3rd ed.). Pittsburgh: PIA/GATF.

- Deshpande, M. (2011). Printing Papers: Sizing and its Role. Journal of Engineering Research and Studies. 2(2), 17-21.
- Diana, M., Vjesnik, Borovic, J. and Davor, D. (2011). The ISO QMS implementation in the Printing House. 7th Research/ Expert Conference with International Participations, Quality 2011, Neum, B&H.
- Dietz, F.M. (1942). Make-Ready. The Musical Quarterly, Oxford University Press, 28(4), 393-394.
- Envirowise. (2004). Key environmental performance indicators in the printing sector.
- FAO. (2014). Survey of World Pulp and Paper Capacities 2013-2018. FAO Forestry Department Rome, Italy.
- Forestindustries. (2013). Global Paper Consumption is growing. Paper production and consumption growing in Asia.
- Forrester,R. (2020). History of Printing: From Gutenberg to the Laser Printer, (pp 1-5).
- Gammarano, R. (2018).Decent work and the Sustainable Development Goals: A Guidebook on SDG Labour Market Indicators. International Organization.
- Giampiero, M. (2010). Recovered Paper Market in 2010.Bureau of International Recycling (BIR) Paper Division. Brussels, Belgium.
- Gornam, M. (2019). Productivity Enhancement: Top 7 Tips for an Employer. Business Productivity.
- Graphic Arts Collection. (2016). Litho Stone. Princeton University.
- Groover, M.P. (2008). Automation, Production Systems, and Computer-integrated Manufacturing (3rd ed.). Pearson Education, New Jersey.
- Gross, J. (2018). How can training help in increasing employee productivity? Your training edge.
- Hashmicro. (2022). How to Improve Your Manufacturing Productivity. Business Tech.
- Heidelberg. (2016).Understanding Overall Equipment Effectiveness.
- HWEI, ONG, M. (2014). Improving Production Workflow Processes in Printing Industry using Simulation. Faculty of Technology, University Malaysia,Pahang.
- Kalpana, R. (2019).Factors influencing industrial productivity (Six Factors). Business Management.
- Kareem, Abdulazeez, M. (2015). Sheet-Fed Offset Press Operating: Importance of Strategic Operation Management. Proceedings of the 8th WSEAS Int. Conf. on Electronics, Hardware, Wireless and Optical Communications.

- Kew. (2018). Paper (pp 1-3).
- Kipphan, H. (2001). Handbook of Print Media. Heidelberg, Berlin. Springer.
- Konopka, J. & Trybula, W. (1996). Overall equipment effectiveness (OEE) and cost measurement semiconductor manufacturing. Nineteenth IEEE/CPMT Electronics Manufacturing Technology Symposium (pp 137-140).
- Kulshrestha, P. & Pant, V. (2014). Importance of machinery maintenance. Ahmedabad Textile Industry's Research Association (ATIRA).
- Lundberg, M., & Wallin, Casper, M. (2016). Reducing Paper Waste to Improve Resource Efficiency at a Swedish Printing and Packaging Company. Chalmers University of Technology, Gothenburg, Sweden.
- Maiervidorno. (2023). Paper and Print Sector Overview.
- Maiervidorno. (2022). Printer Manufacturers in India Embracing Innovation.
- Maiervidorno. (2020). Printing Industry Set to Drive Further Growth.
- Martin, Sam. (2004). Paper Chase. Ecology Communications, Inc.
- Mauro, James, J. (2007). JDF-based Print Production Workflow. Heidelberg USA, Inc.
- Michael. (2020). 8 Ways to Increase Productivity at Your Manufacturing Plant. Delta Regis.
- Misterek, S., Dooley, K. & Anderson, J. (1992). Productivity as a performance measure. International Journal of Operations and Production Management, vol. 12, pp 29-45.
- Nicholas, John, M. (1997).Competitive Manufacturing Management: Continuous Improvement, Lean Production and Customer Focused Quality. Irwin Professional/McGraw-Hill series, USA.
- Offset Pressman. (2021). Make Your Make-ready More Efficient.
- Offset Pressman. (2012). Take Control of Waste in Your Pressroom.
- Offset Pressman. (2014). Make Your Offset Press Make-ready Faster.
- Offset Pressman. (2019). The Future of Offset Printing.
- Oxford Dictionaries. (2023). Papyrus.
- Poksinska, B. (2010). When does ISO 9000 lead to improvements. International Journal of Productivity and Quality Management, 5(2), 124-136.
- Prepressure. (2012). The History of Printing.
- Printing Tips. (2023). Glossary of Printing Terms. Make-ready.
- Research and Markets. (2020). Commercial Printing Market-Growth, Trends and Forecasts (2020-2025).

- Ryan, V. (2020). Computer- integrated Manufacturing (CIM) explained.....clearly. Armagard.
- Salman, Mustafa, R. Brady, M. & Geraghty, J. (2008). Productivity Improvement Methodologies: A Comparison. Enterprise Process Research Centre, School of Mechanical & Manufacturing Engineering, Dublin City University, Ireland.
- Sarokin, D. (2020). Definition of increased Productivity. Chron.
- Sciencephotolibrary. (2023). Alois Senefelder.
- Shabat, B. (2019). 10 Ways to Improve Manufacturing Productivity. Become Blog.
- Shadiya, O. O., Satish, V. & High, K.A. (2012). Process enhancement through waste minimization and multi objective optimization. Journal of Cleaner Production, vol. 31. pp 137-149.
- Shital, M. (2018). Productivity: Meaning, Concept, Formulas, Techniques, Measurement and Advantages. Economics Discussion.
- Singh, H. Motwani, J. & Kumar, A. (2000). A review and analysis of the state-of-the-art research on productivity measurement. Industrial Management and Data Systems, vol 100, pp 234-41.
- Smithers. (2023). The Future of Global Printing to 2024.
- Smithsonian. (2016). Lithographic offset press, Rubel. National Museum of American History.
- Smyth, S. (2003). The Print & Production Manual. (9th ed.). Pira International Ltd.
- Sneed, H. & Verhoef, C. (2001). Reengineering the Corporation-A Manifesto for IT Evolution. University of Amsterdam, Department of Mathematics and Computer Science, Amsterdam, Netherland (pp. 1-22).
- Statista. (2023). Value of the printing industry in India 2007-2022.
- Subramaniam, Siva, K., Husin, Siti Huzaimah, B., Yusop, Yusmarnita, B. & Hamidon, Abdul Hamid, B. (2007). The production performance monitoring system. In 6th WSEAS International Conference on Circuits, Systems, Electronics, Control & Signal Processing (CSECS'07) World Scientific and Engineering Academy and Society (pp. 185-190).
- Subramaniam, Siva K., Husin, Siti Huzaimah B., Yusop, Yusmarnita B. and Hamidon, Abdul Hamid B. (2014). Machine efficiency and man power utilization on production lines. Universiti Teknikal Malaysia Melaka, Malaysia.

- Tangen, S. (2002). Understanding the concept of productivity. In Proceedings of the 7th Asia Pacific Industrial Engineering and Management Systems Conference, Dept. of Production Engineering. The Royal Institute of Technology Stockholm, Sweden.
- Thompson, C. (2014). Challenges for the Printing Industry Globally in 2015.
- Thornhill, T. (2014). Turning the printing industry green-Tips. Auditel.
- Tom, P. (2006). Overall Equipment Effectiveness & Real-Time Visual Management Critical Lean Tools. Intelligent Manufacturing Solutions (pp. 1-18).
- Tomljanovic, S. (2015). Graphic Design and Print Production Fundamentals. Chapter 7, Web2print, Graphic Communications Open Textbook Collective.
- University of Houston. (2019). The History of Lithography.
- Uribe, J. (2008). Print Productivity: A System dynamics approach. RIT.

www.ingramcontent.com/pod-product-compliance
Lightning Source LLC
LaVergne TN
LVHW082338200926
848481LV00012B/3379